November 2004.

Ninette,
Just as a reminder....
Ginny.

PEAK DISTRICT MOODS

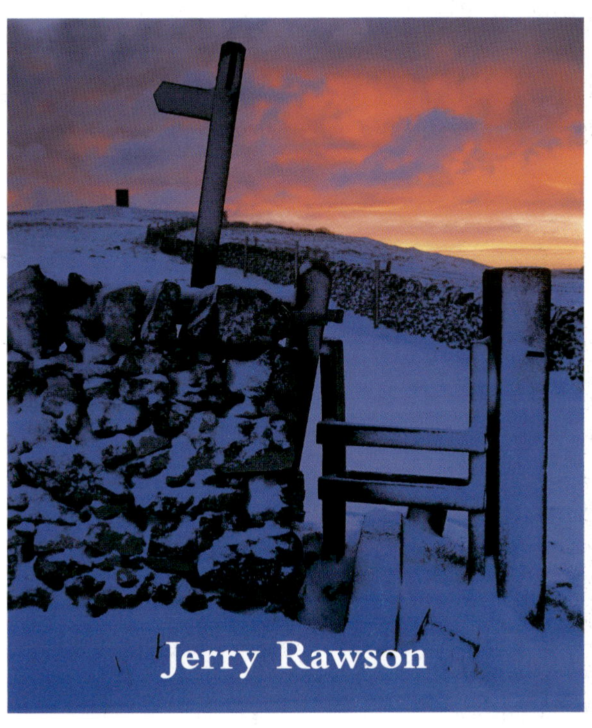

Jerry Rawson

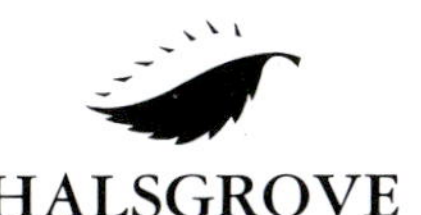

HALSGROVE

First published in Great Britain in 2003

British Library Cataloguing-in-Publication Data
A CIP record for this title is available from the British Library

ISBN 1 84114 270 0

HALSGROVE

Halsgrove House
Lower Moor Way
Tiverton, Devon EX16 6SS
Tel: 01884 243242
Fax: 01884 243325
email: sales@halsgrove.com
website: www.halsgrove.com

Printed by D'Auria Industrie Grafiche Spa, Italy

INTRODUCTION

The 555 square miles (1438 square km) of the Peak District National Park, the first to be designated way back in 1951, lie at the southern end of the Pennines and form a marked transition between the soft green lowlands and the harsh moorland uplands. Surrounded by the conurbations of Manchester, Sheffield and the Midlands, it's not surprising that the park is the most popular in the UK.

The Peak landscape consists of two clearly defined types of scenery produced by different rocks. The high, bleak gritstone moorland forms a horseshoe known as the Dark Peak, and enclosed within this inverted 'U' is the rolling limestone area of the White Peak, an undulating plateau of high pastureland split by dramatic dales.

This varied landscape offers great opportunities to landscape photographers and each season has its own beauty. This ranges from the colourful display of wild flowers in Dovedale during springtime; the purple-clad heather moors of Bleaklow in high summer; the golden autumnal colours of the trees below the eastern edges; to the Arctic-like snowy wastes of Kinder Scout.

Chasing the light across this precious landscape can be very rewarding but also requires great patience – sitting on the top of a hill waiting for the sun to rise only to find a bank of cloud rolling in from the east blocking out the magical dawn light, or sheltering behind rocks waiting for heavy rain to pass over and leave dramatic clouds, sunbeams and rainbows. In rapidly changing light, pictures can appear and disappear in seconds.

You will find some pictures in the book with azure skies and bright sunshine, but I prefer the impact of dramatic light, stormy conditions and especially around dawn and dusk when the light can be a revelation transforming a mundane landscape into something quite sublime; capturing a fleeting moment of perfection.

The choice of pictures and their order are purely personal and take you on a photographic odyssey capturing the energy and moods of the Peak District landscape throughout all the seasons. We start along the river courses of the Dove, Wye, Manifold and Lathkill through the limestone dales of the White Peak and also explore the surrounding limestone plateau. Our photographic journey then continues in marked contrast across the broad, rocky ridges and rolling gritstone moors of the western flanks of the Peak District to the high, wild moors of Bleaklow and Kinder Scout. Finally, we return along the Derwent Valley with its crag-rimmed skyline, ancient oak and silver birch woodlands and heather moors.

Jerry Rawson

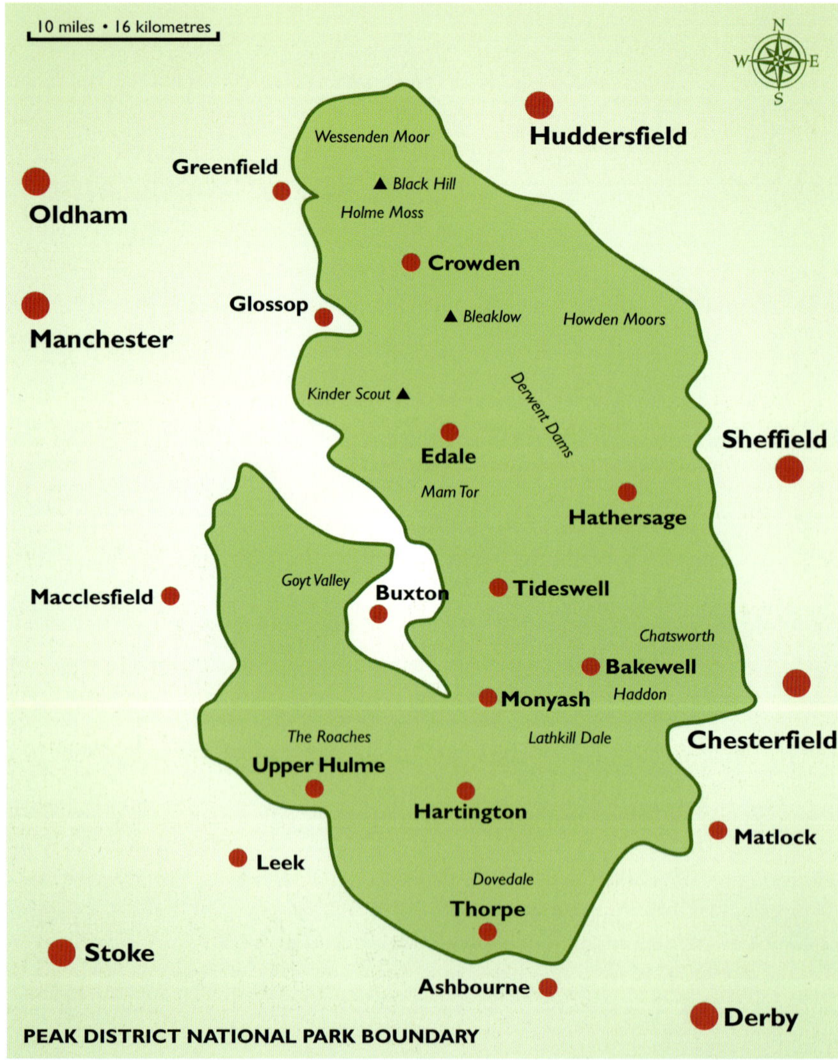

ACKNOWLEDGEMENTS

I wish to thank Katy Rawson for all her help and support and also Roly Smith, editorial manager for Halsgrove and president of the Outdoor Writers' Guild for his guidance and editorial help.

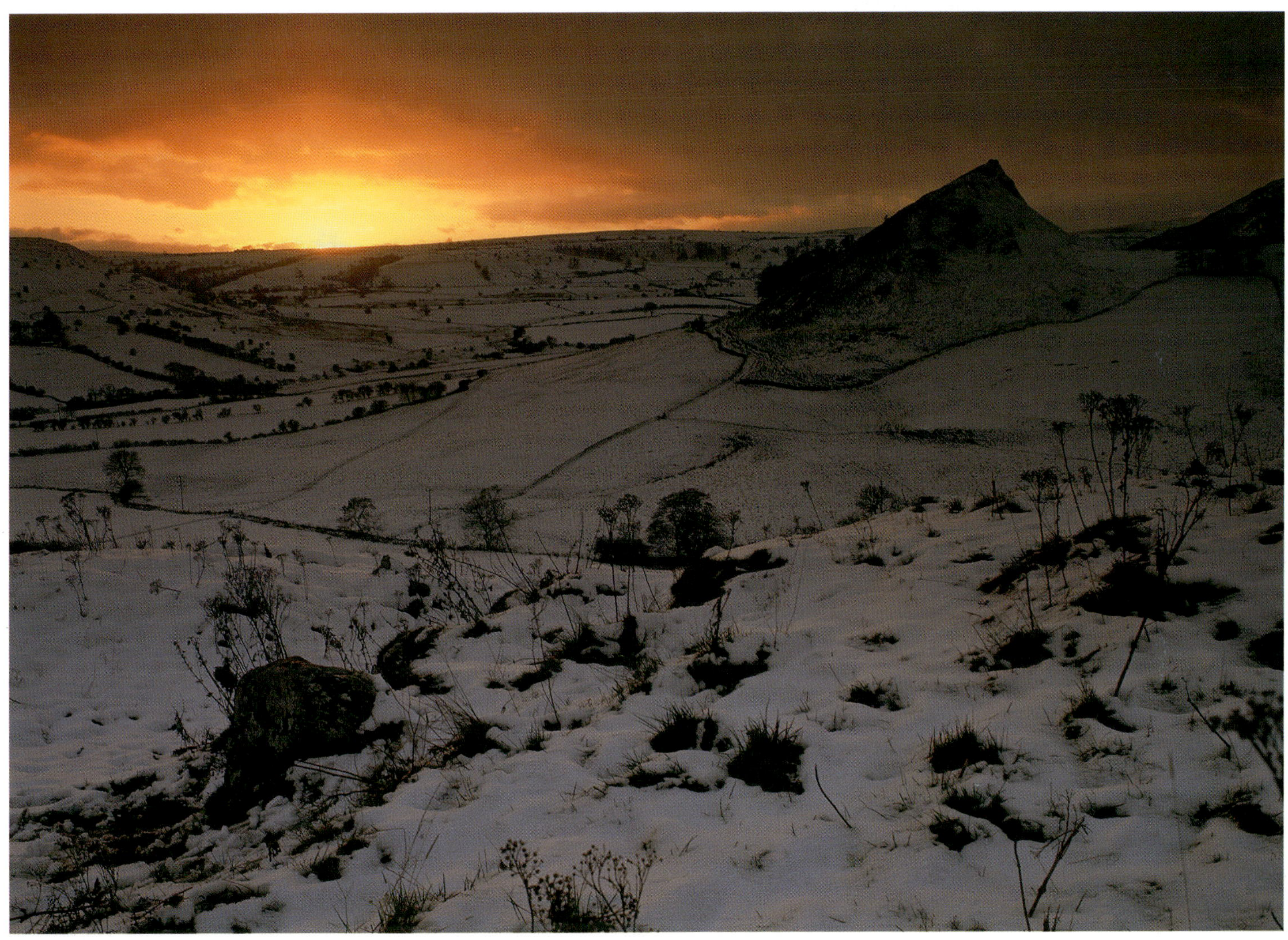

Sunset over the Dove
Snow adorns the Upper Dove Valley with the last rays of the setting sun forming a gold band over the distant Morridge moors.

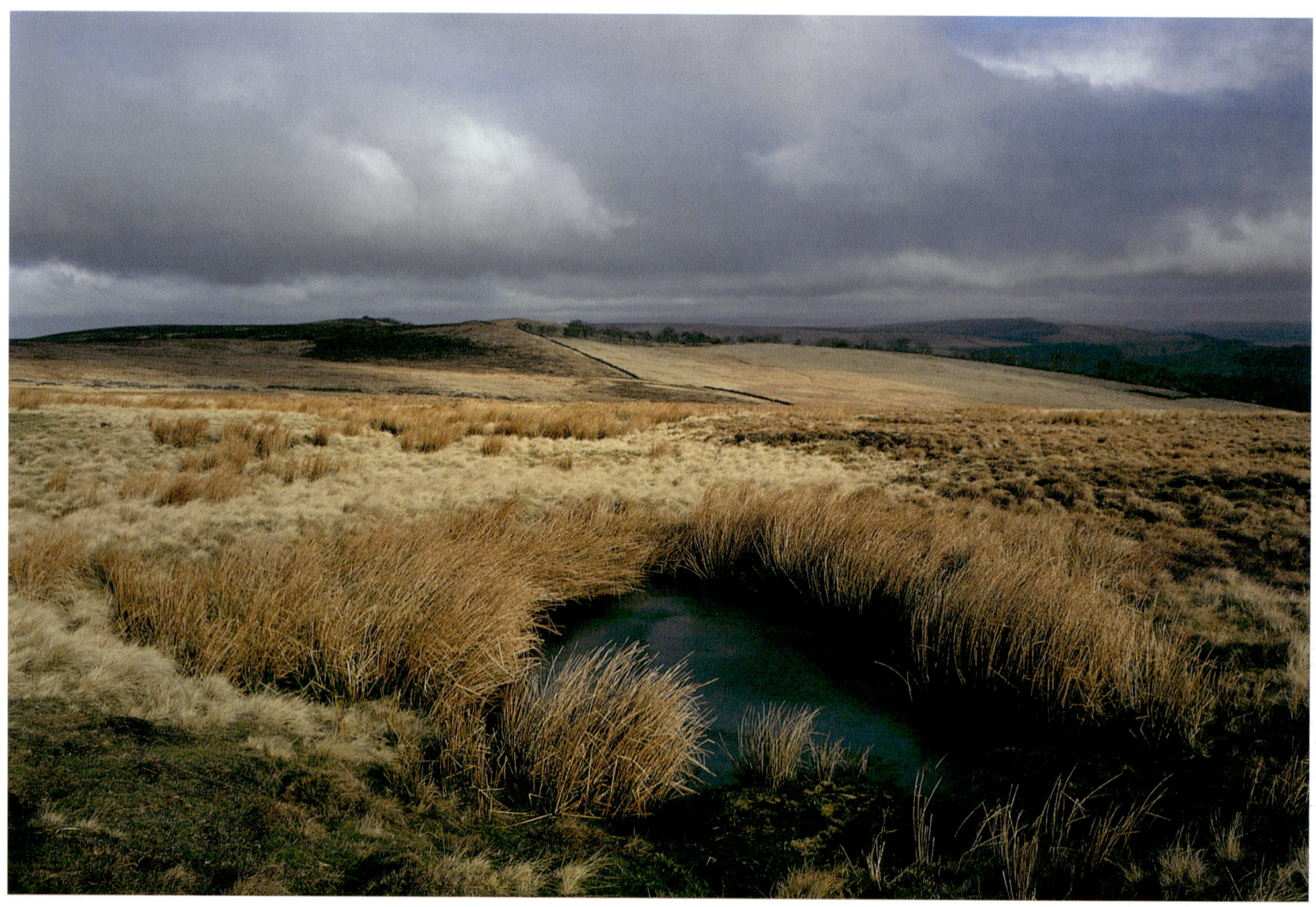

Birthplace of rivers
The gritstone moors of Axe Edge near Buxton give birth to the major Peak District rivers of the Dane, Goyt, Wye, Manifold and Dove.

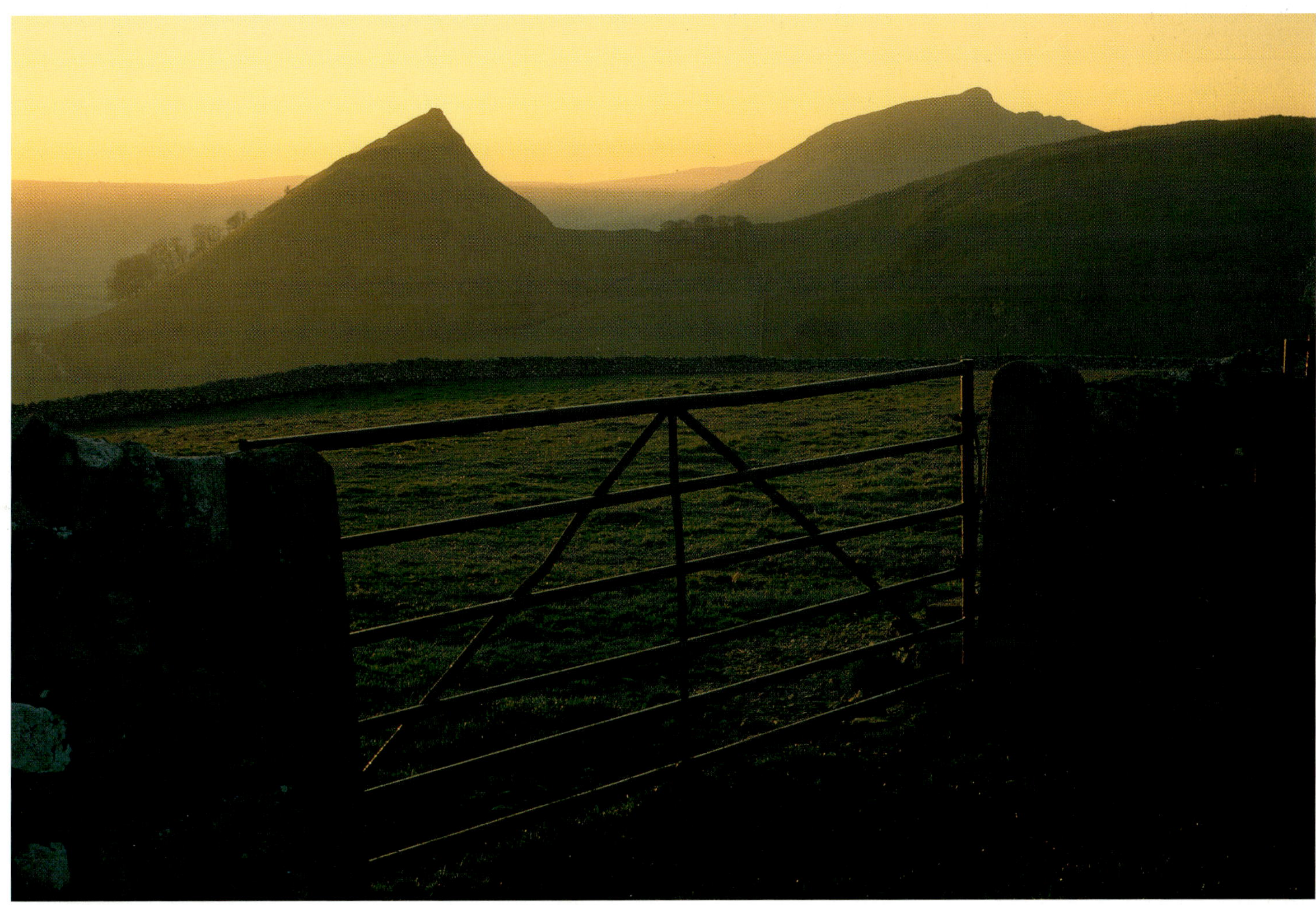

Gateway to the Dove
The pale light of an autumn evening adds shape and form to Parkhouse Hill and Chrome Hill, below which the infant Dove flows, near Earl Sterndale.

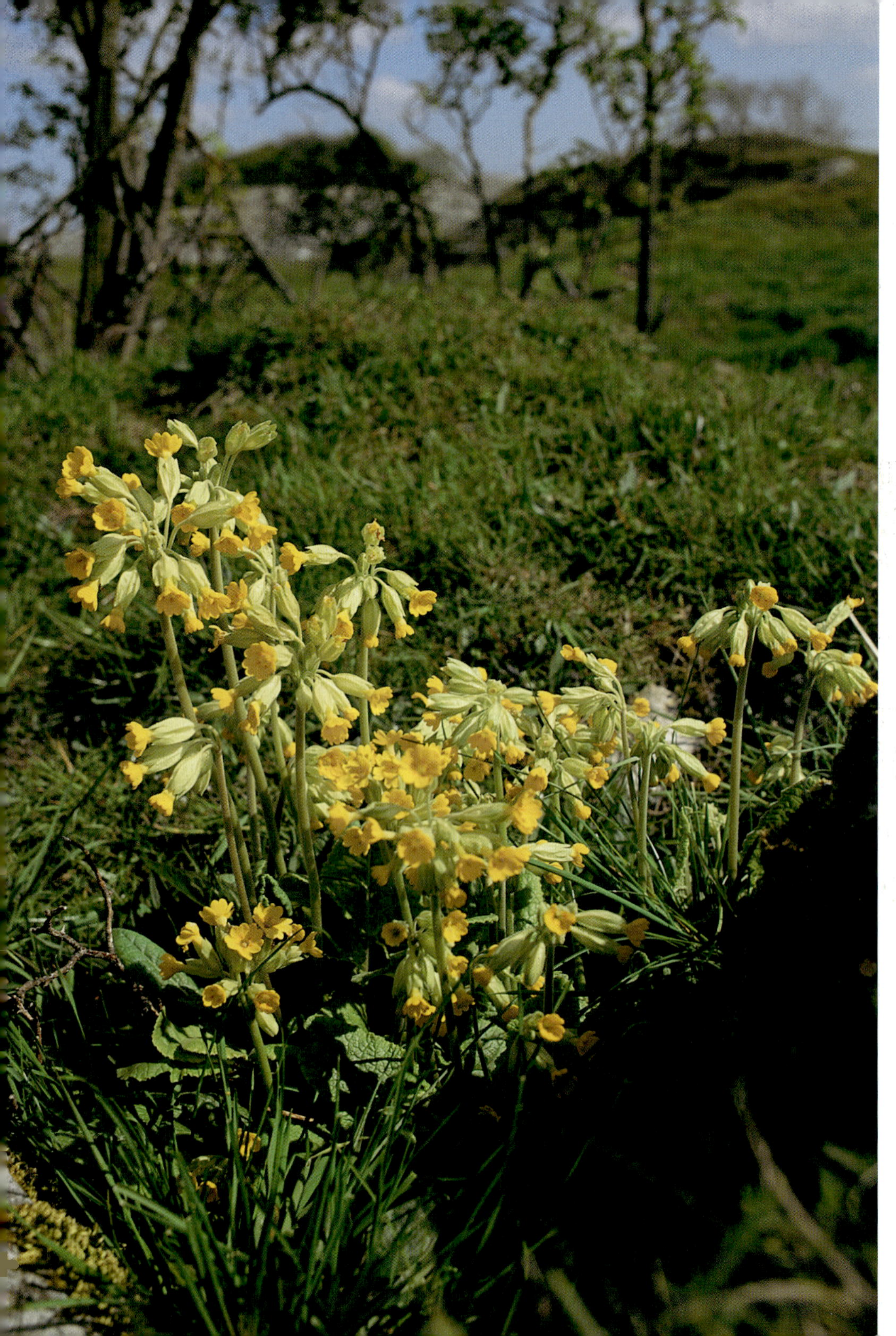

Colourful cowslips
The drooping yellow flowers of the cowslip add a welcome touch of colour to the limestone plateau of the White Peak.

Misty dragon

The undulating crest of Chrome Hill, known locally as the Dragon's Back, rises above the early morning mist in the Upper Dove Valley.

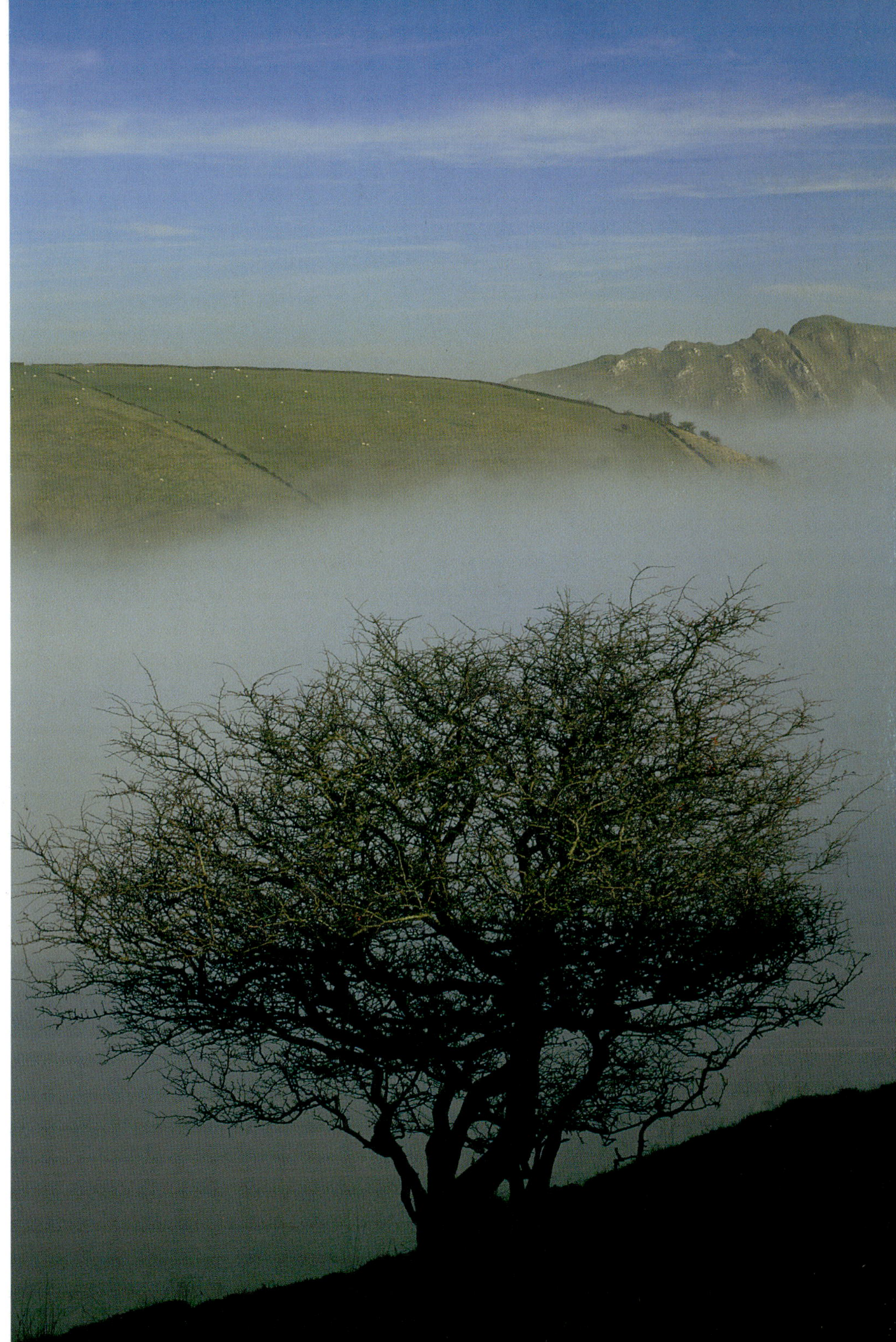

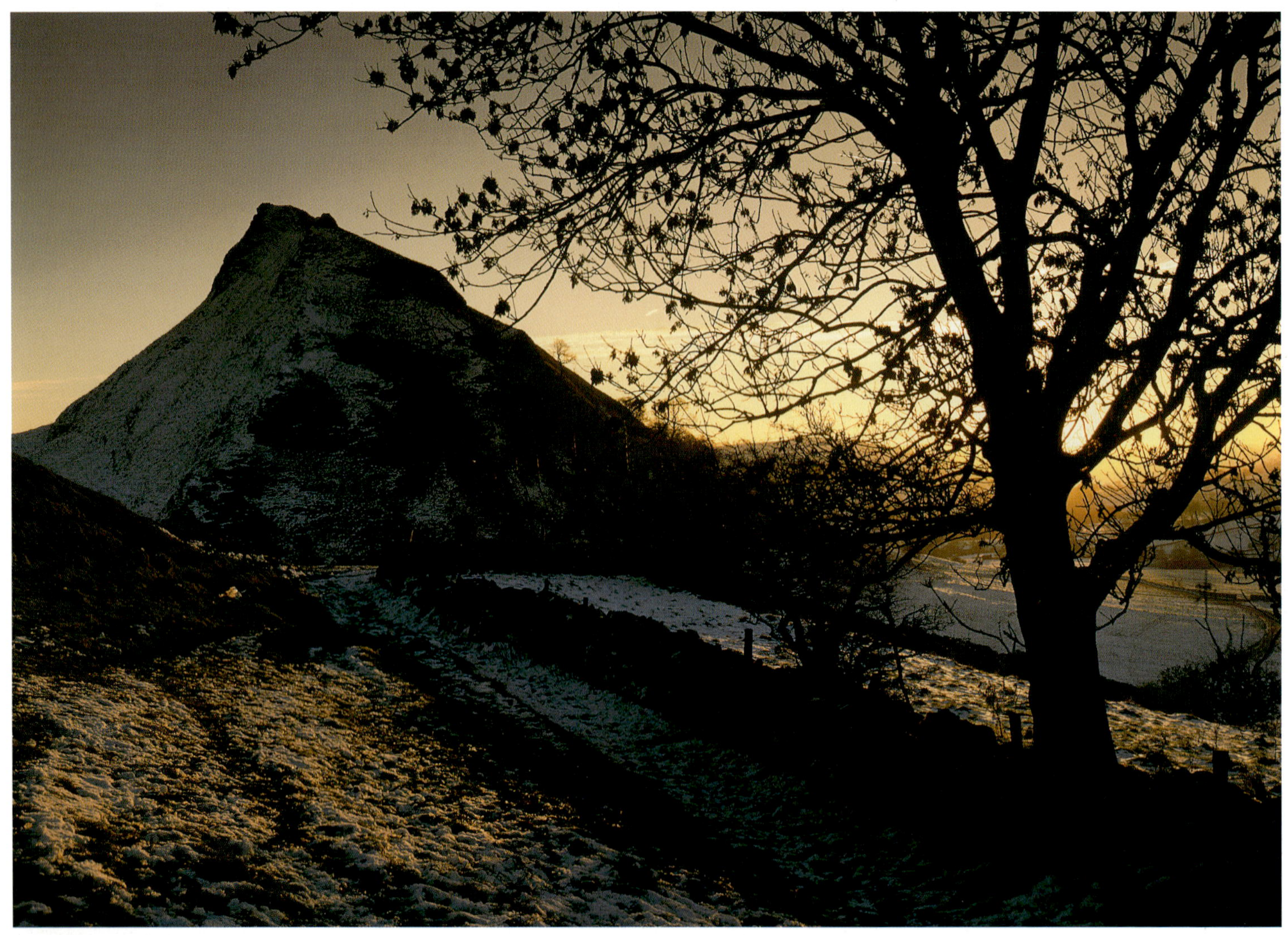

Shark's fin
A weak dawn sun rises behind the shark's fin of Parkhouse Hill, in the Upper Dove Valley, surely one of the shapeliest peaks in the district.

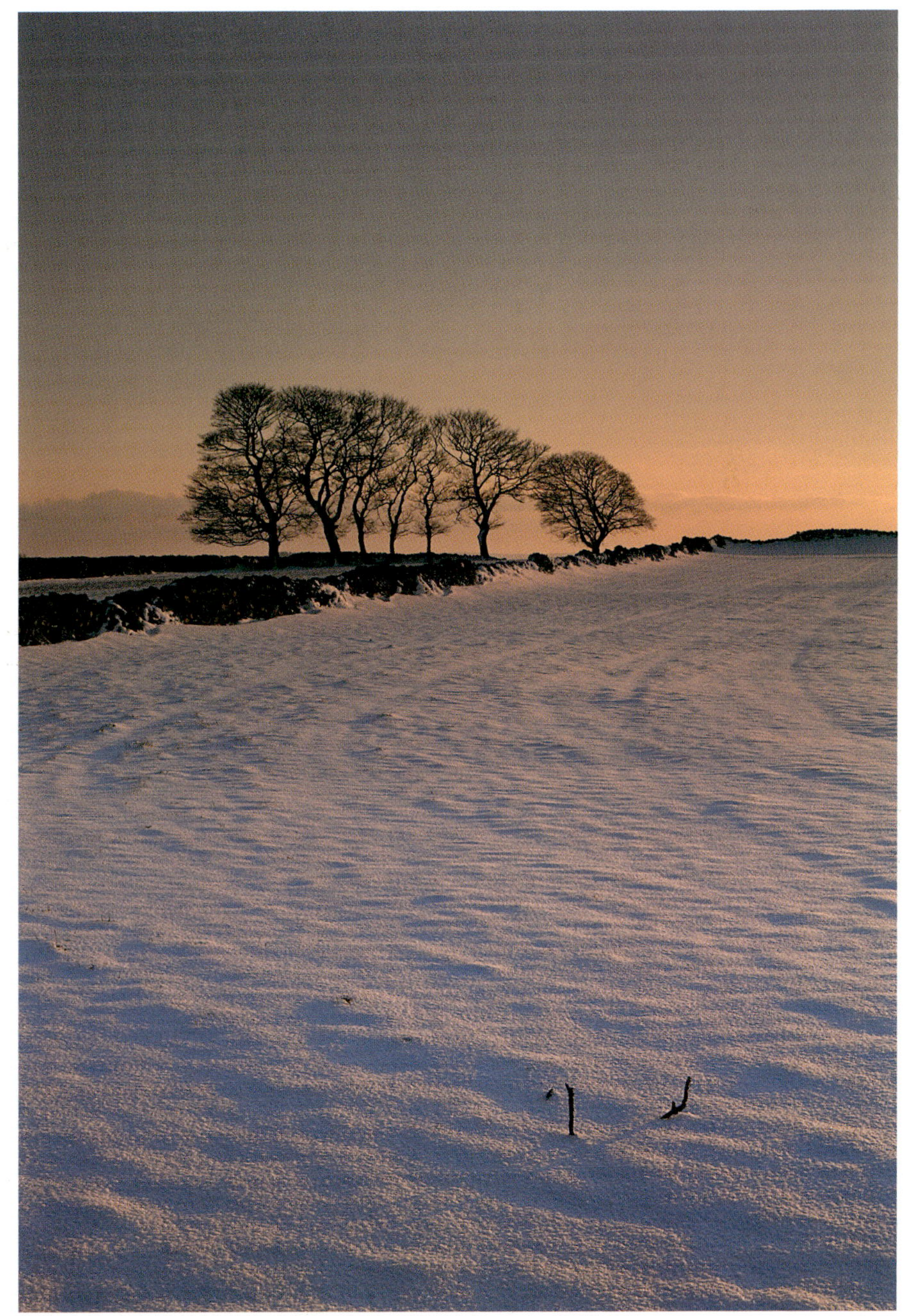

Winter dusk
The last rays of the winter sun add warmth to this snowy scene on the White Peak plateau above Hartington.

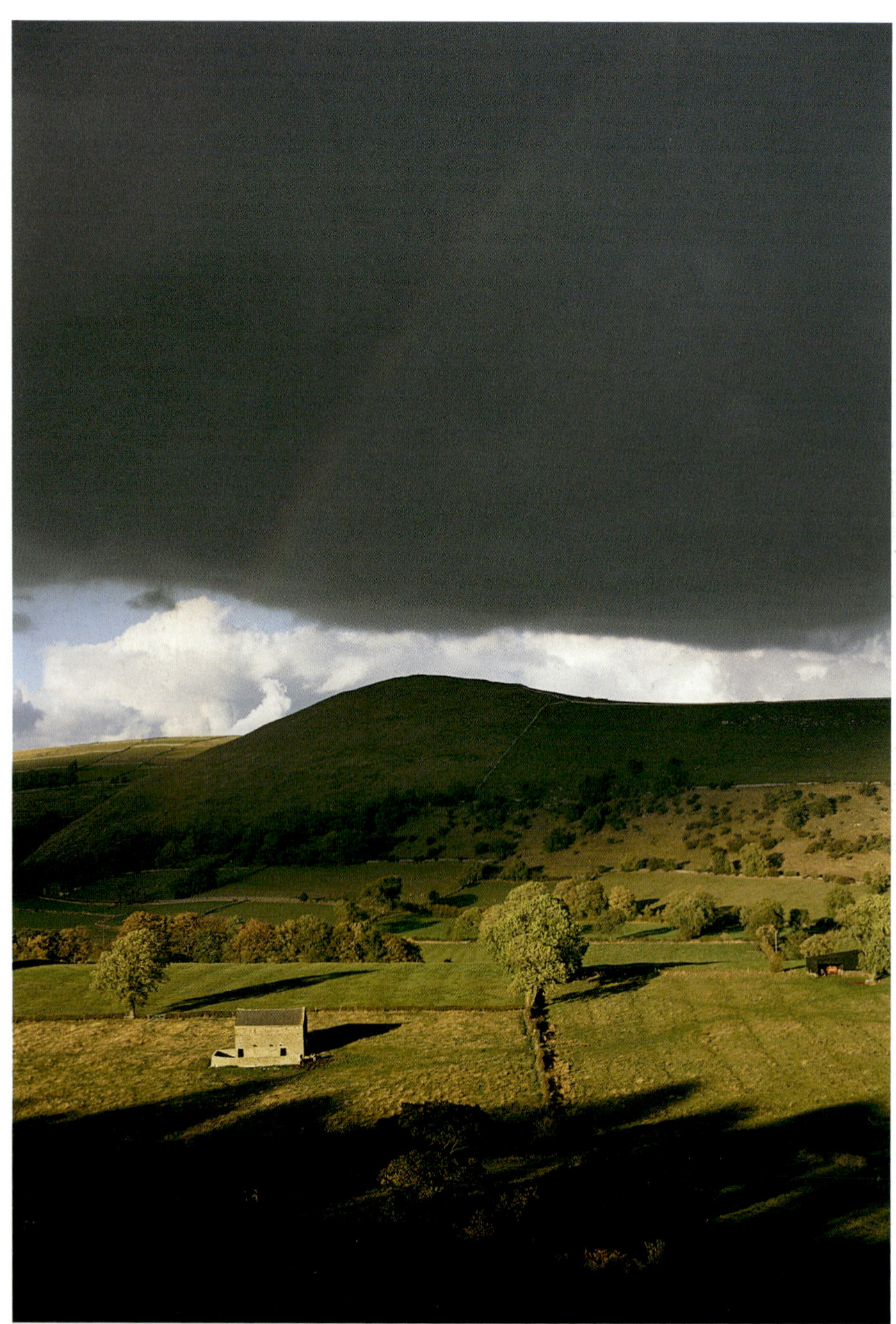

Storm over Crowdecote
Dramatic storm clouds drift across the White Peak landscape near the village of Crowdecote on the banks of the Upper Dove.

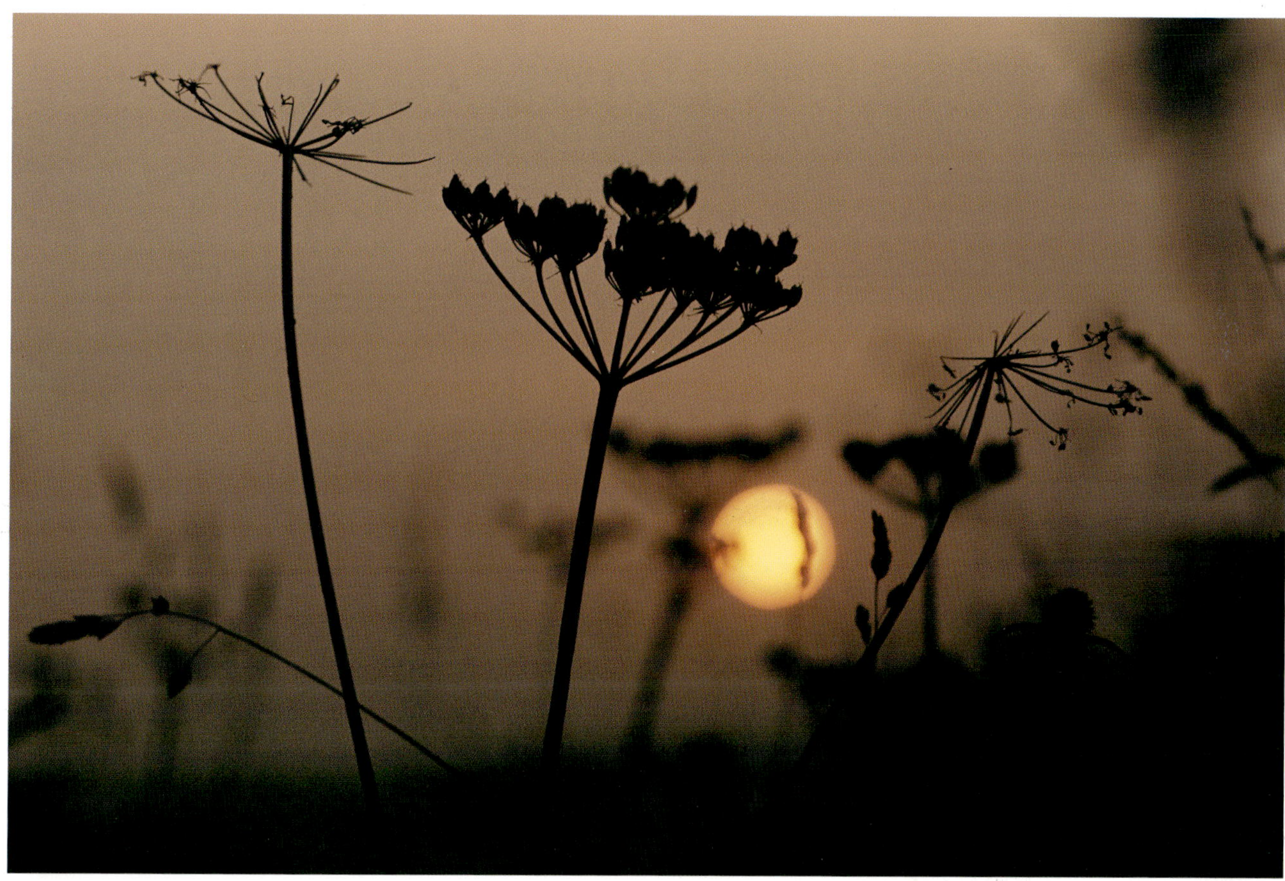

Sunny silhouette
The setting sun creates a silhouette of late summer grasses and cow parsley in the fields near Hartington.

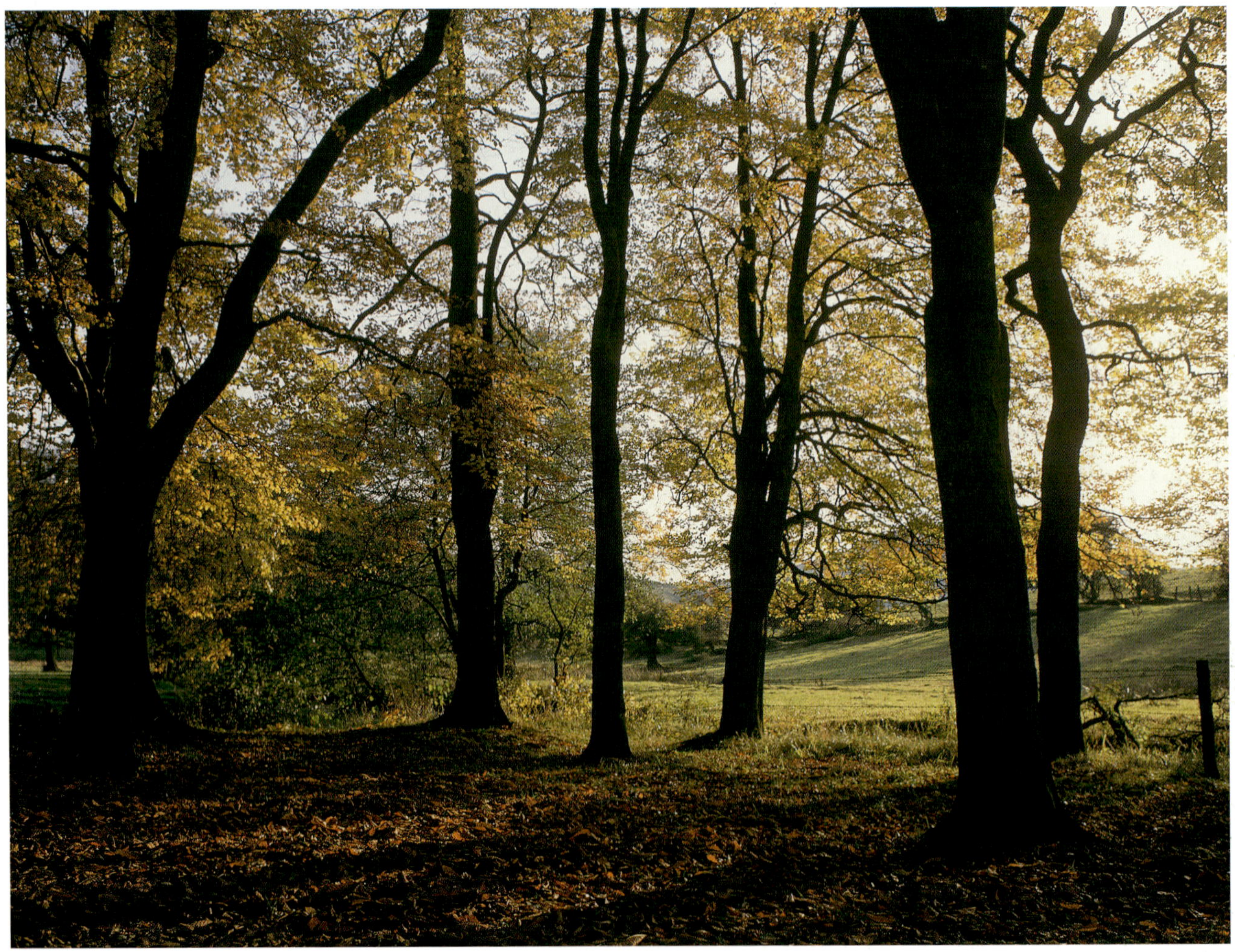

Autumn gold

A small copse of beech trees in their autumn colours in Beresford Dale, which was made famous in the seventeenth century by the fishing duo Izaak Walton and Charles Cotton's *The Compleat Angler.*

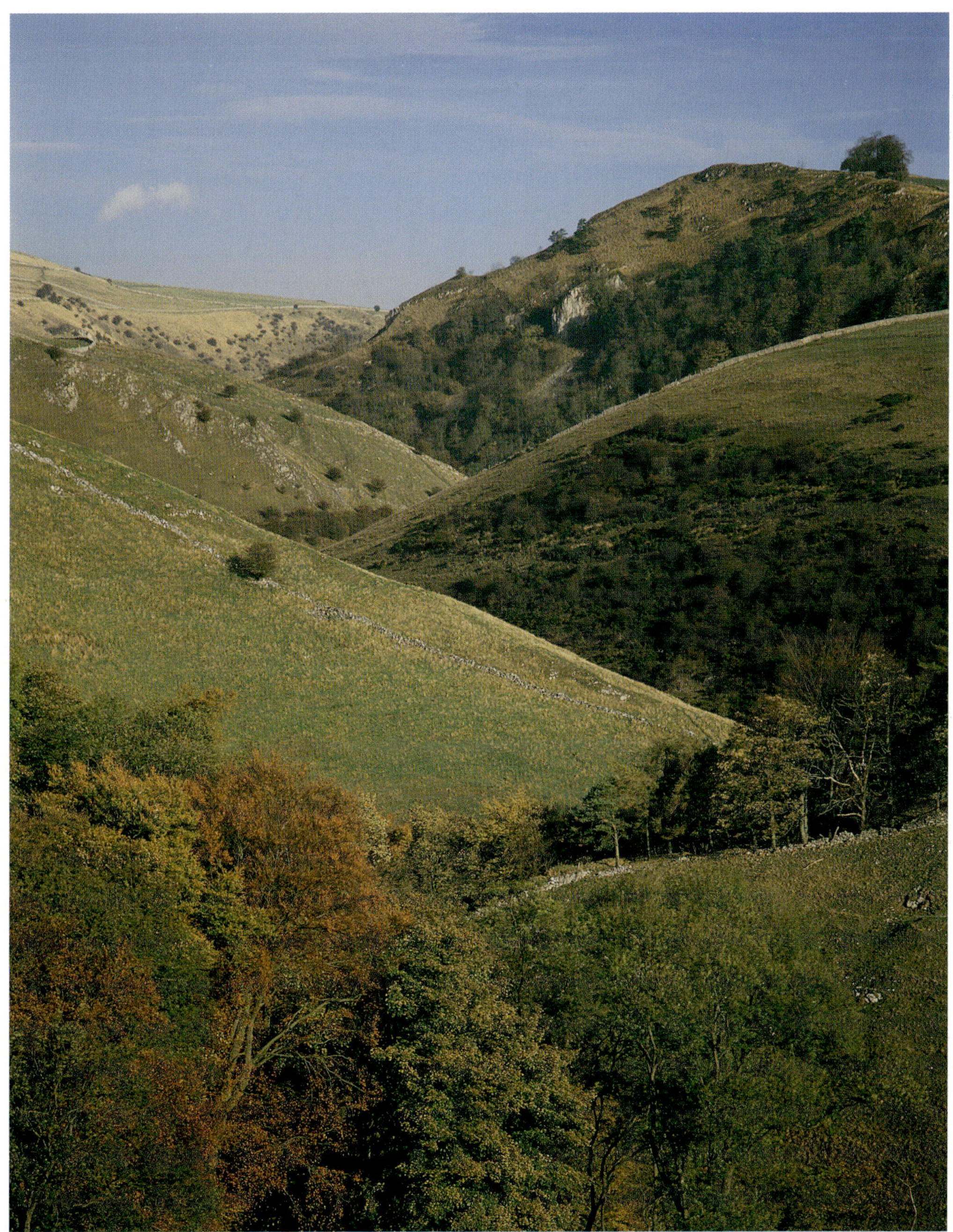

Wolfscote Dale

The autumn colours of the foreground add texture and colour to this view north up Wolfscote Dale, through which the Dove follows a zig-zag course.

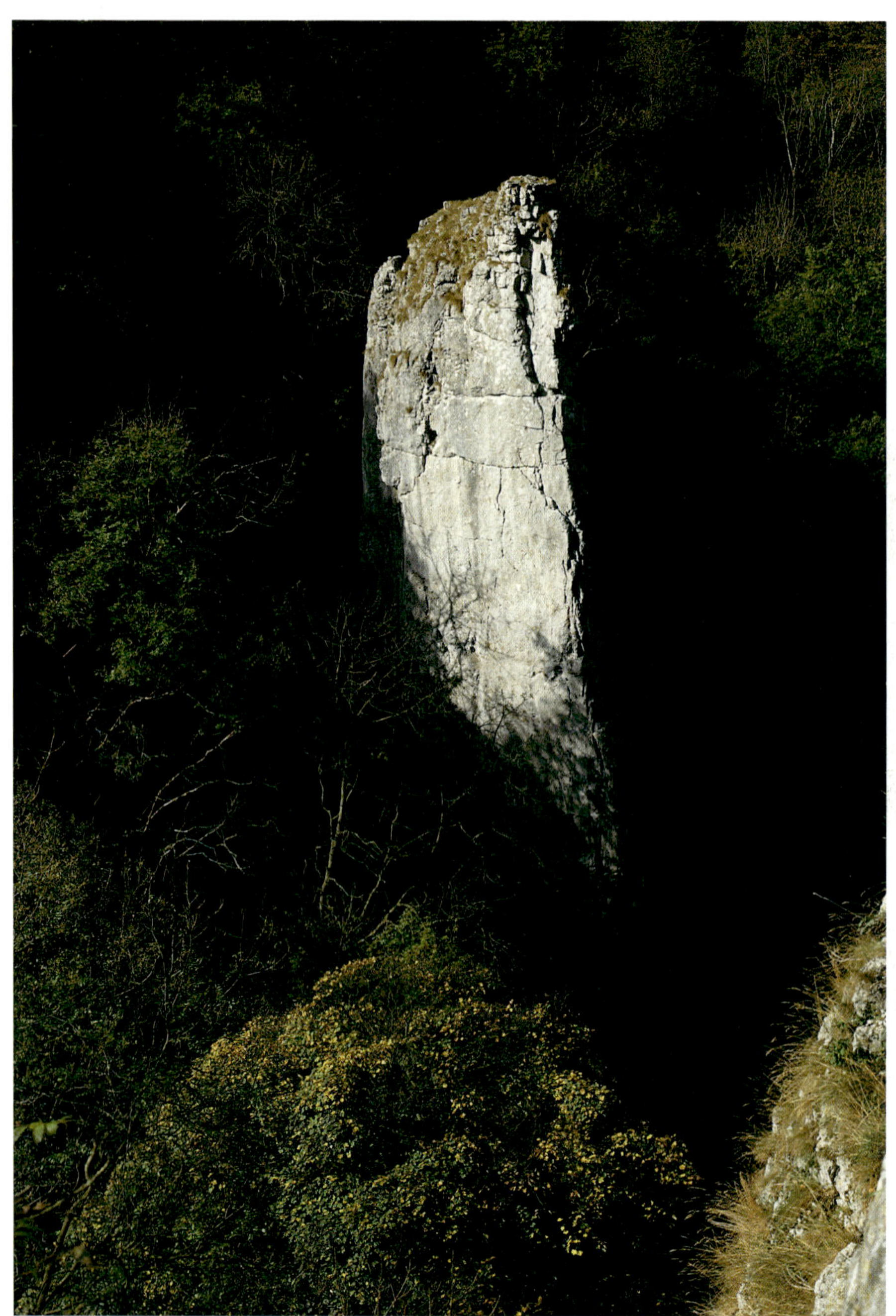

White fang
The slender reef limestone monolith of Ilam Rock rises through the trees on the banks of the River Dove.

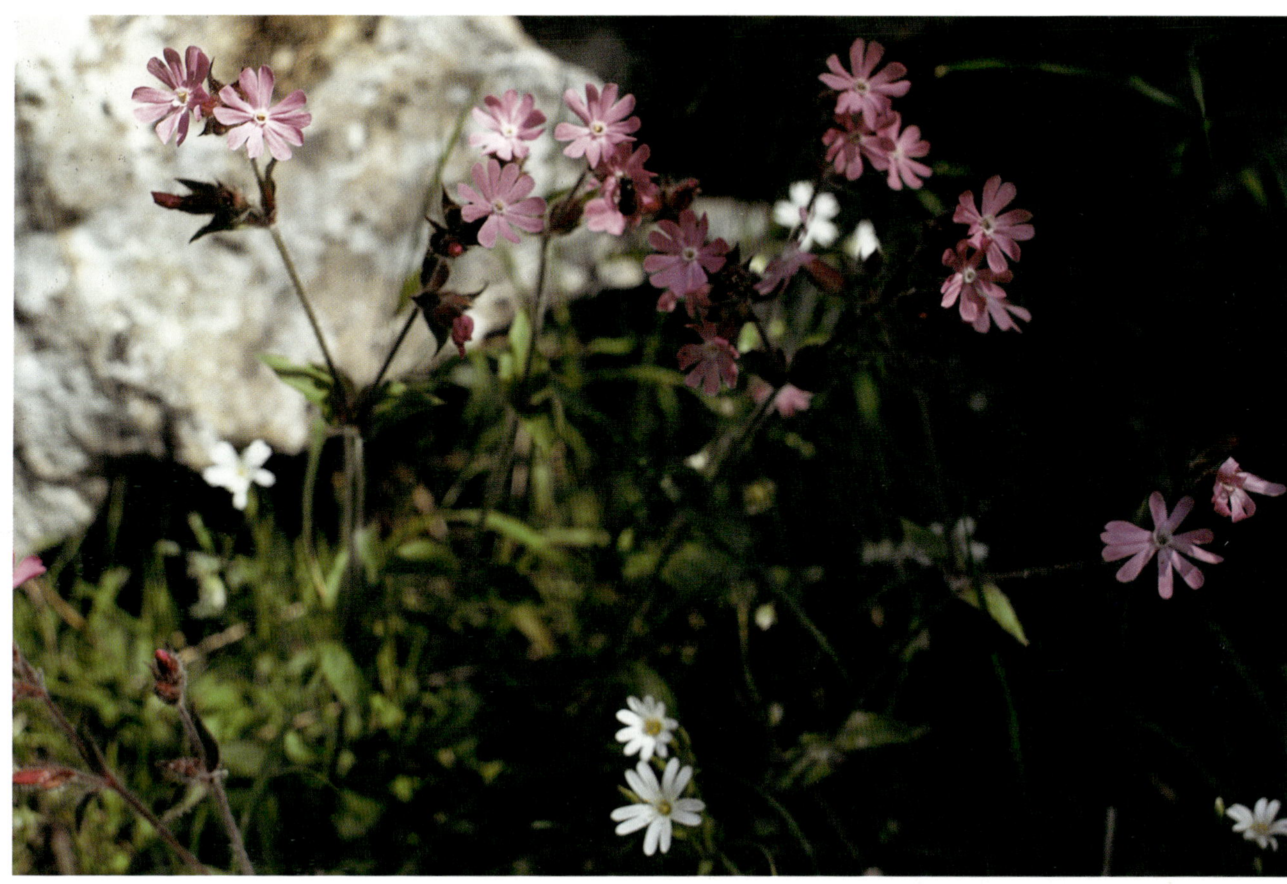

Summer flowers

The bright summer flowers of red campion enlivens the grassy banks, scree slopes and cliff ledges in Dovedale.

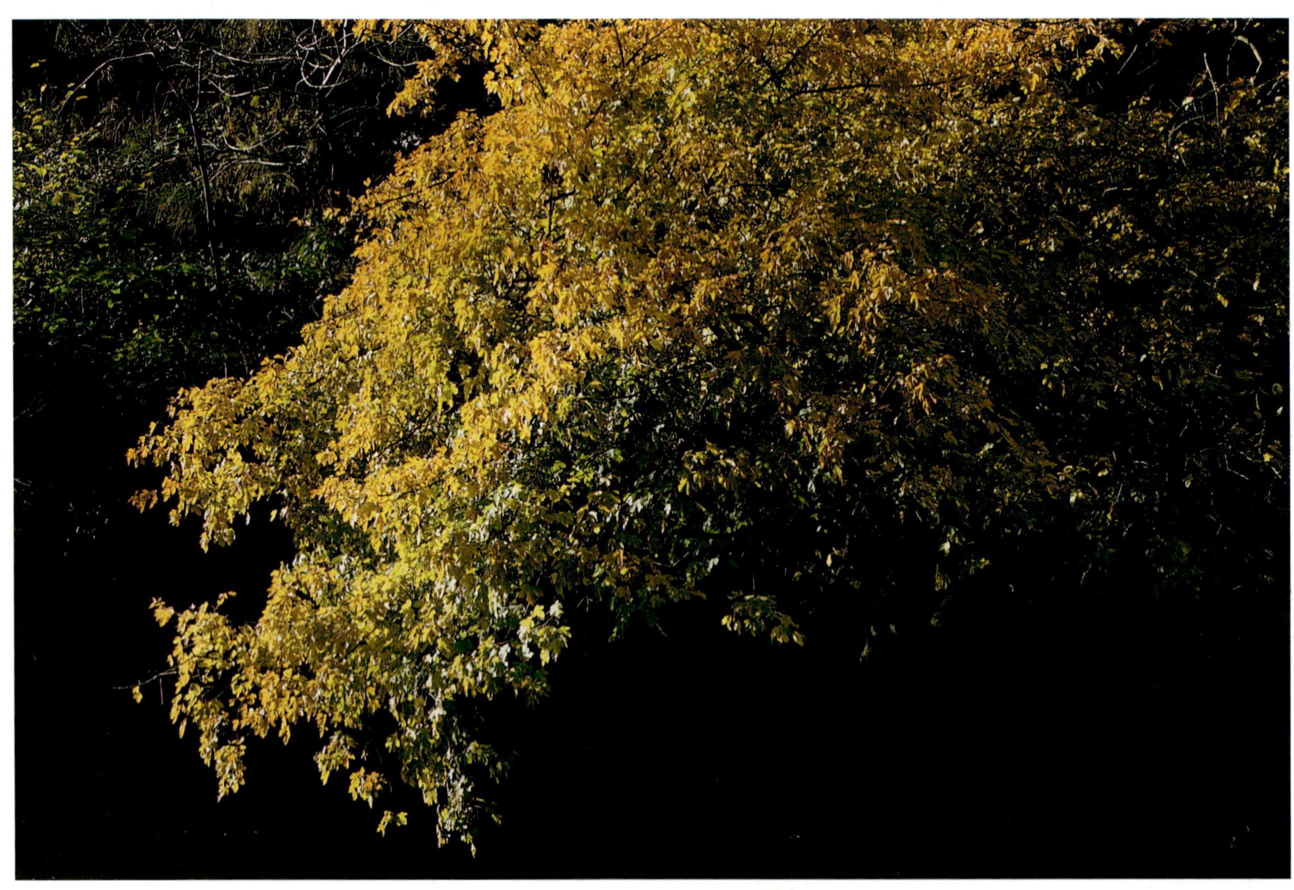

Golden burst
A burst of golden autumn colours on trees overhanging the River Dove.

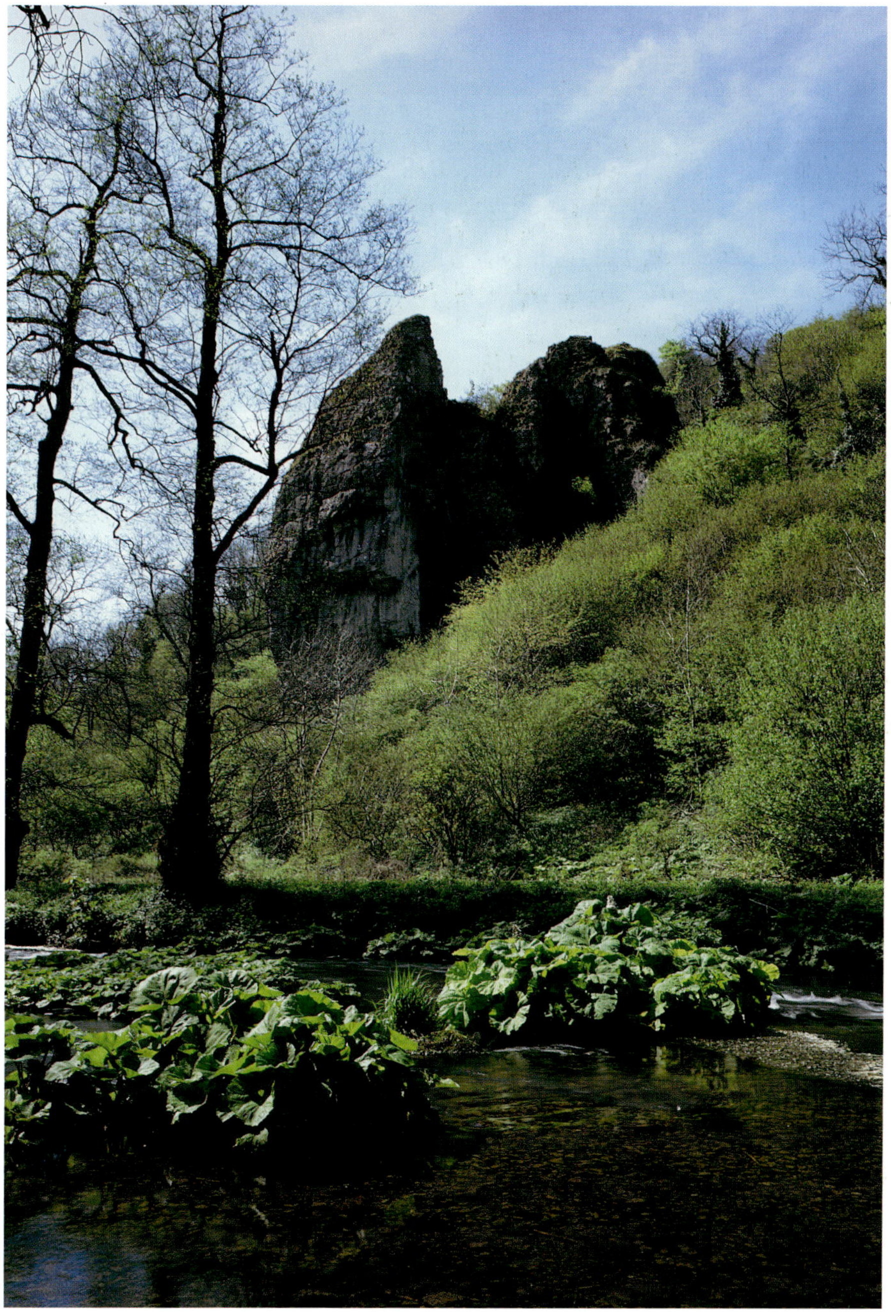

Dovedale spring

Early morning spring sunshine brings myriad shades of fresh green to this view of the limestone buttresses of Dovedale Church, overlooking the tranquil waters of the Dove.

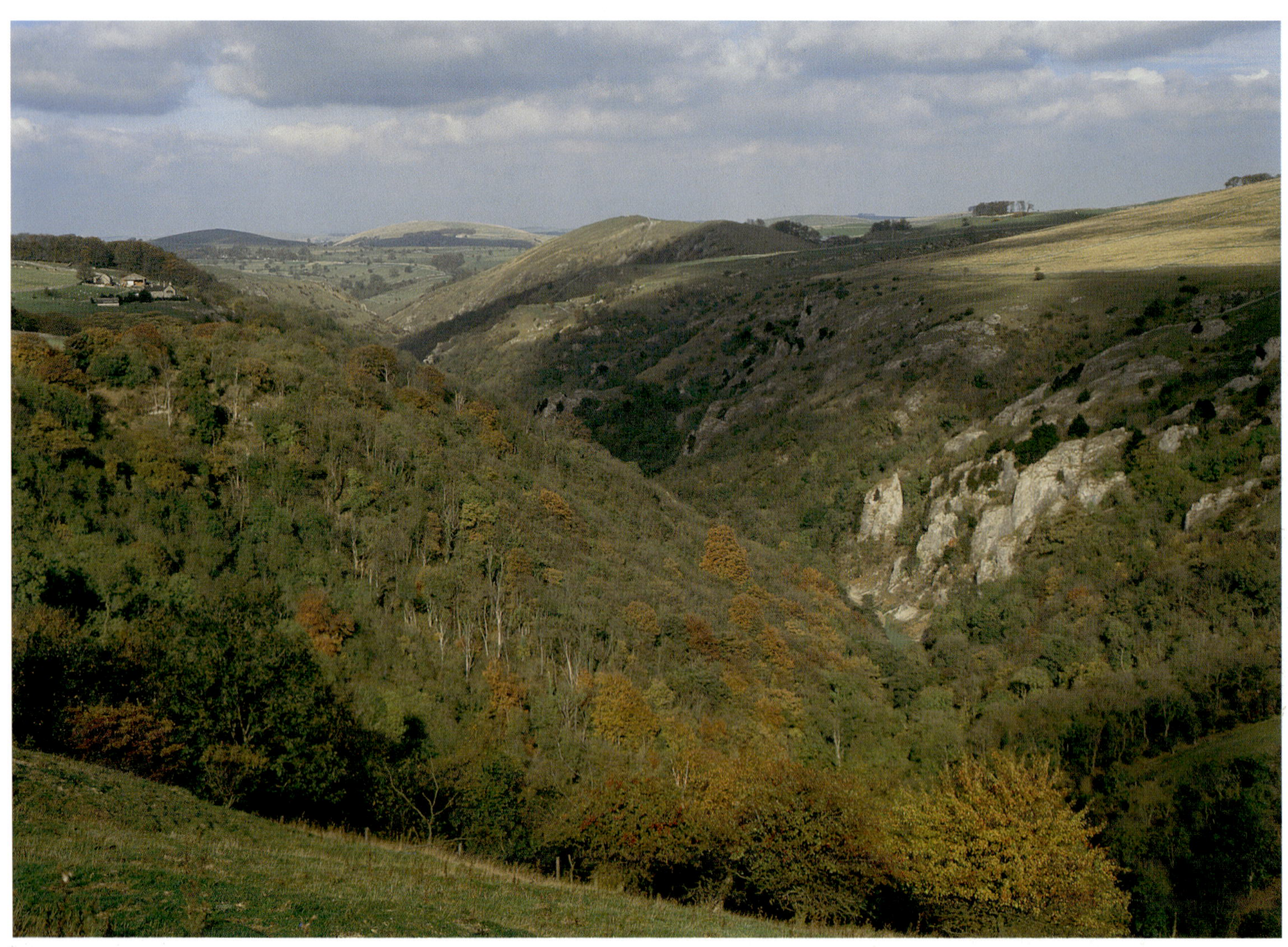

Dovedale and Tissington Spires
Bunster Hill provides a lovely view across the steep wooded slopes of Dovedale to the limestone pinnacles of Tissington Spires.

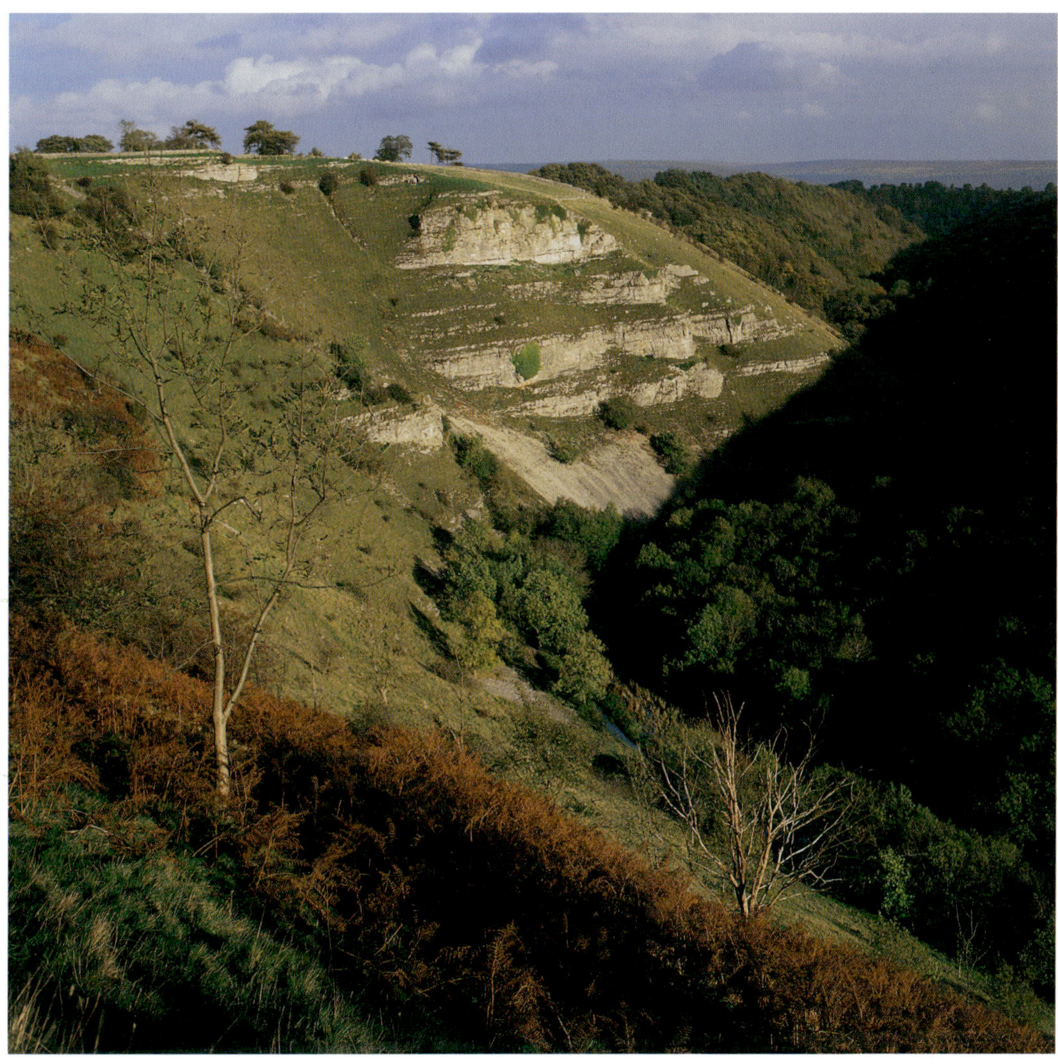

Lathkill Dale
The decaying bracken adds a touch of colour to the green, ash-tree-clad slopes in Lathkill Dale near Monyash.

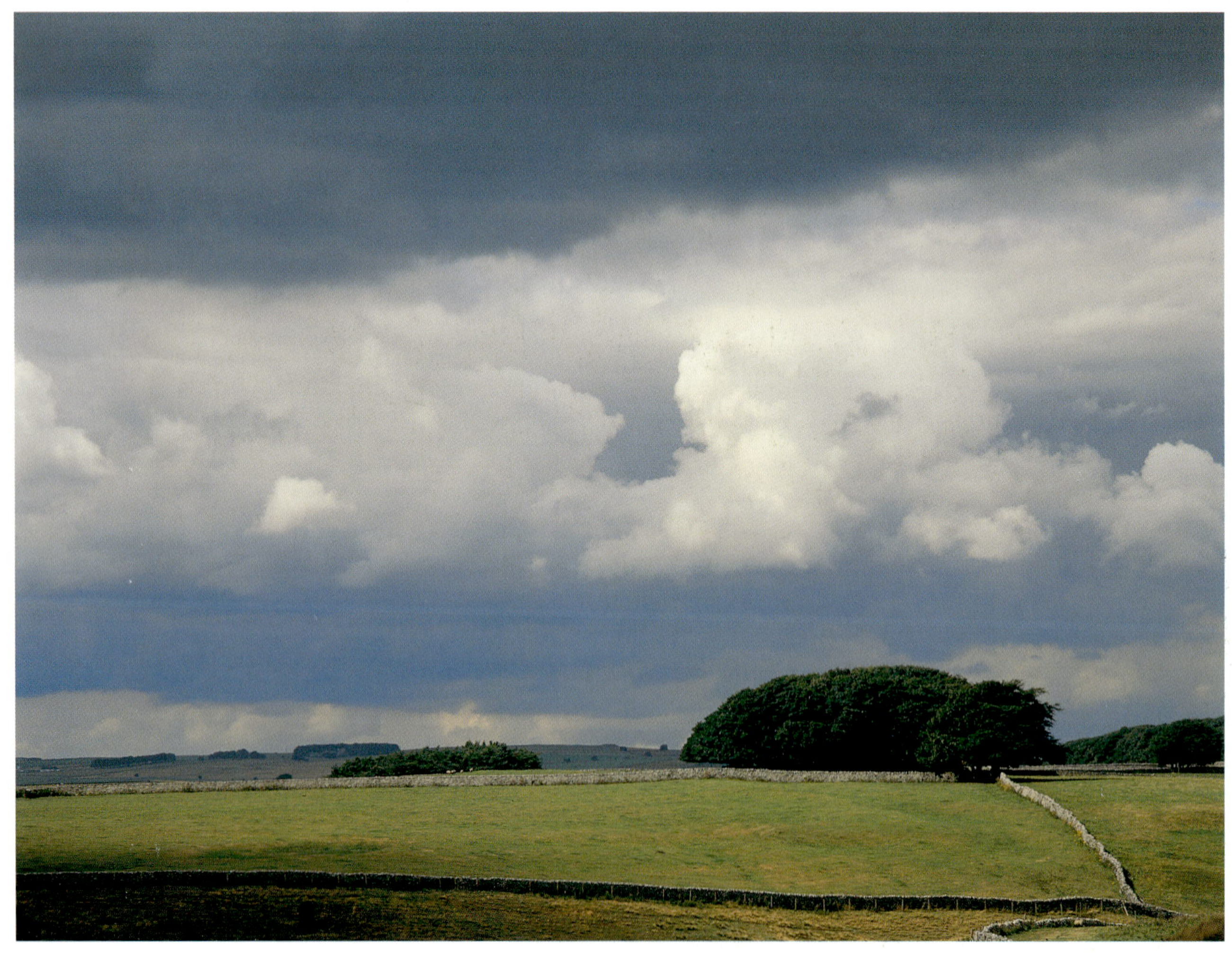

Storm clouds
A summer storm breaks over the White Peak plateau near Monyash at the northern end of Lathkill Dale.

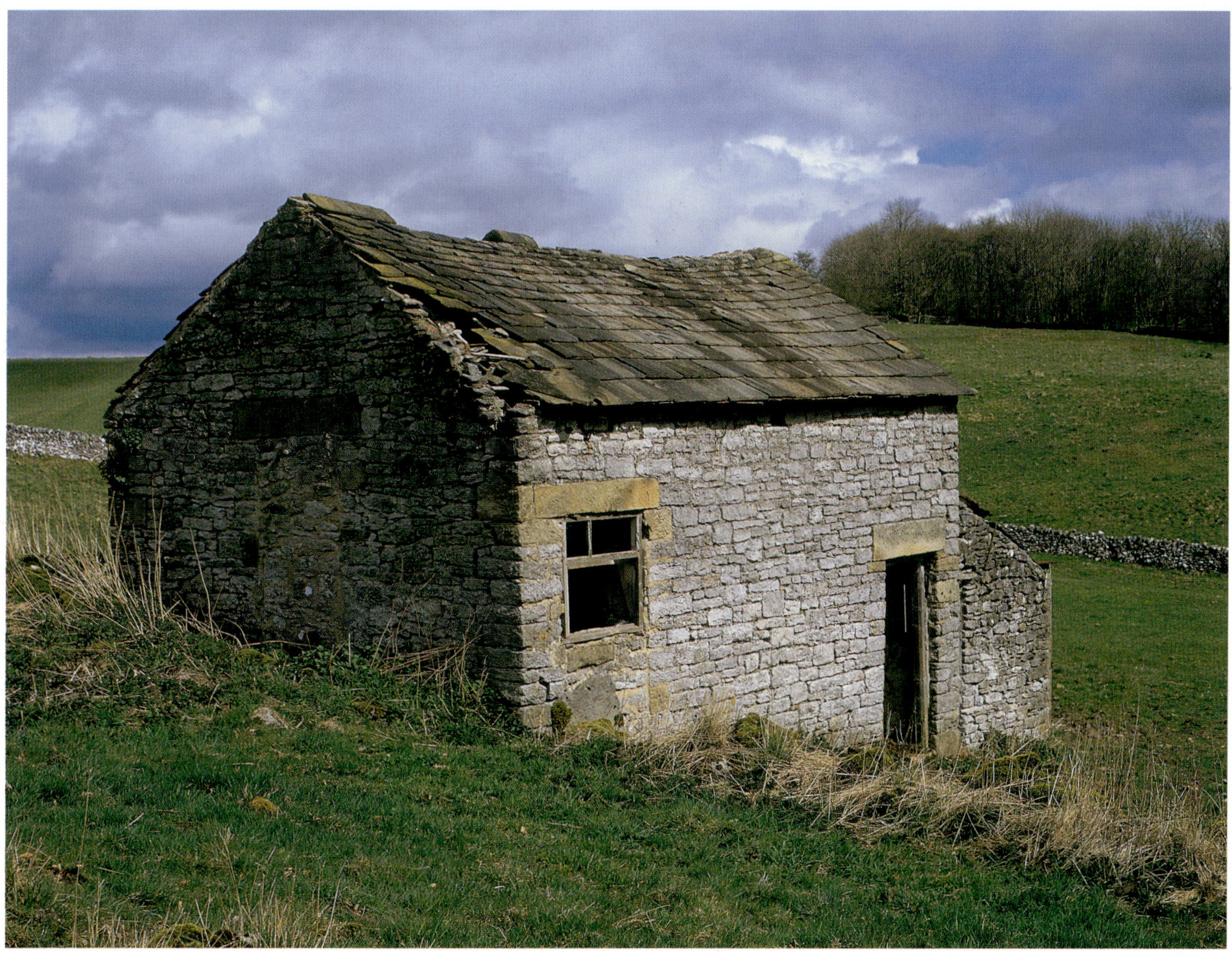

Seeking a new use
Stone barns like this one near Youlgreave form an important feature in the White Peak landscape, although many have been allowed to fall into dereliction.

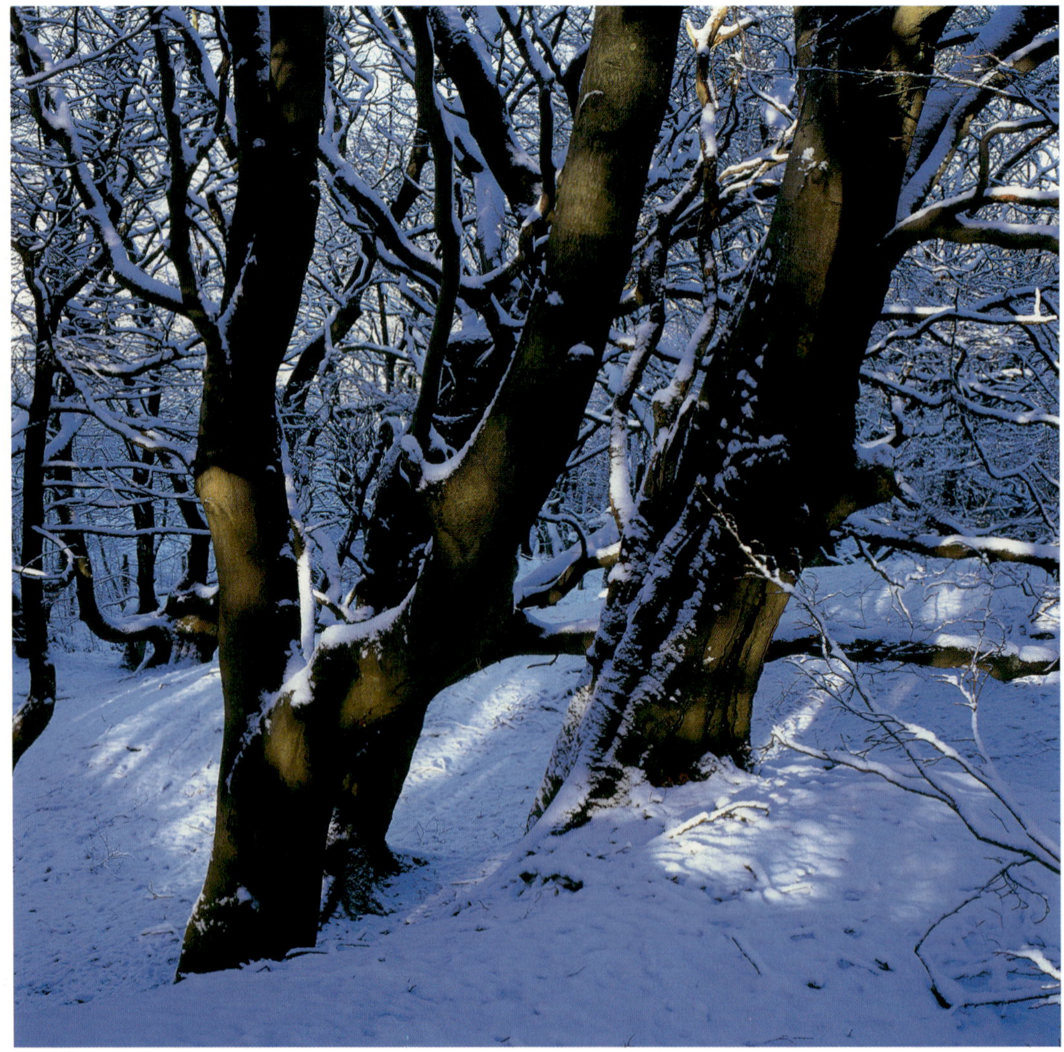

Sunlit trunks
Winter sunshine picks out the trunks of beech trees, in marked contrast with the background of snow-laden trees.

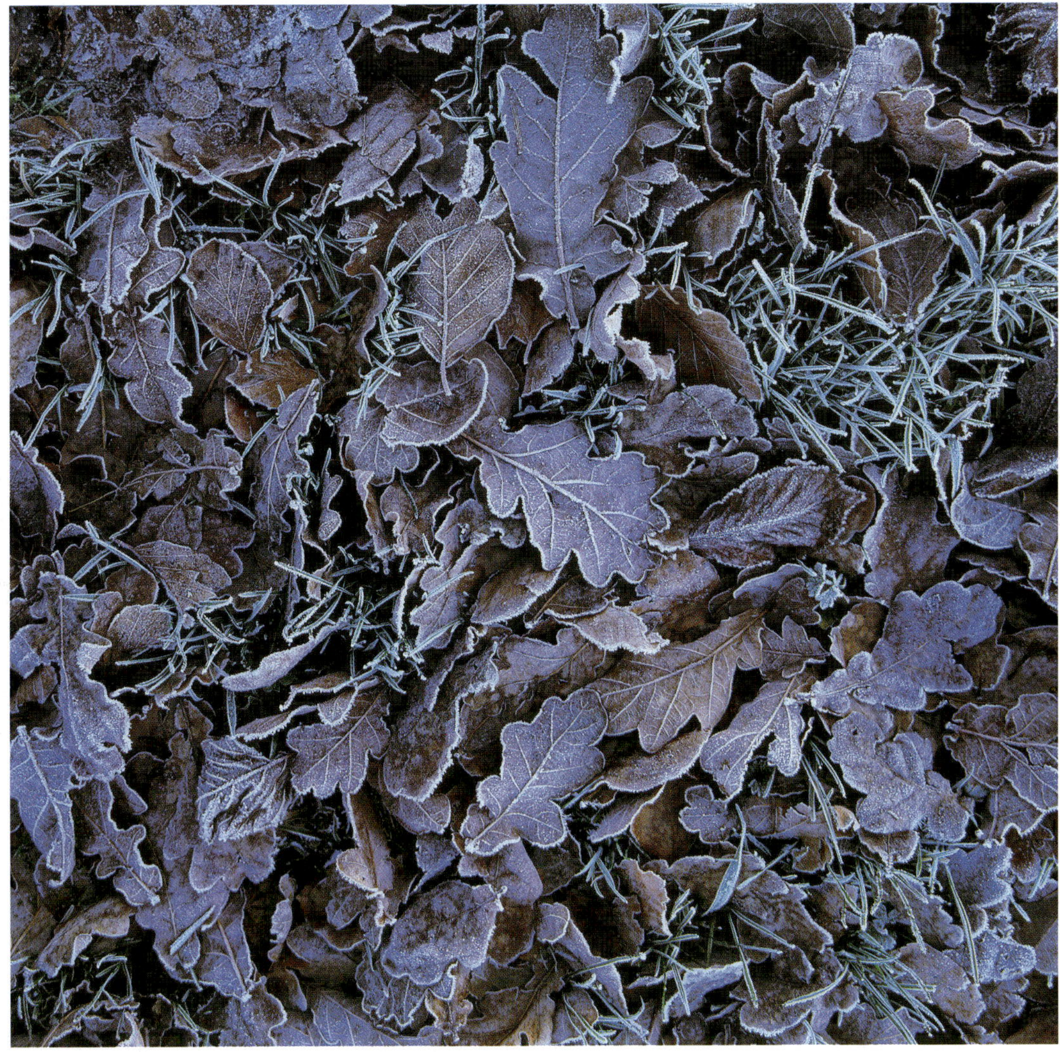

Frozen leaves
Scattered on the woodland floor, the richly-coloured autumn leaves are etched by morning frost.

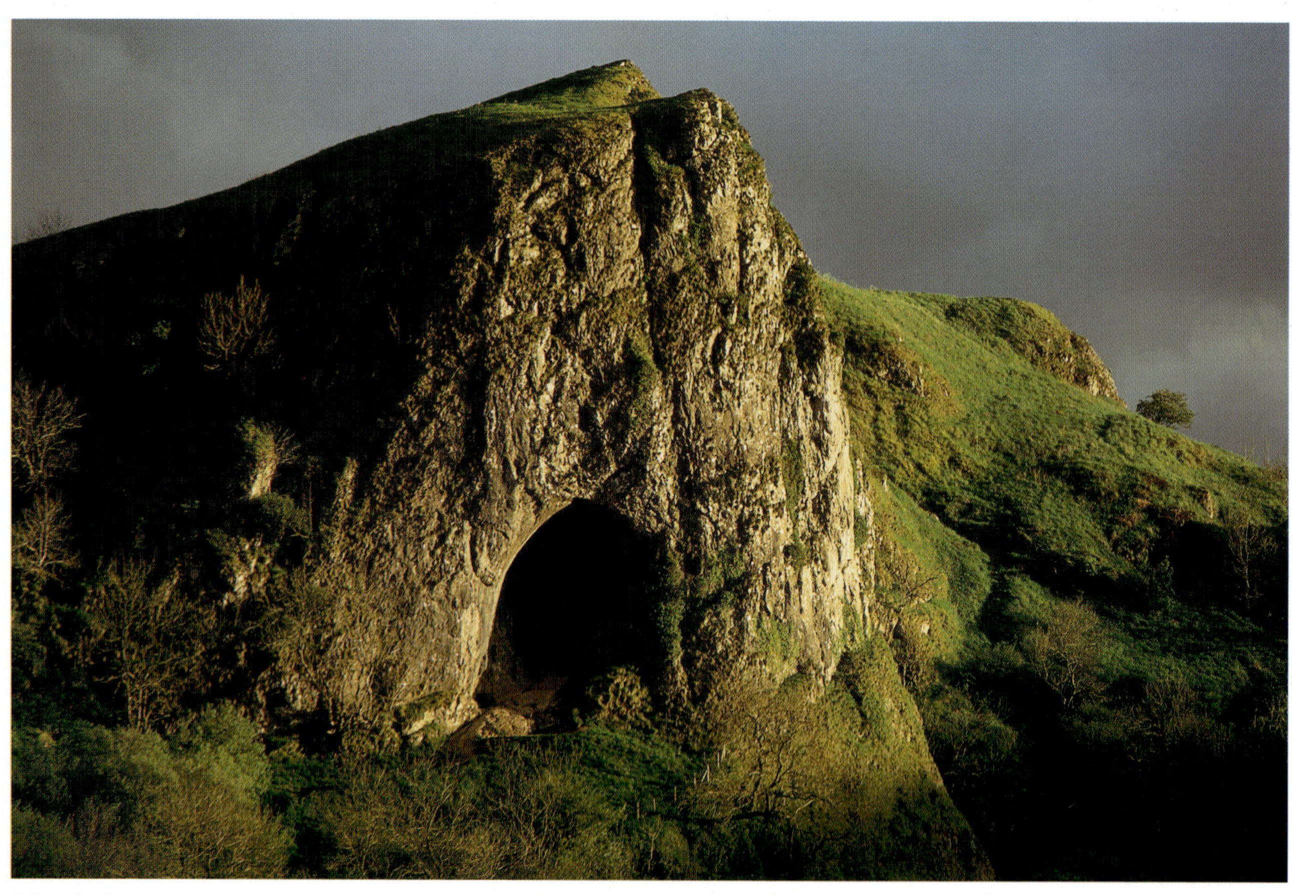

Thor's Cave

Evening summer sunshine illuminates the huge cathedral-like entrance to Thor's Cave in the Manifold Valley.

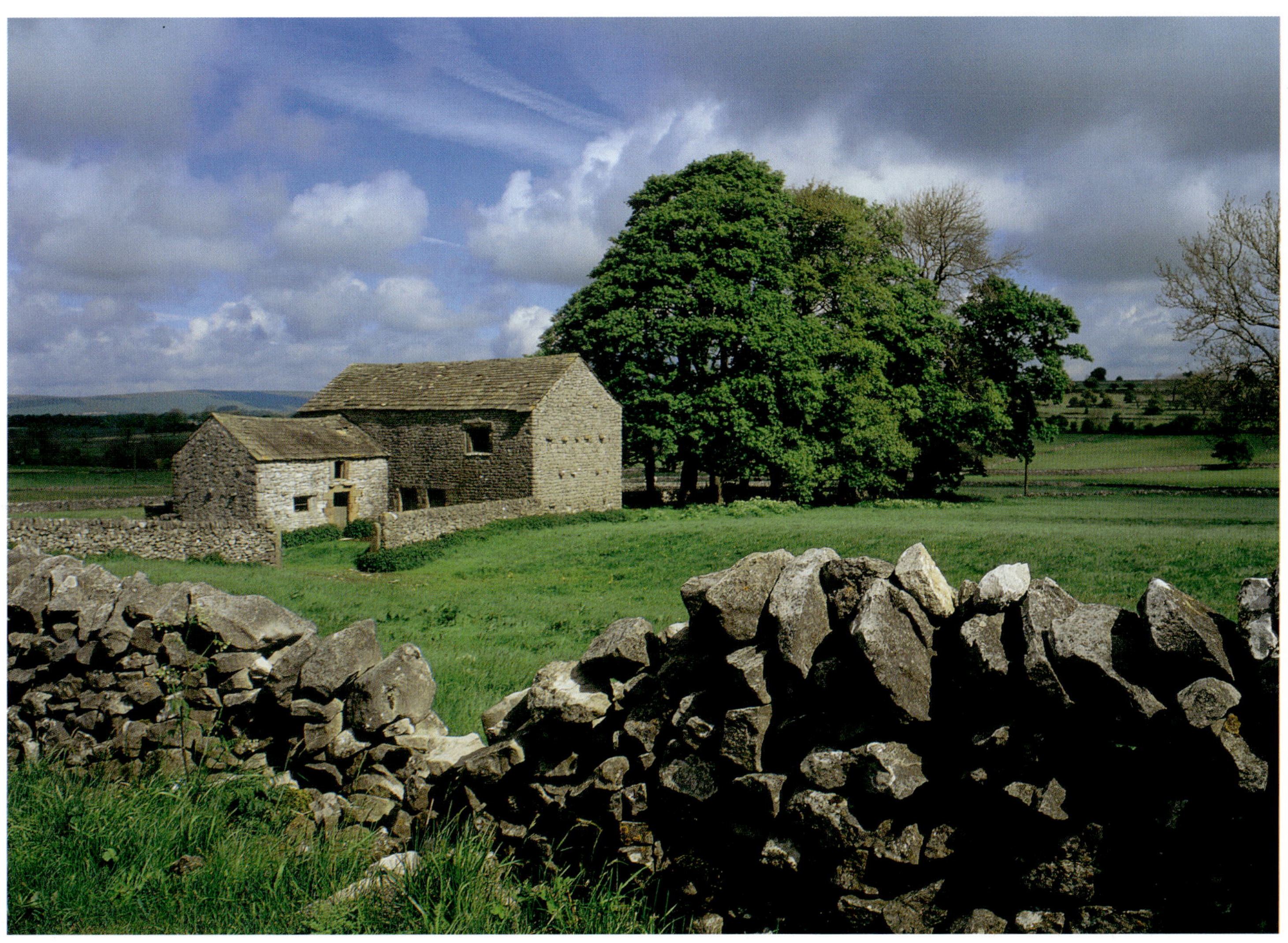

Stone barn at Chelmorton
Spring sunshine warms a stone barn on the edge of the village of Chelmorton.

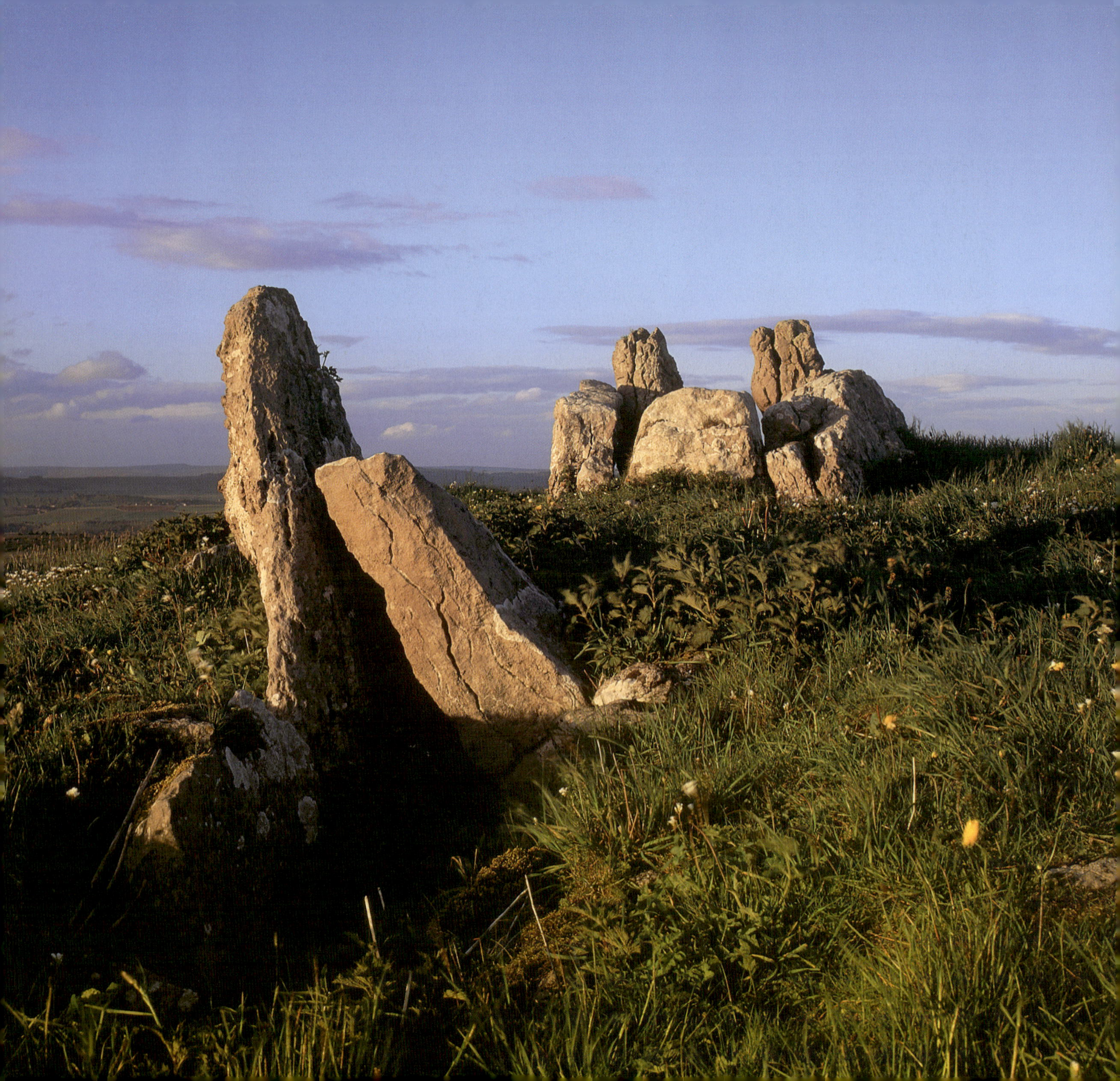

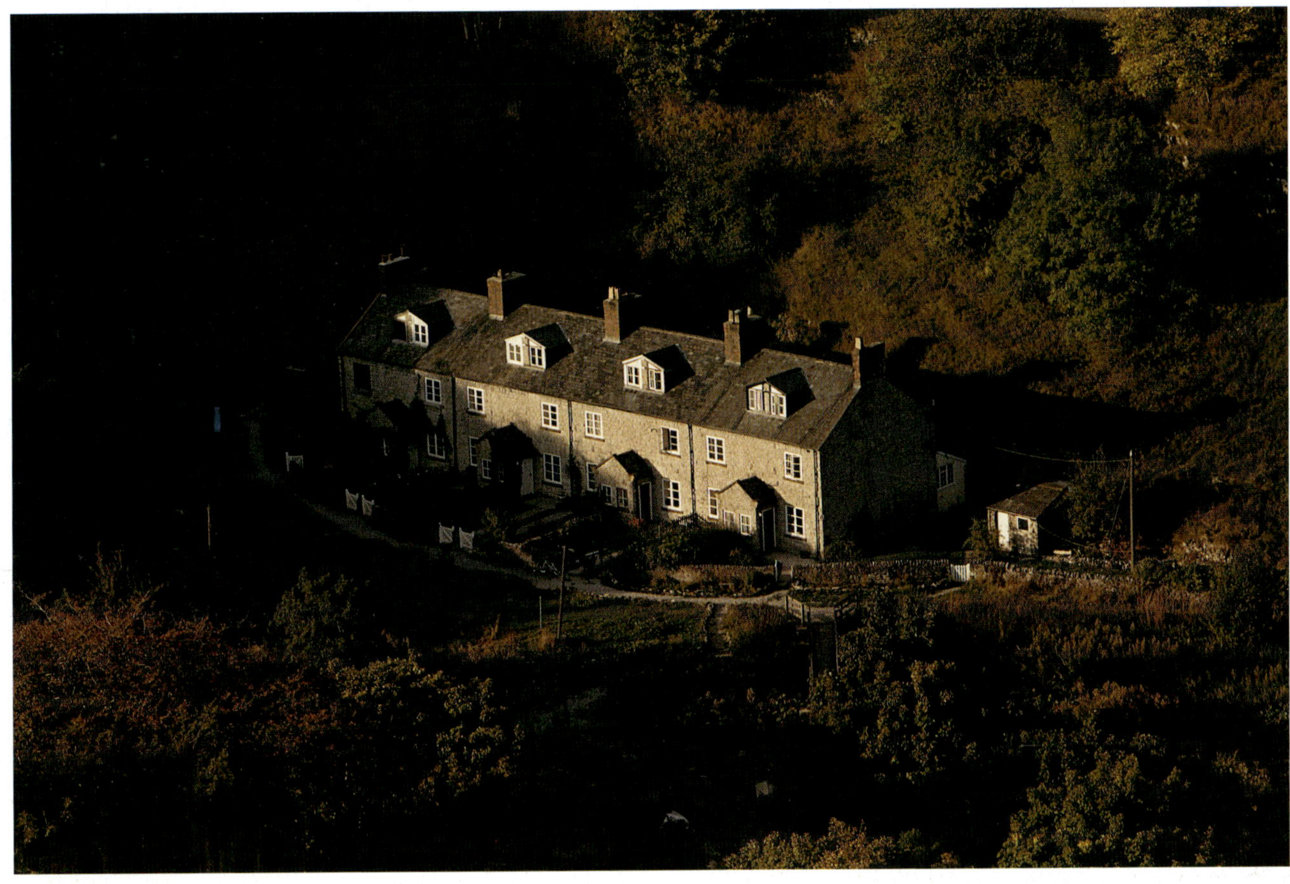

Home station
Evening sunshine on a row of former railwaymen's cottages at the western entrance to Chee Dale near Buxton.

Left: **Five Wells Tomb**
The rays of the setting sun illuminate the Five Wells Neolithic chambered tomb – one of the highest chambered tombs in England – overlooking the Wye Valley near Taddington.

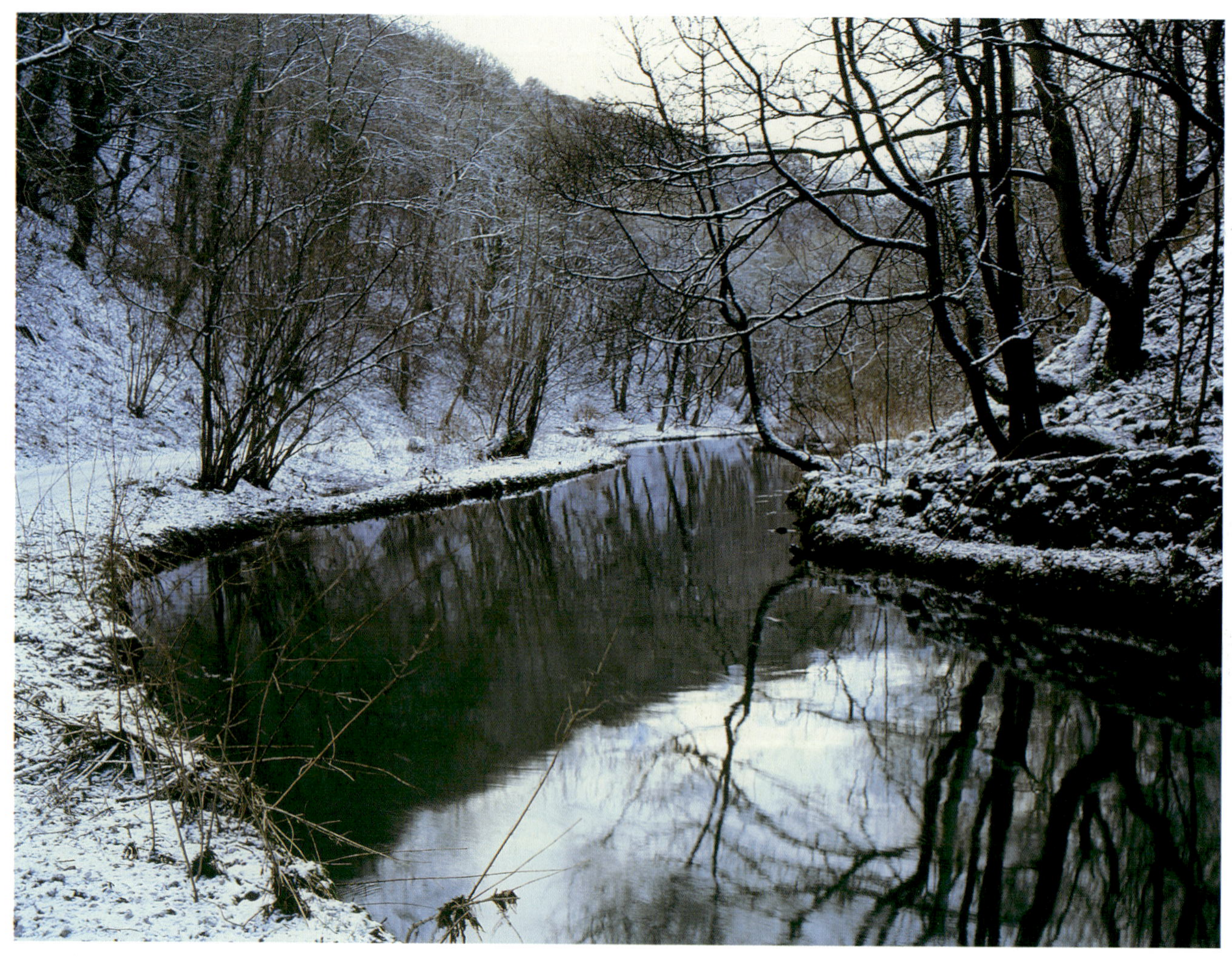

Wandering with the Wye
A January morning along the River Wye, which wanders through the White Peak to join the Derwent at Rowsley.

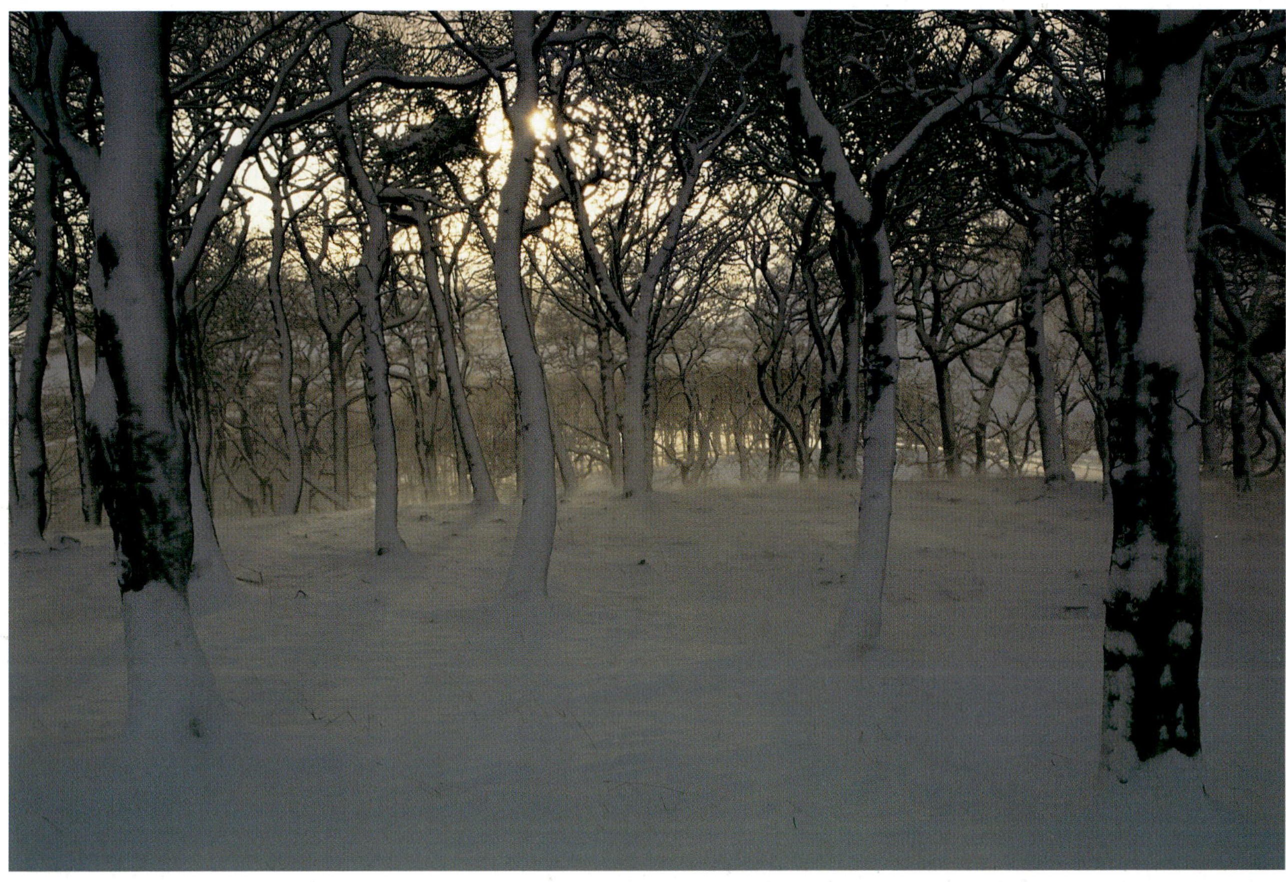

Winter sunrise

The light from the rising sun highlights the windblown snow, creating long shadows in this small copse above the Wye Valley.

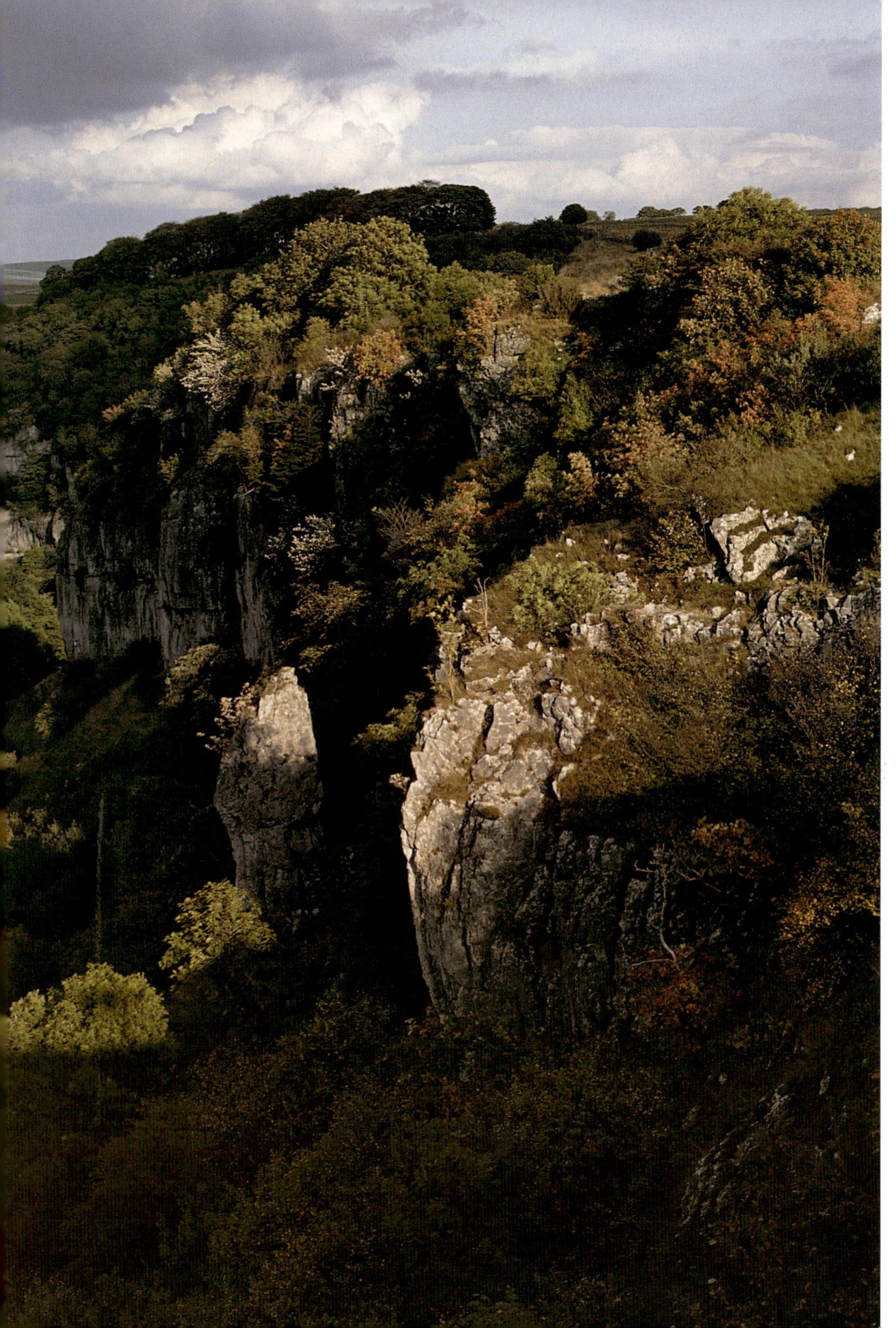

Chee Dale
The autumnal colours of the trees contrast with the grey limestone cliffs on the steep slopes overlooking the River Wye in Cheedale.

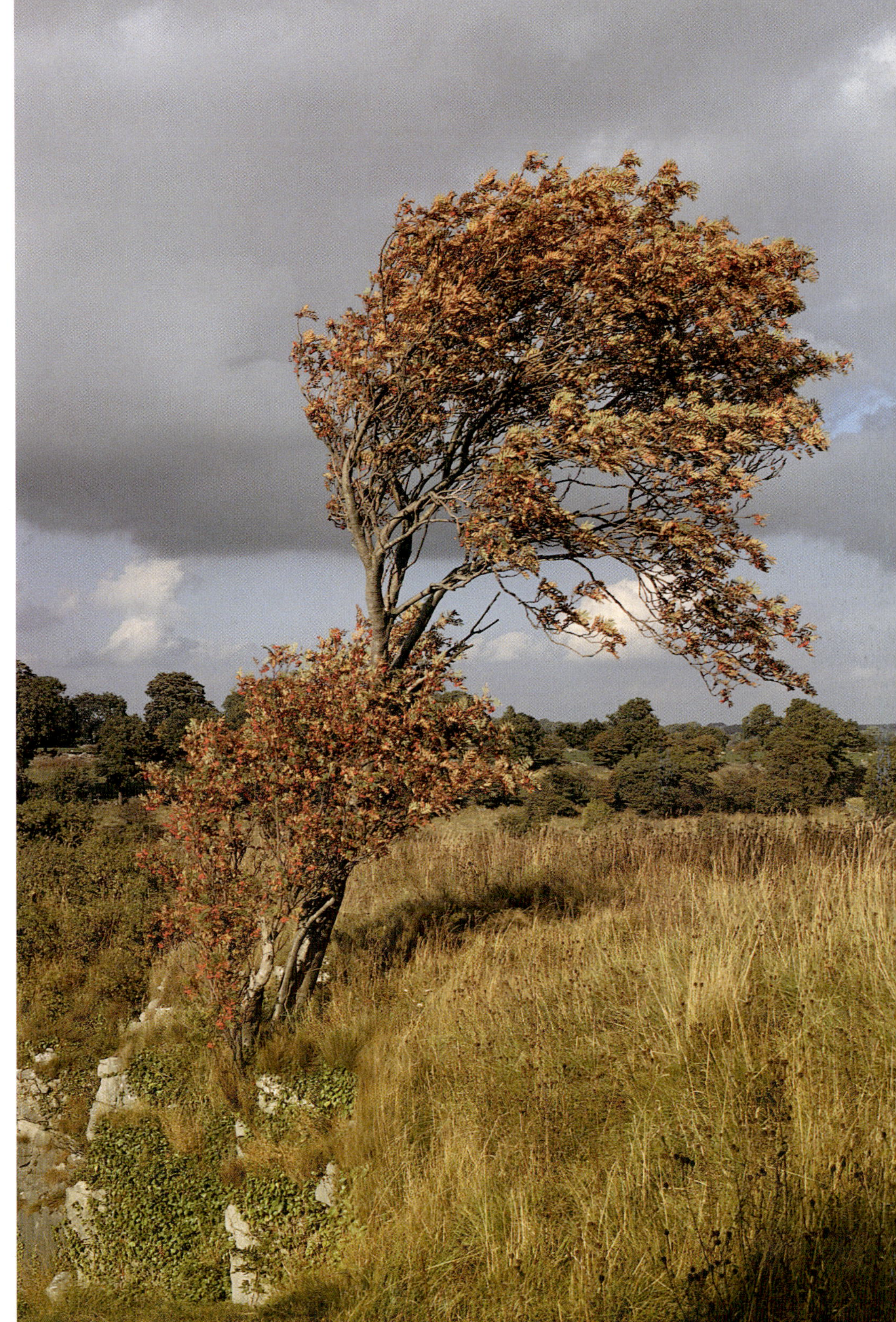

Lone tree
A lone, windblown rowan tree struggles for survival on the edge of the steep limestone cliffs in Chee Dale.

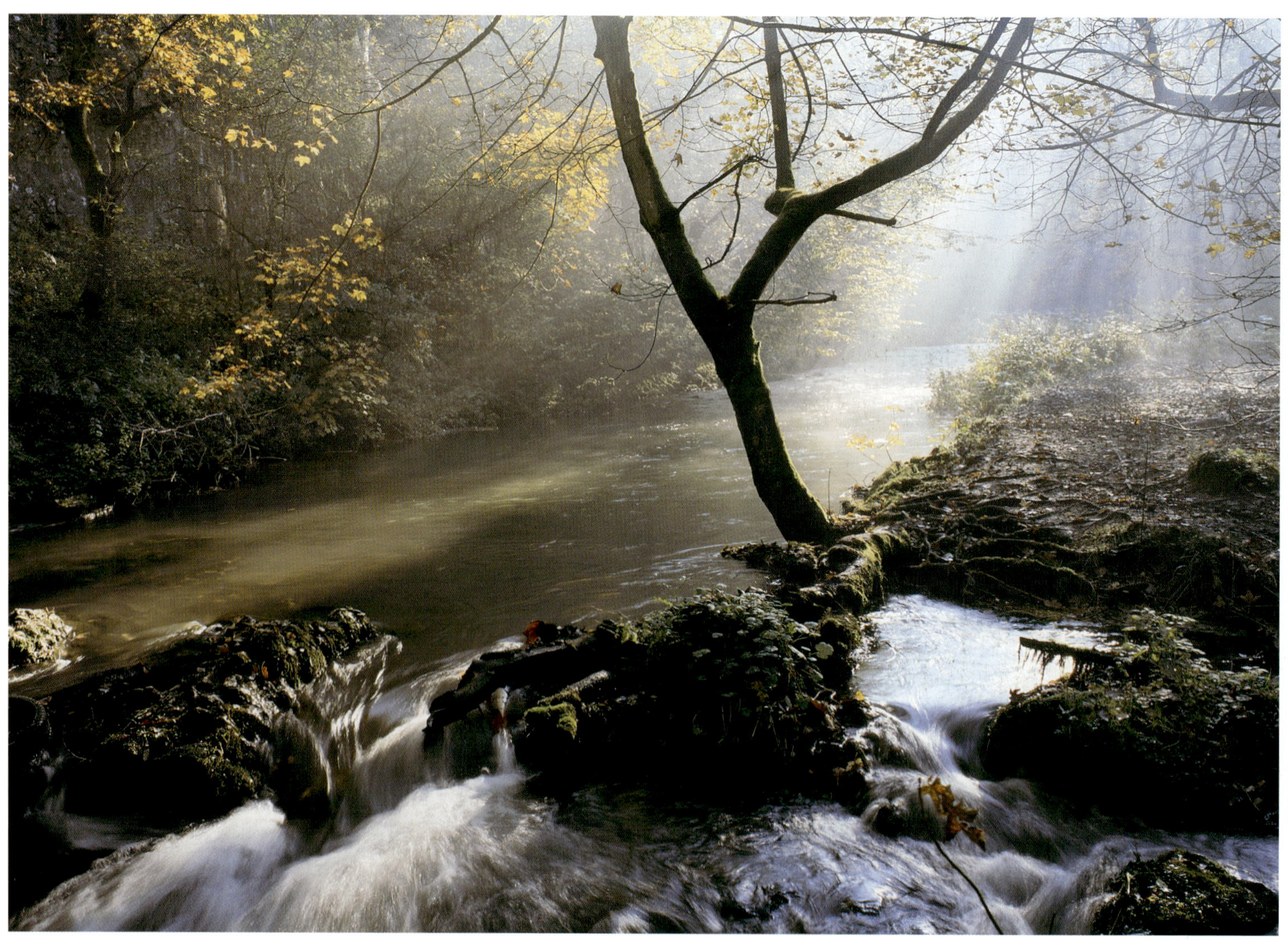

Mist on the Wye
Early morning mist rises from the Wye as it weaves its way through Chee Dale.

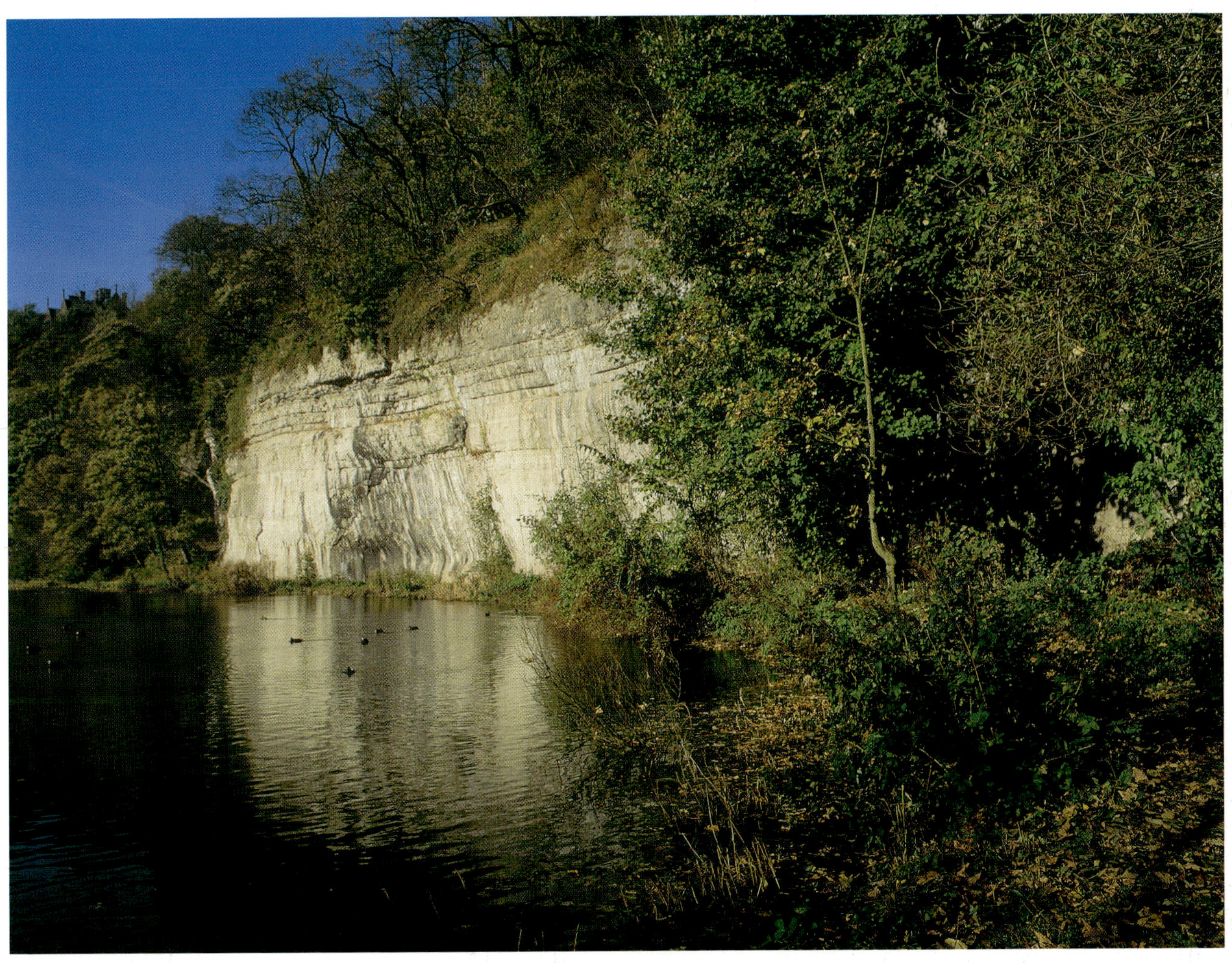

Rubicon Wall
The limestone cliff of Rubicon Wall in Water-cum-Jolly Dale, reflected in the old mill pond, which once provided the water power for Cressbrook Mill.

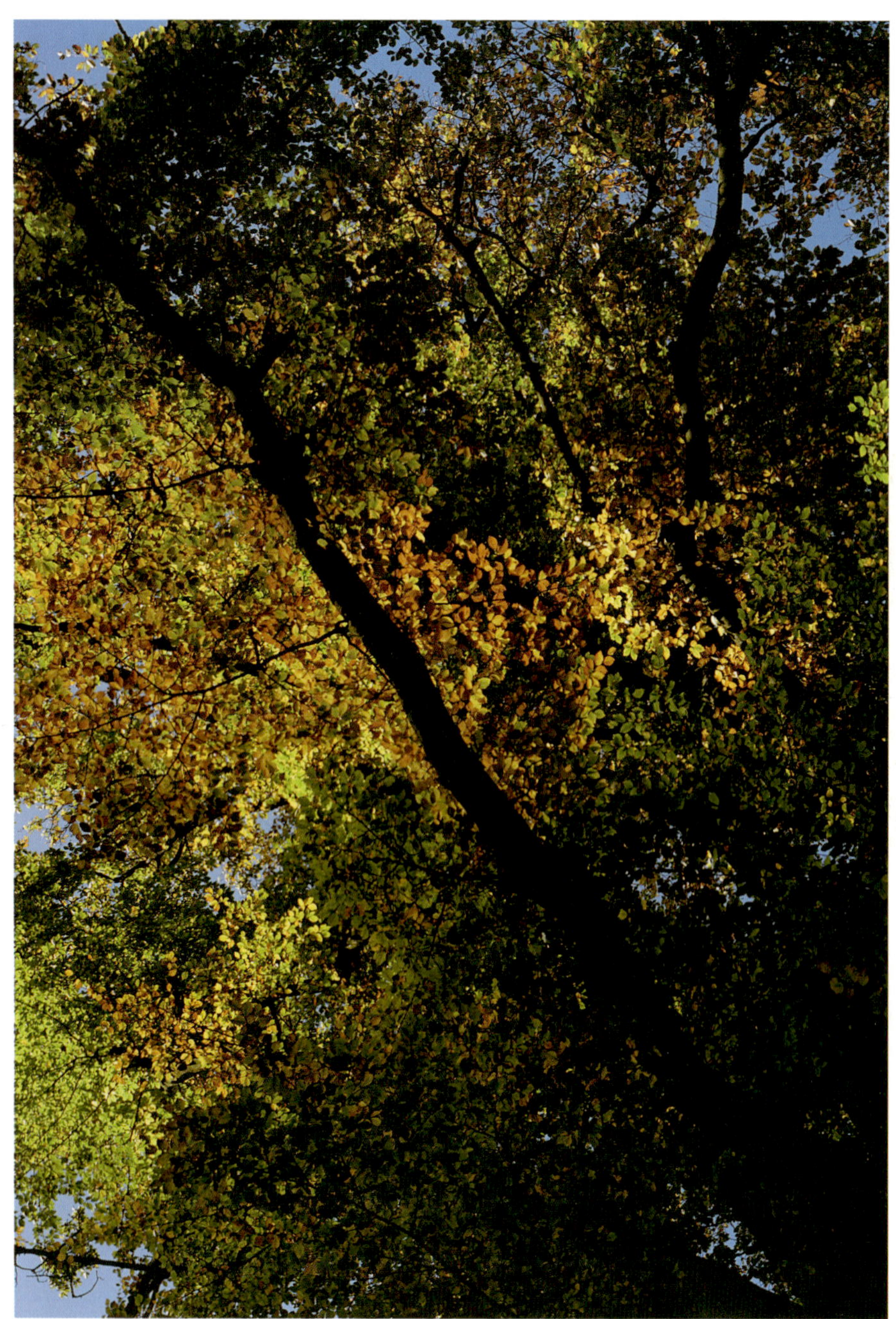

Illuminated leaves
An explosion of autumn colours set against the black veins of a tree overhanging the banks of the Wye.

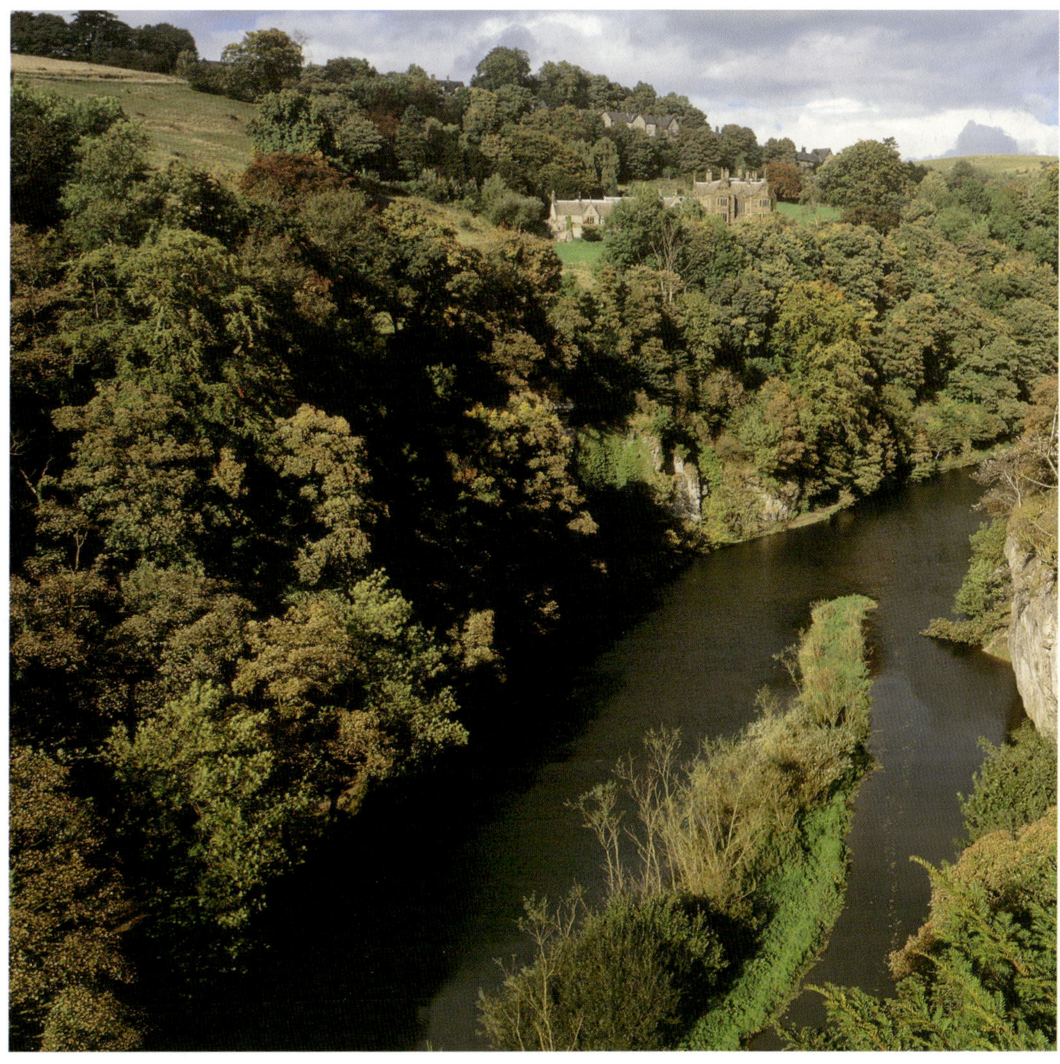

Water-cum-Jolly

The beautiful wooded valley of Water-cum-Jolly Dale, through which the River Wye flows on its journey south.

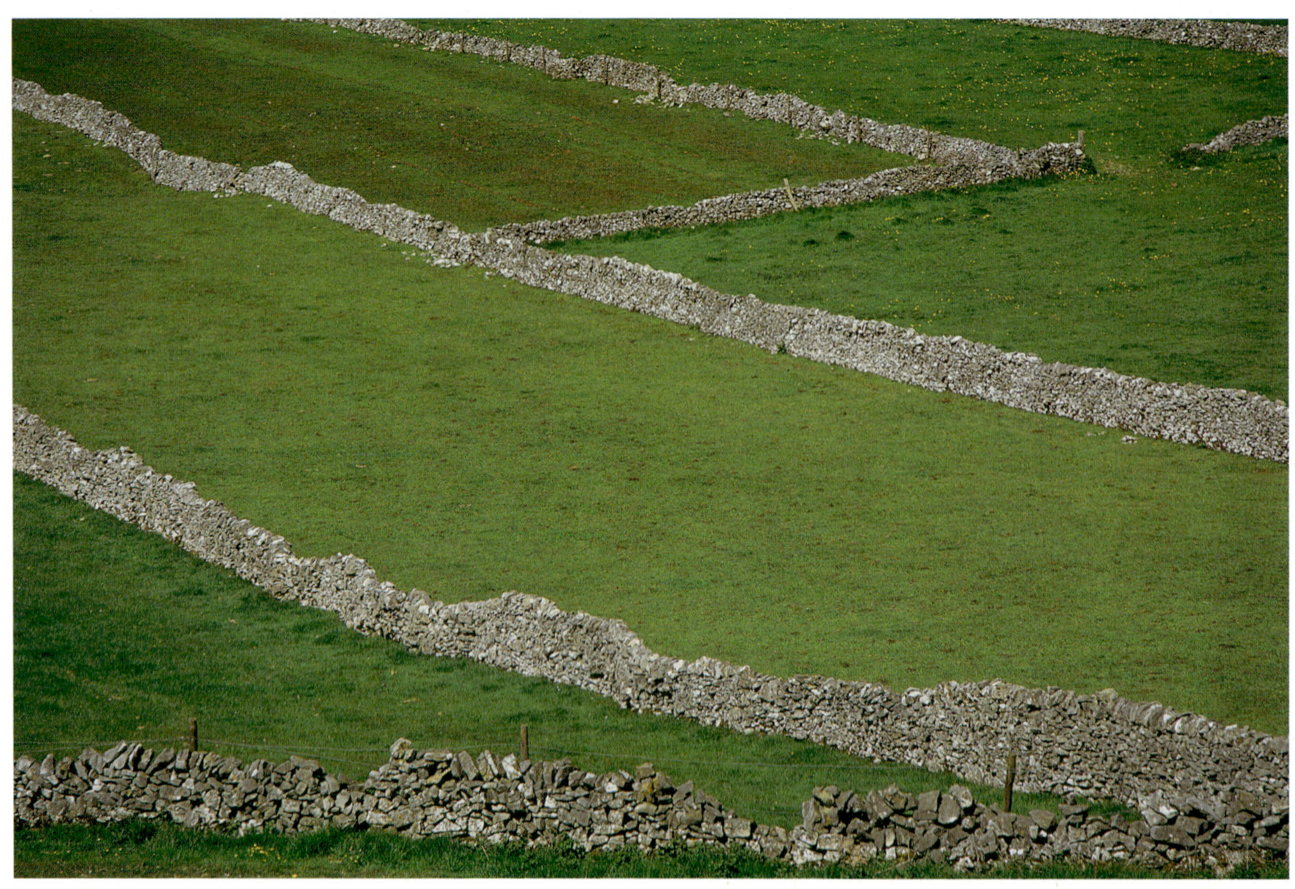

Wall patterns
Limestone wall patterns on the White Peak plateau near Chelmorton. These historic walls preserve the outline of medieval strip fields.

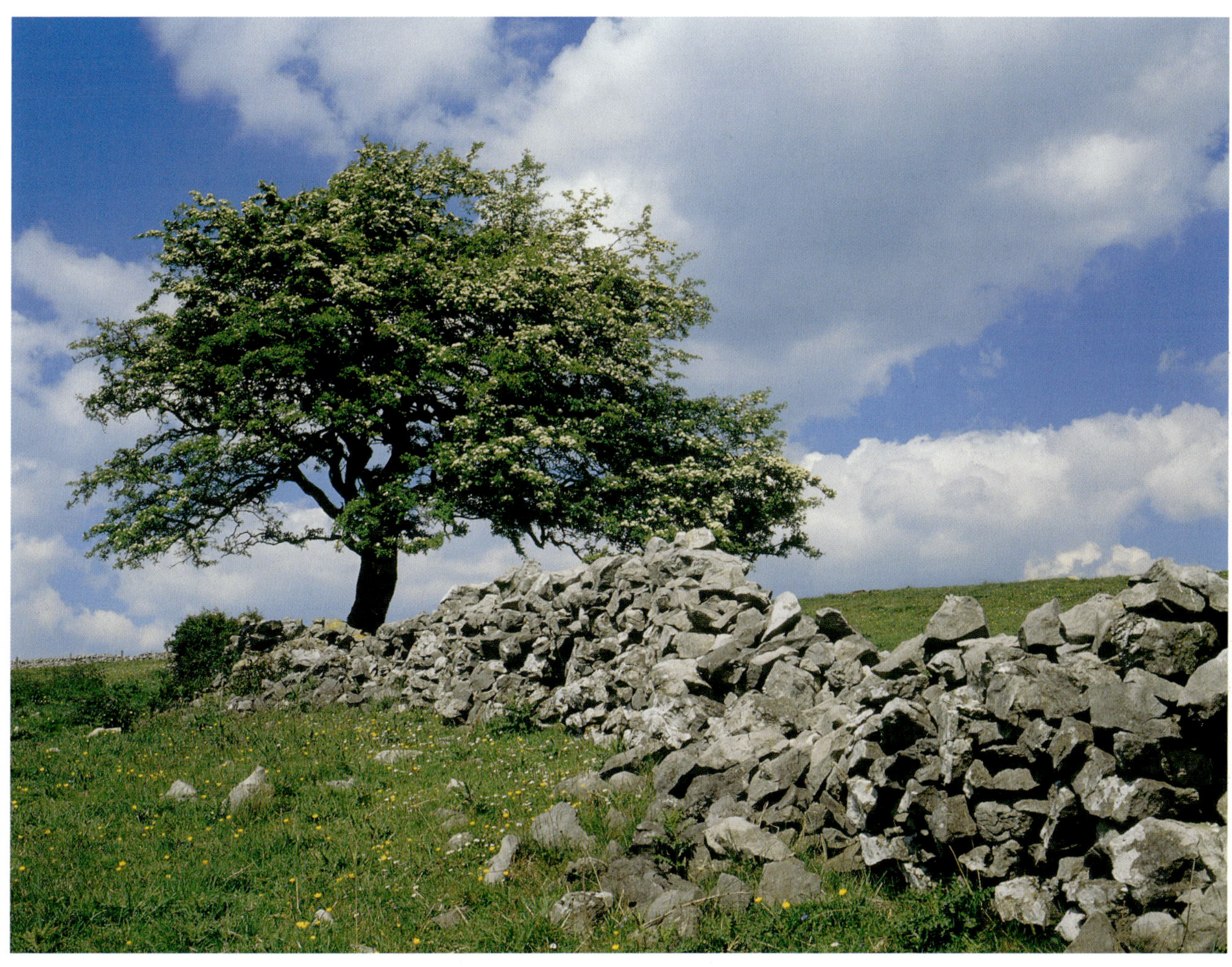

Hawthorn blossom
A lone hawthorn tree in its blossomy spring finery.

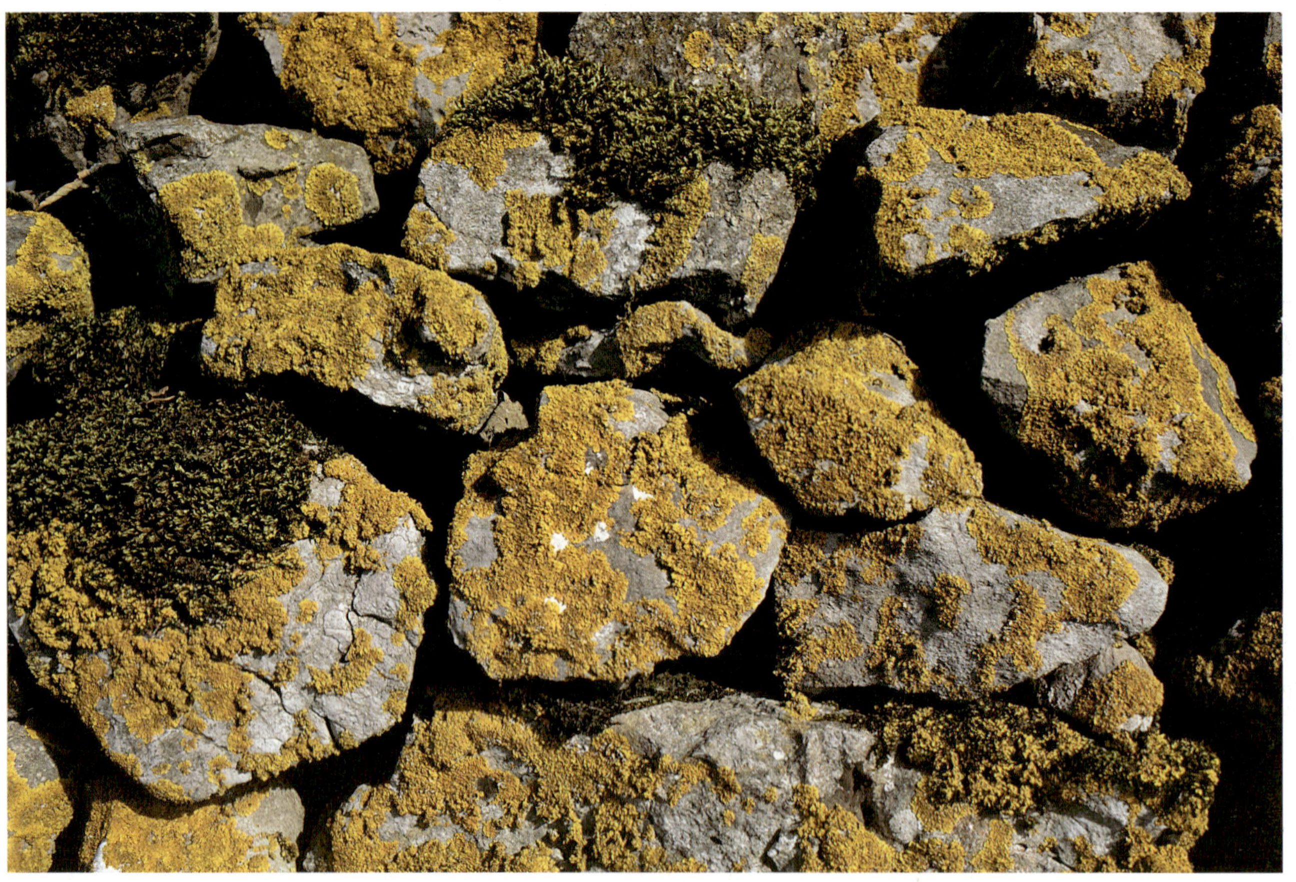

Lichens and mosses
Lichens and mosses add a touch of colour to an ancient limestone wall.

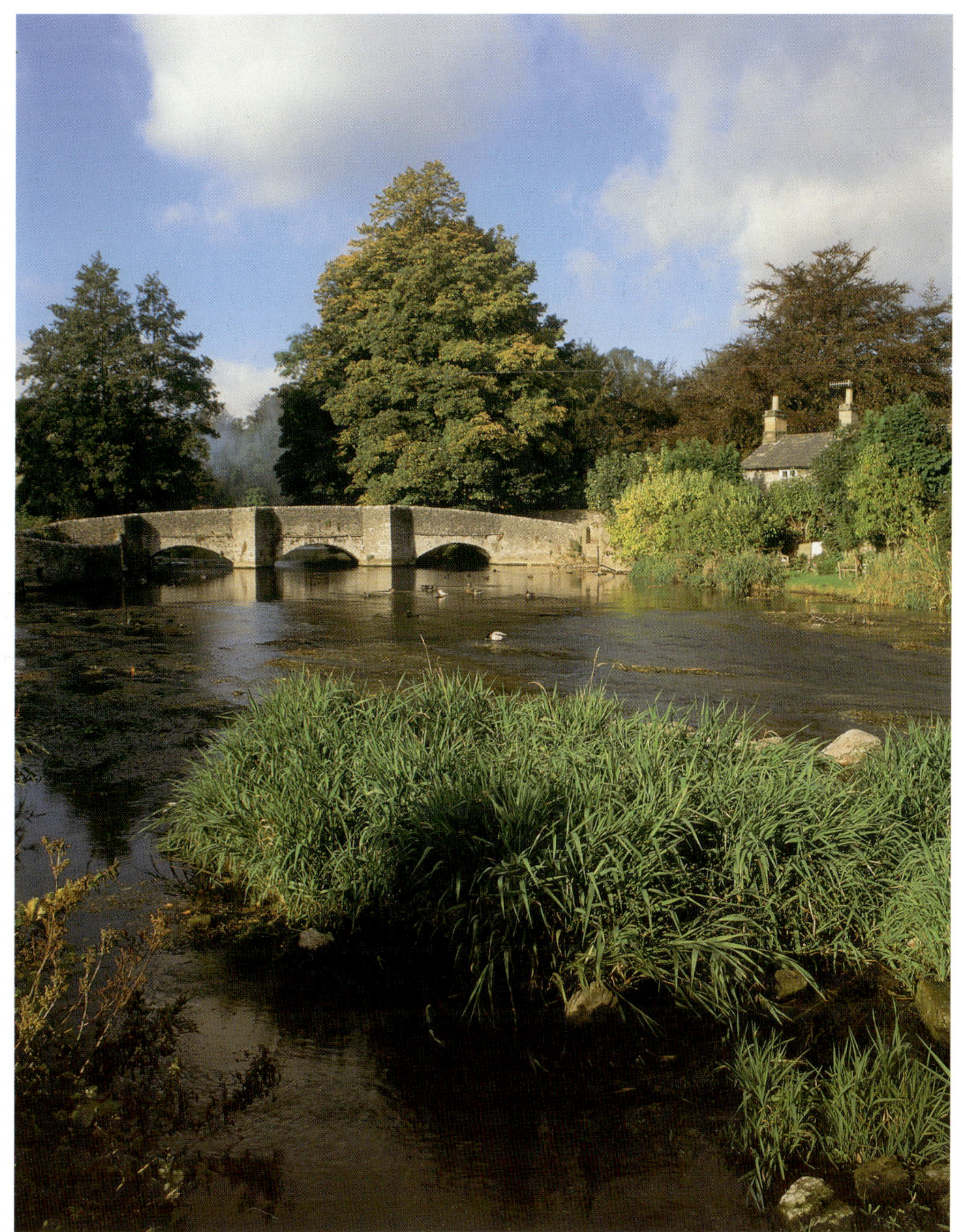

Sheepwash Bridge
The seventeenth century, three-arched Sheepwash Bridge over the River Wye near Ashford-in-the-Water.

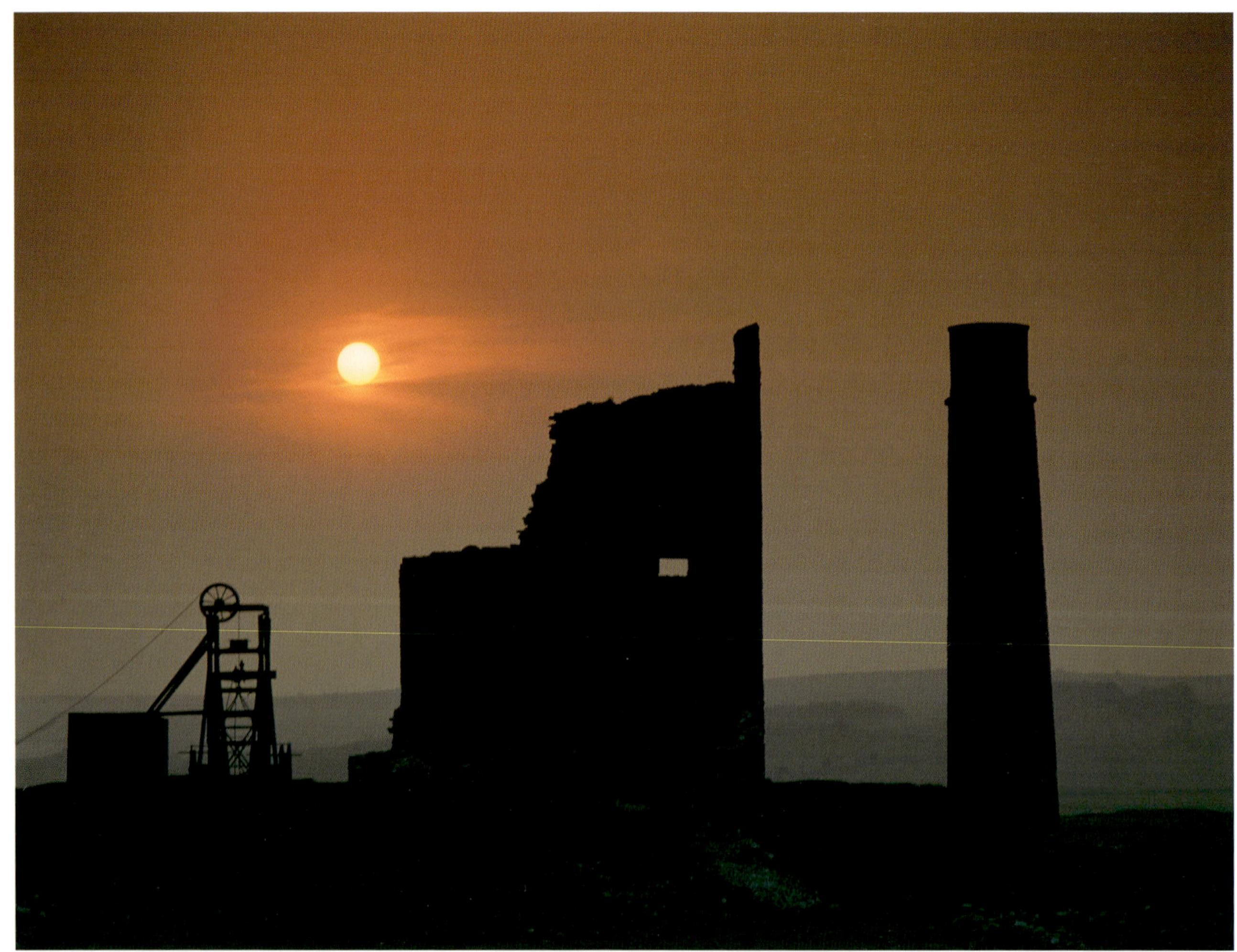

Magpie Mine
The stark outline of the Magpie Mine, the most complete remains of a lead mine in the Peak District.

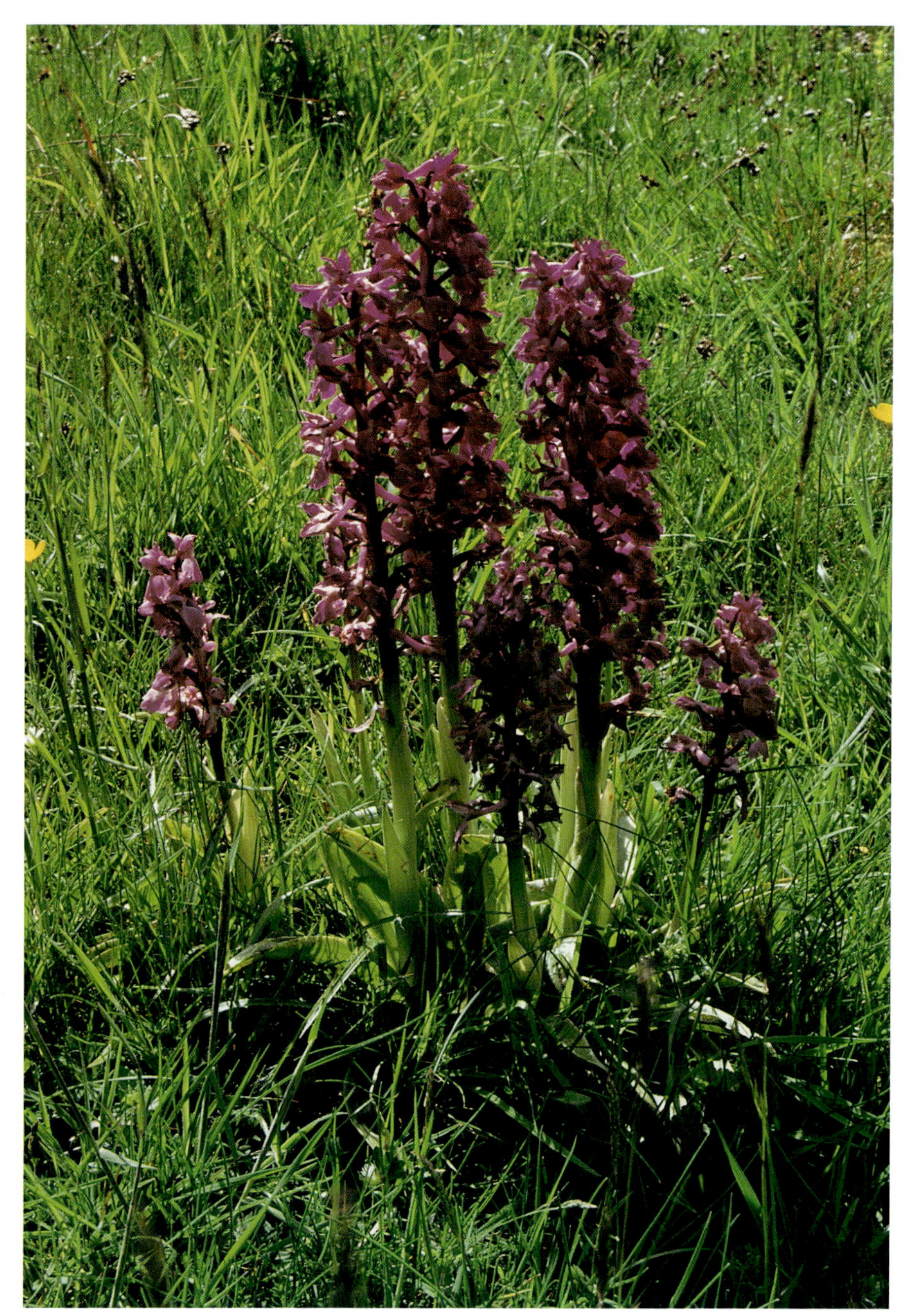

Purple Orchids
Early purple orchids in Deep Dale, near Sheldon.

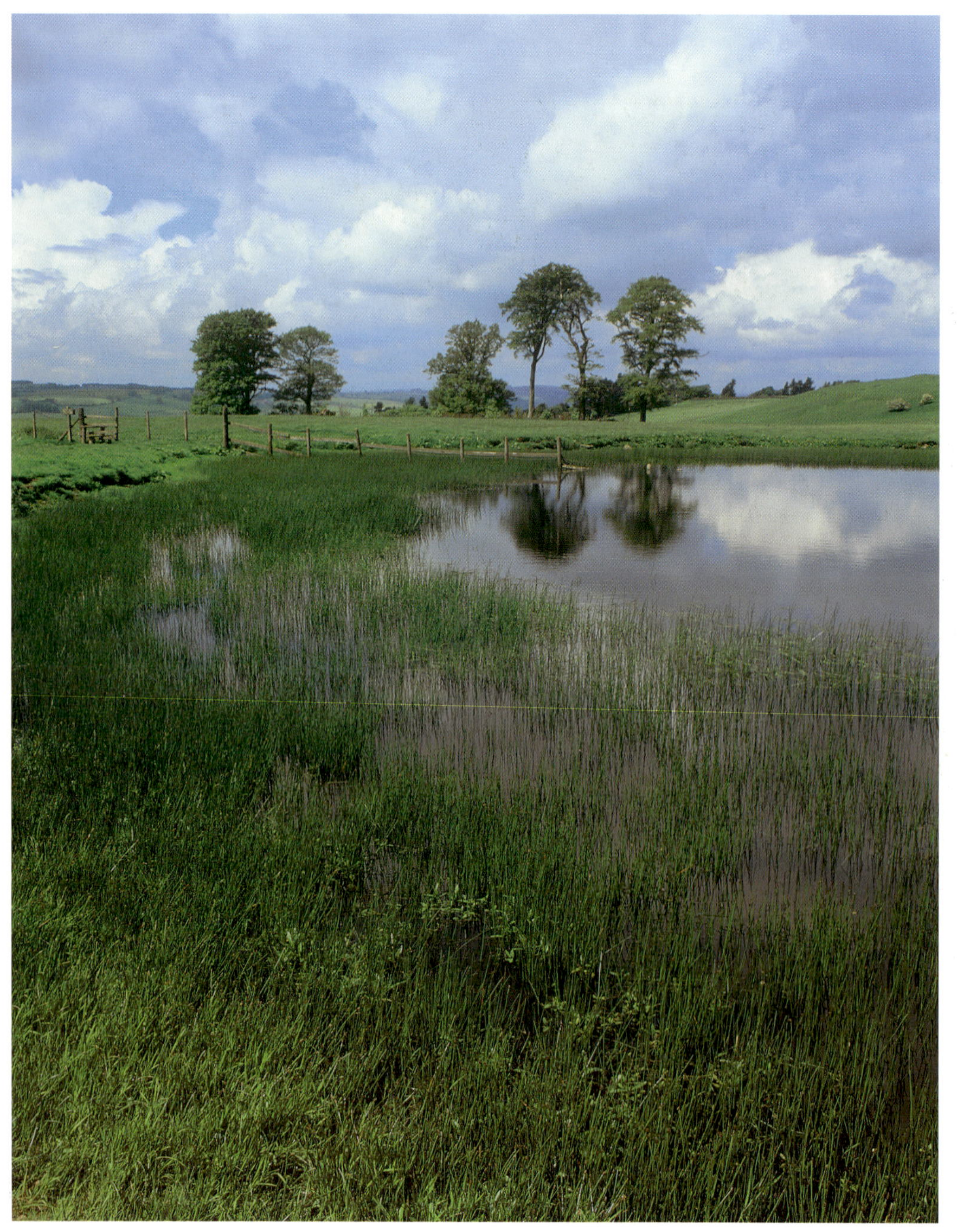

Summer reflections
Reflections in the small tarn on the broad, grassy Calton Pastures above Bakewell.

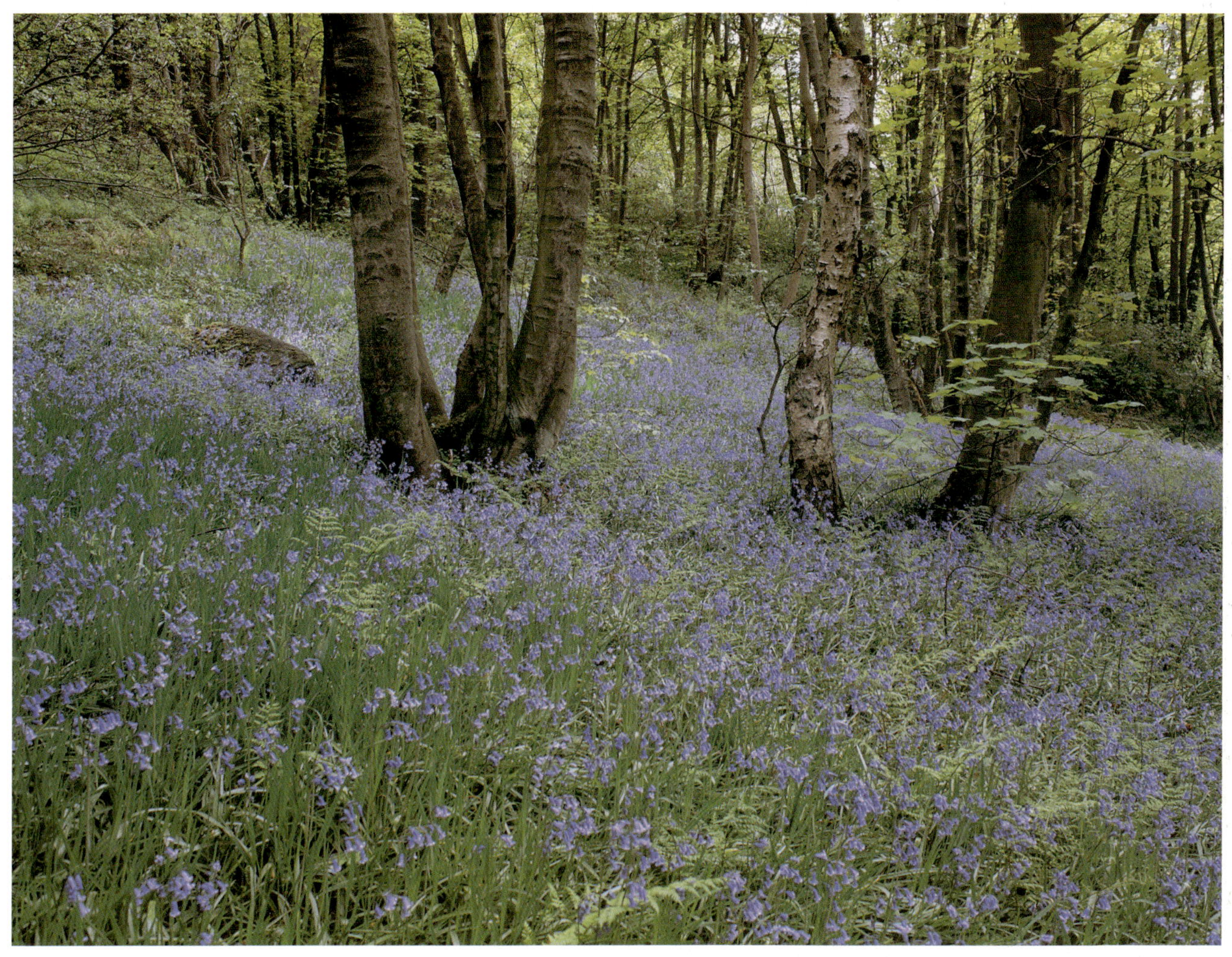

A mist of bluebells

A sea of blue cascades down the grassy slopes in Manners Wood above Bakewell.

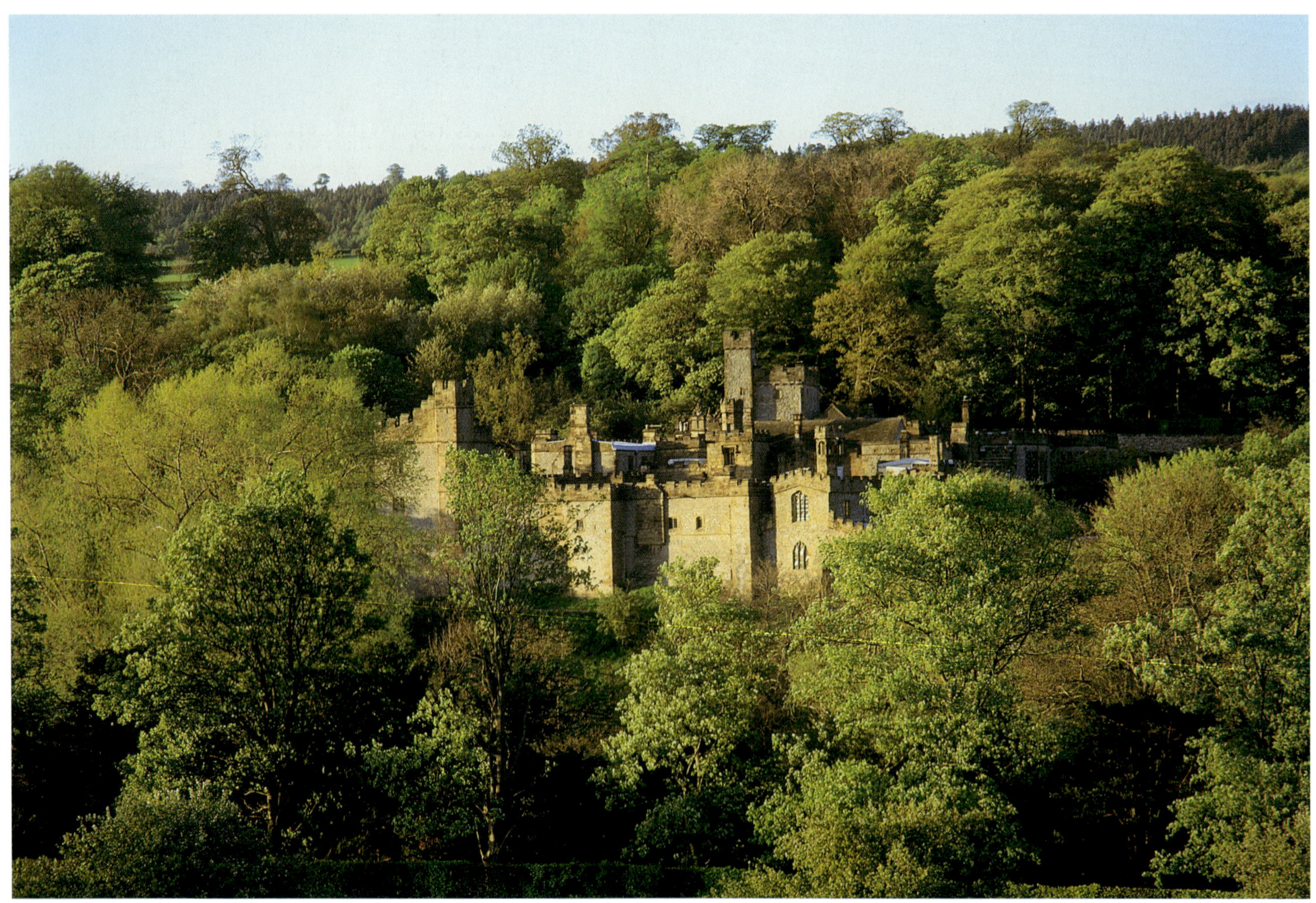

Haddon Hall

In the evening spring sunshine, the warm coloured walls of Haddon Hall, one of the finest medieval houses in England, contrast with the innumerable shades of green of the fresh leaves on the trees overlooking the River Wye.

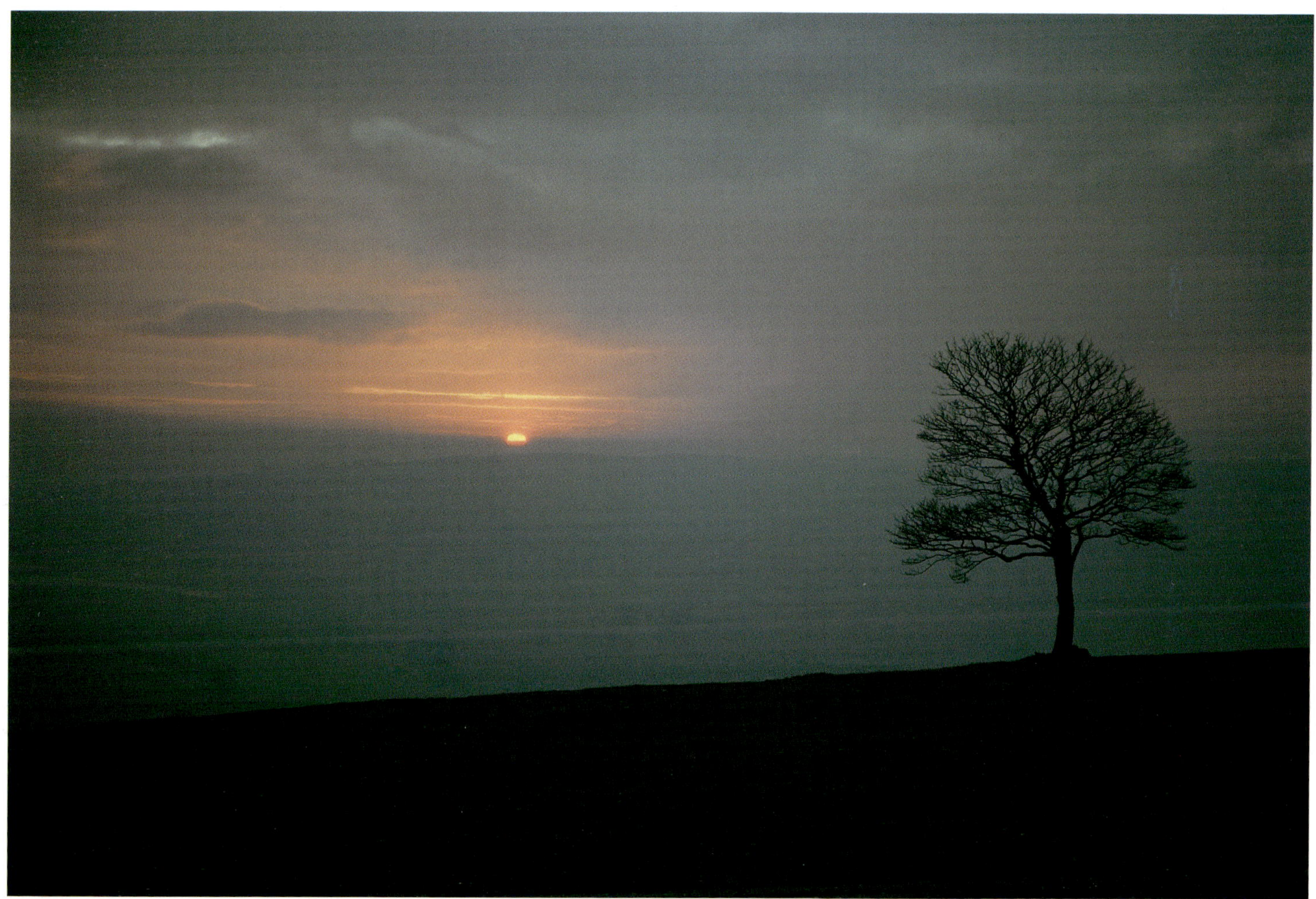

Lone sentinel
This tree acts as a lone sentinel below the Roaches, as the sun sets across the Staffordshire Moors.

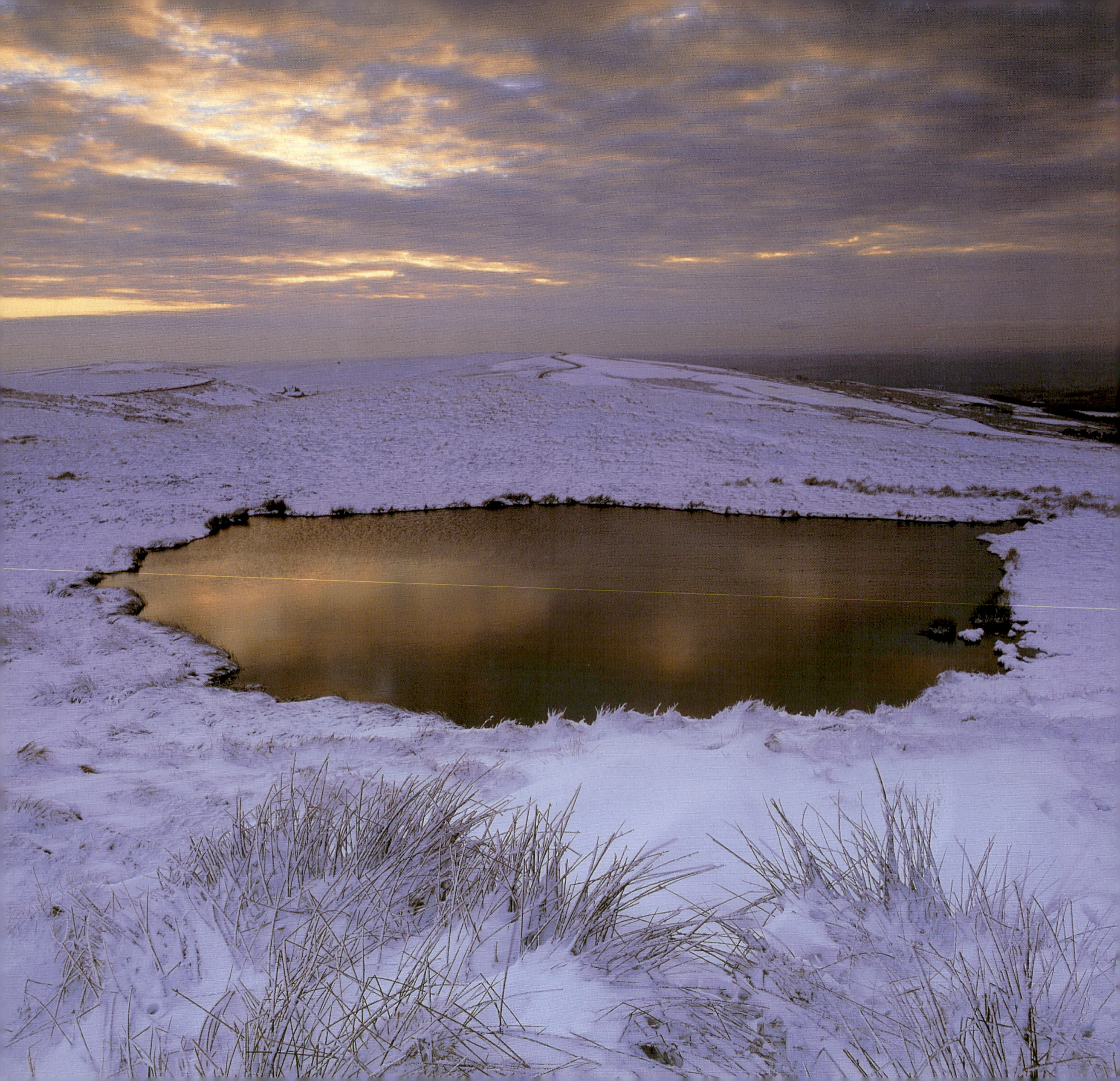

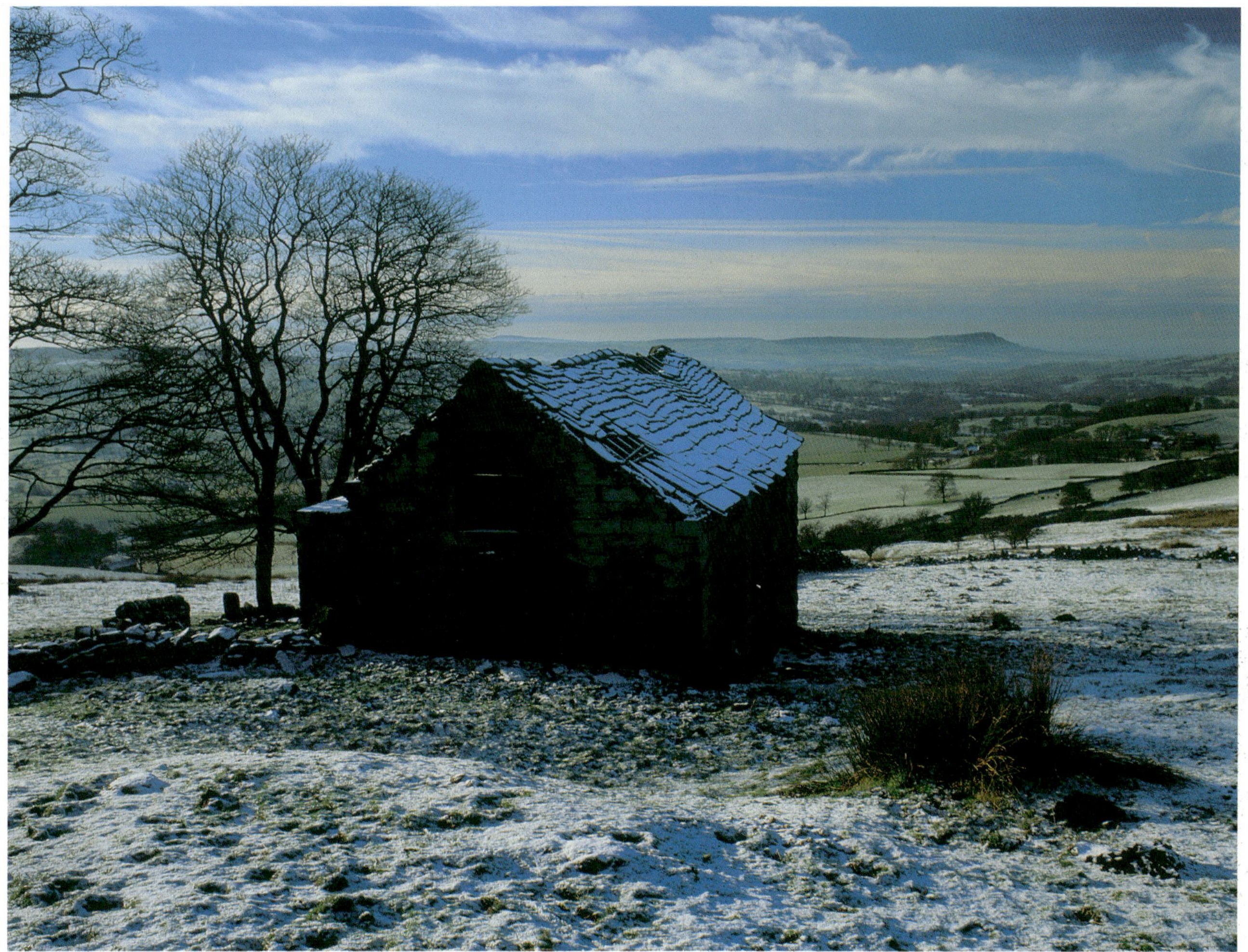

Winter barn
A snow-covered derelict barn forms a dramatic foreground for this view westwards from Roach End.

Left: **Mermaid's Pool**
A winter sunset reflected in Blake Mere, which retains the legend of a mermaid. The pool nestles in a moorland hollow a few miles east of the Roaches, near Warslow.

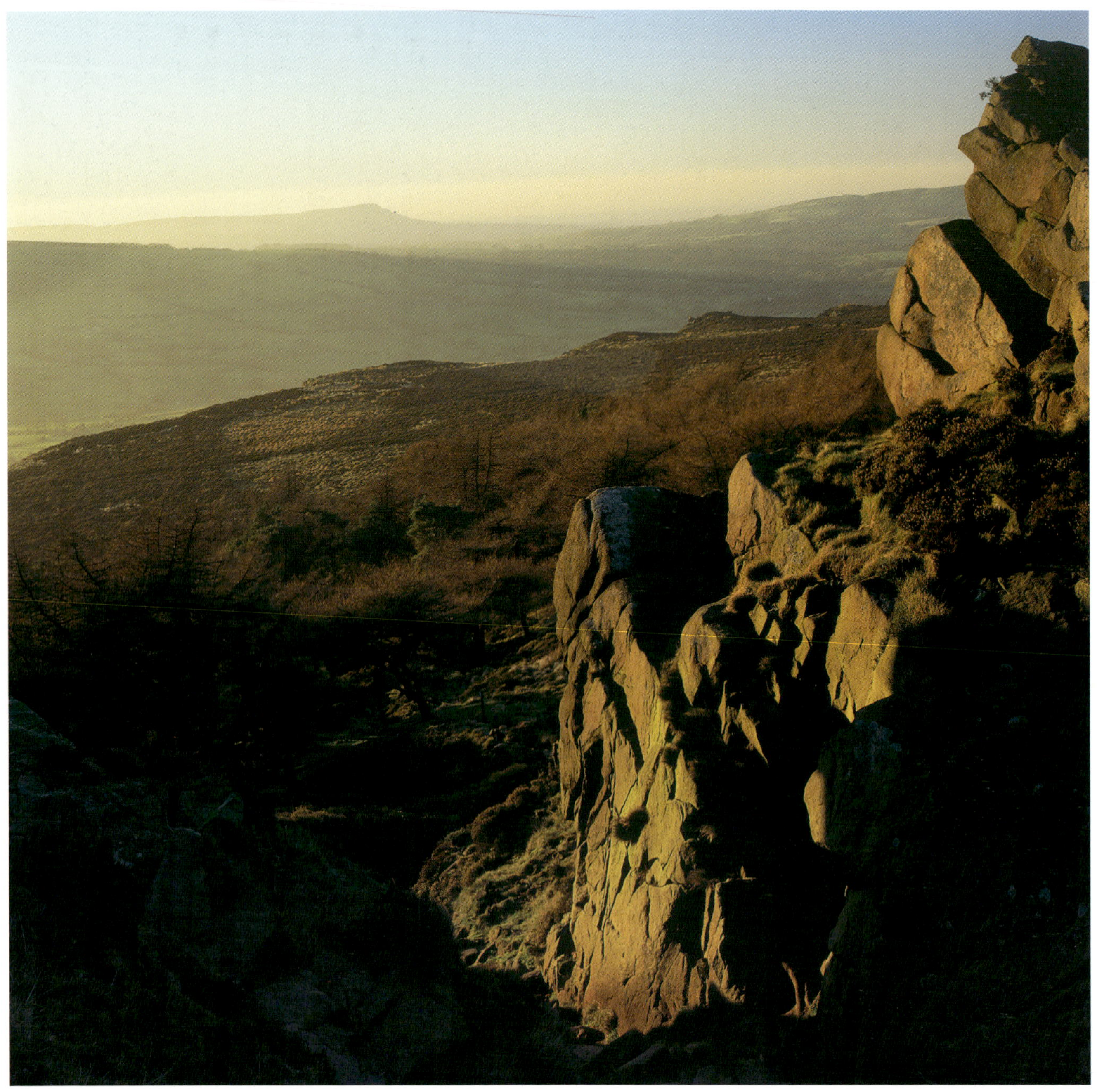

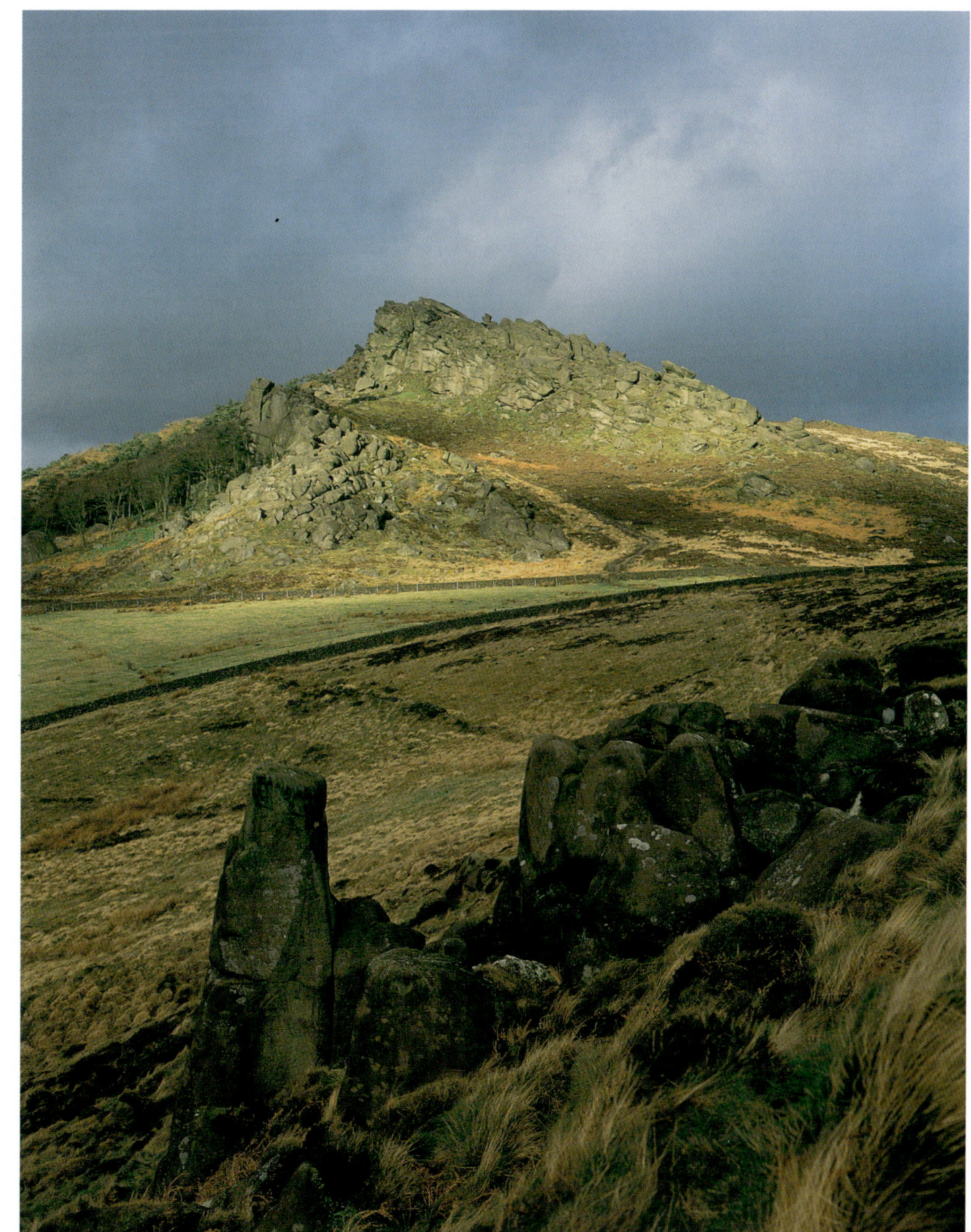

Storm over the Roaches
Seen from the lower slopes of Hen Cloud, storm clouds drift over the craggy skyline of the Roaches.

Left: **Evening glow**
Lingering evening light brings out the warm, rich colours of the grit-stone rocks in this view westwards from the Roaches.

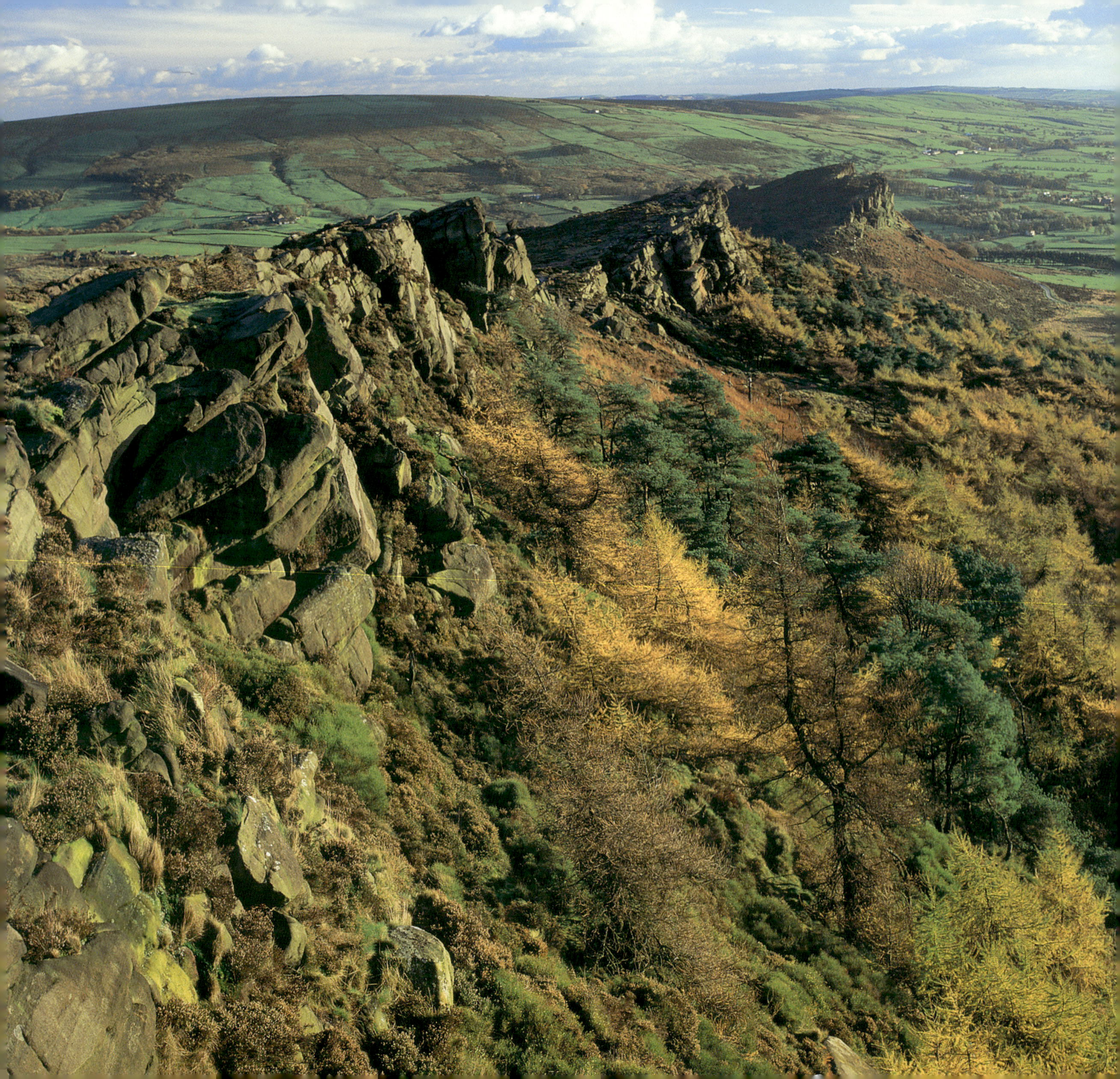

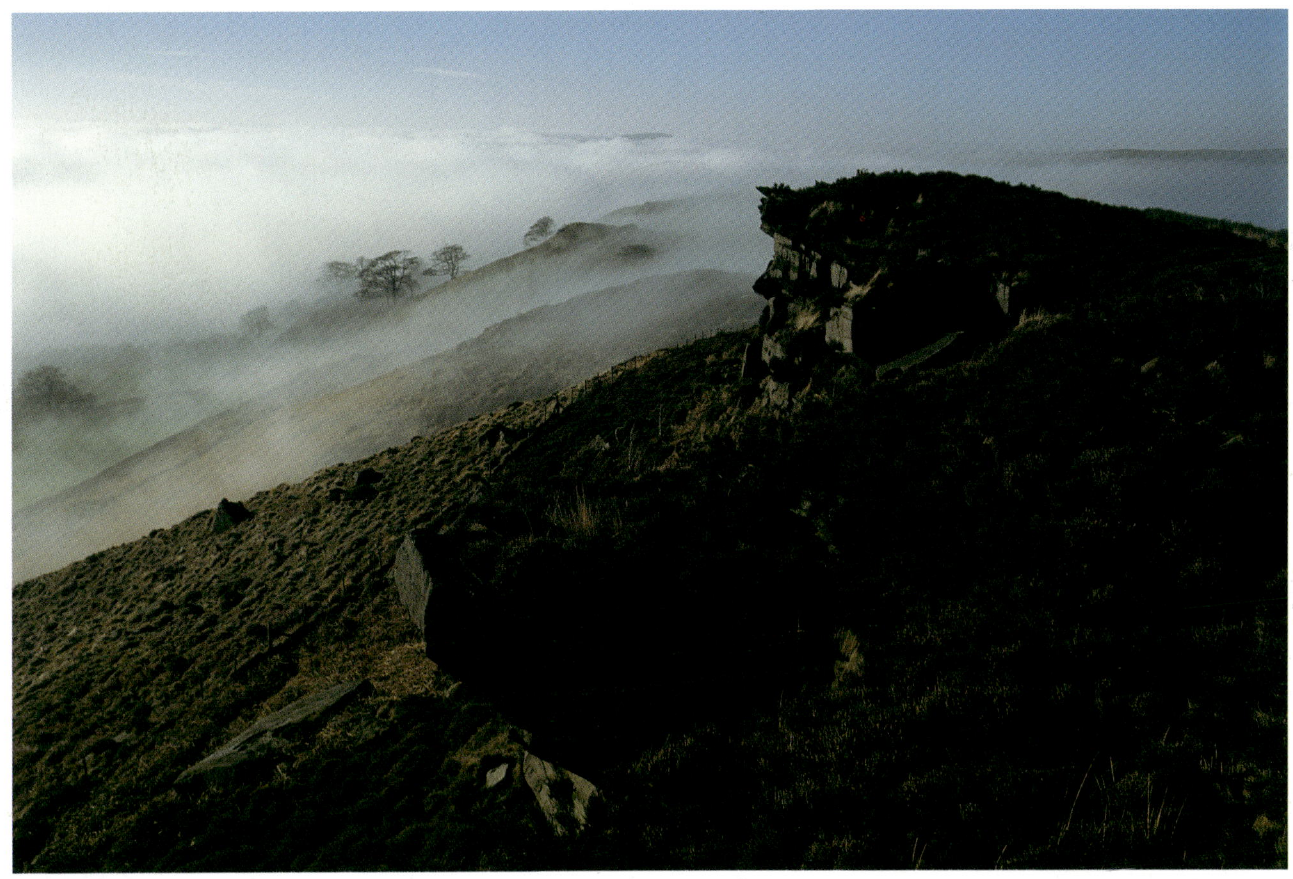

Misty morning
Autumn mist rolls over the Back Forest ridge, a westward extension of the broad Roaches ridge.

Left: **Patchwork of colours**
A vibrant mix of greens and golds below the rearing gritstone buttresses of the Roaches.

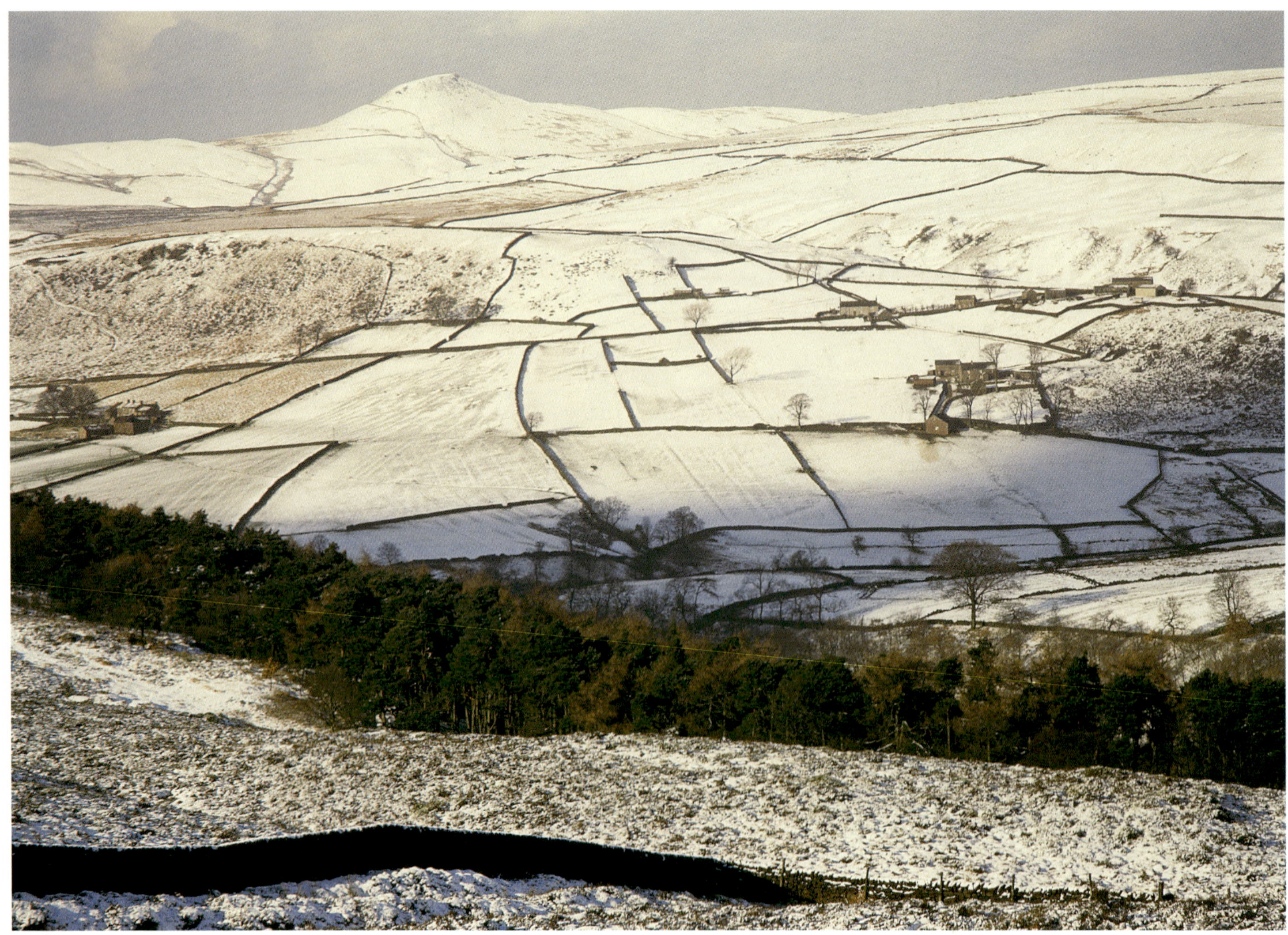

A snowy landscape
A snowy view across Gradbach to the shapely peak of Shutlingsloe, its flanks criss-crossed by gritstone walls.

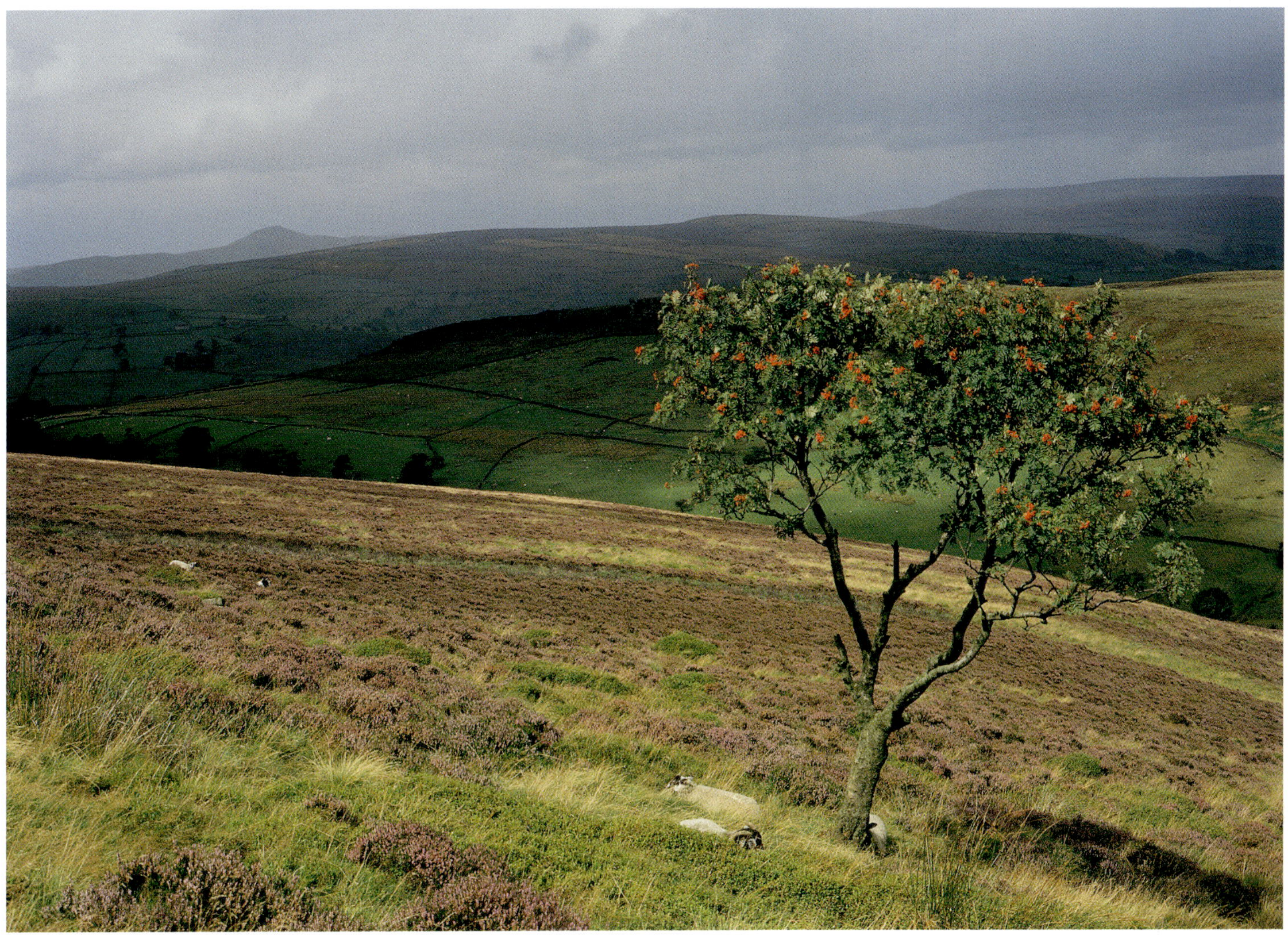

Lone rowan
A lone rowan tree with its red berries set among heather moorland acts as a foreground for this view north over Goldsitch Moss to the dome of Axe Edge.

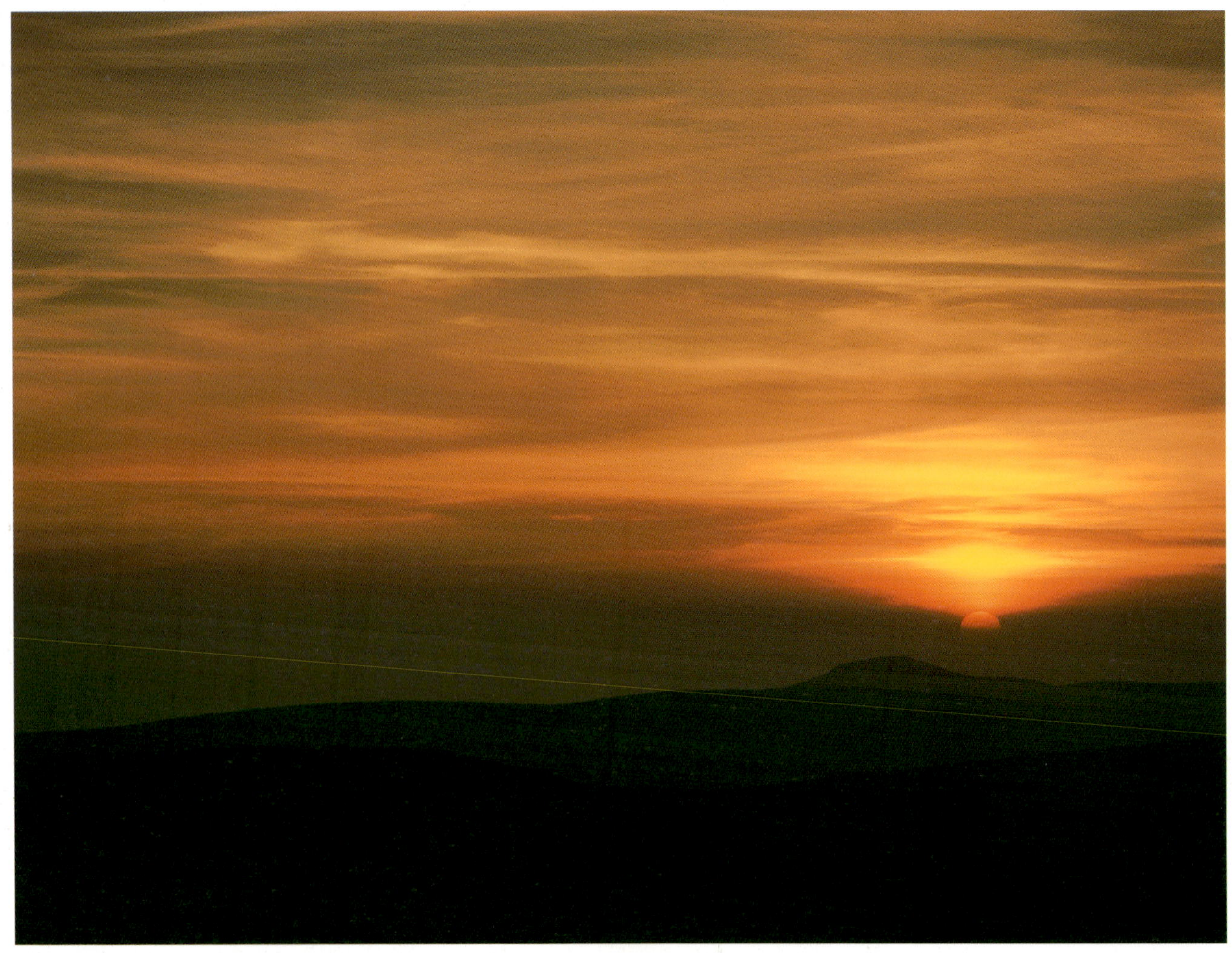

Evening light
Soft light on the western moors as the sun dips beyond Shutlingsloe.

Right: **Ramshaw Rocks**
Evening sunshine highlights the series of eroded boulders and dramatic pinnacles at Ramshaw Rocks, near Leek.

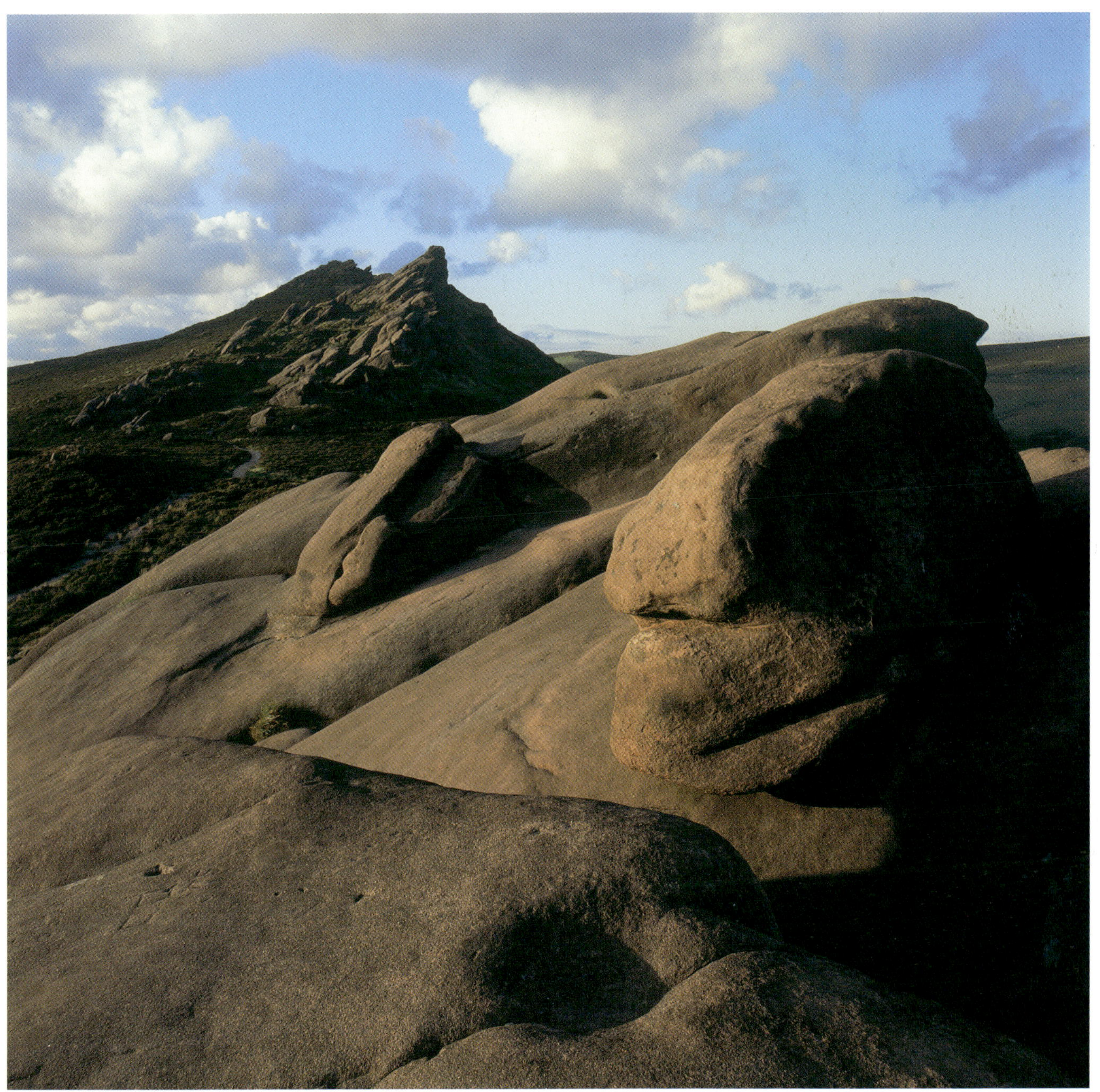

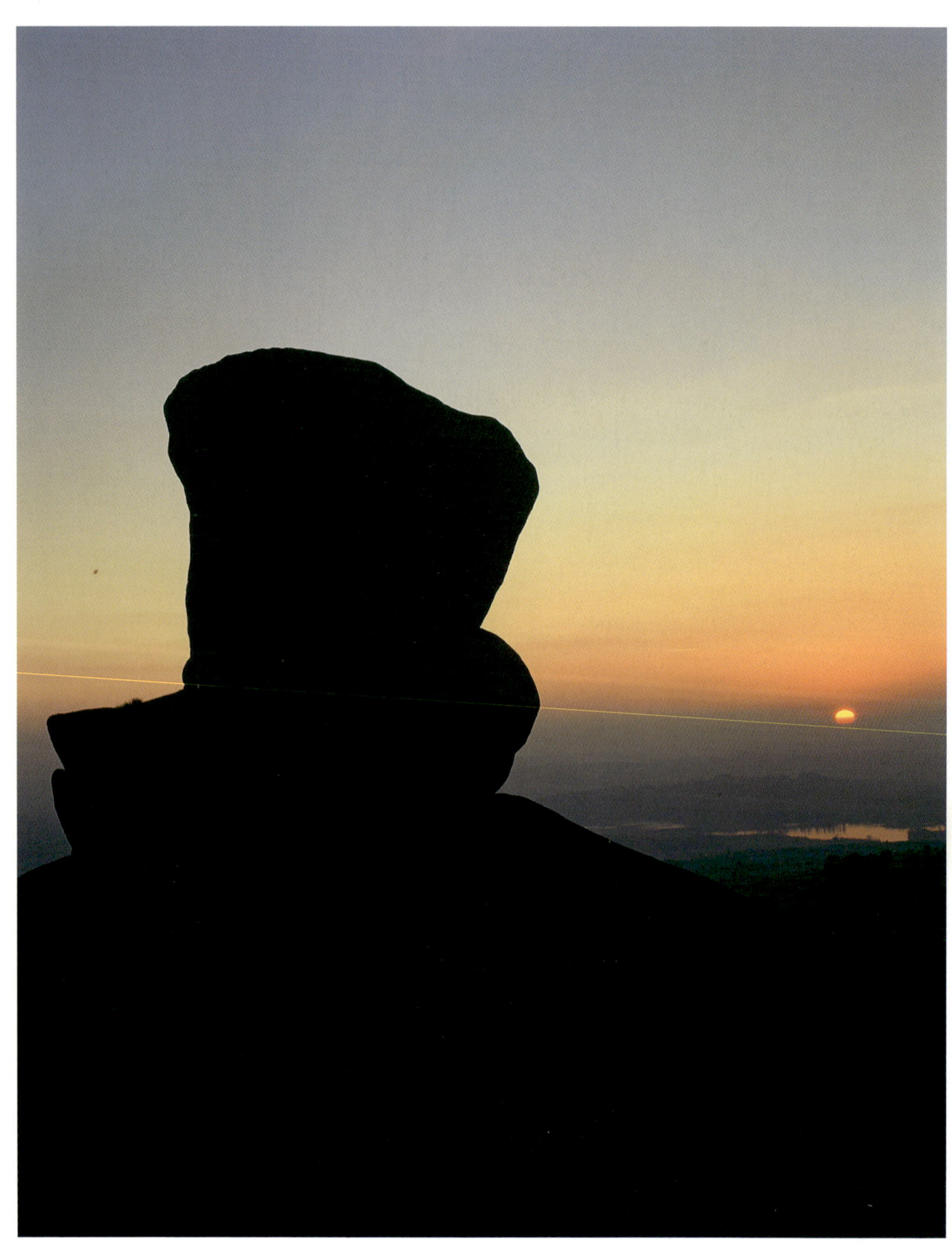

Eroded pinnacles
Weirdly shaped eroded gritstone pinnacles silhouetted against the setting sun. The distant silver strip of light is Tittesworth Reservoir.

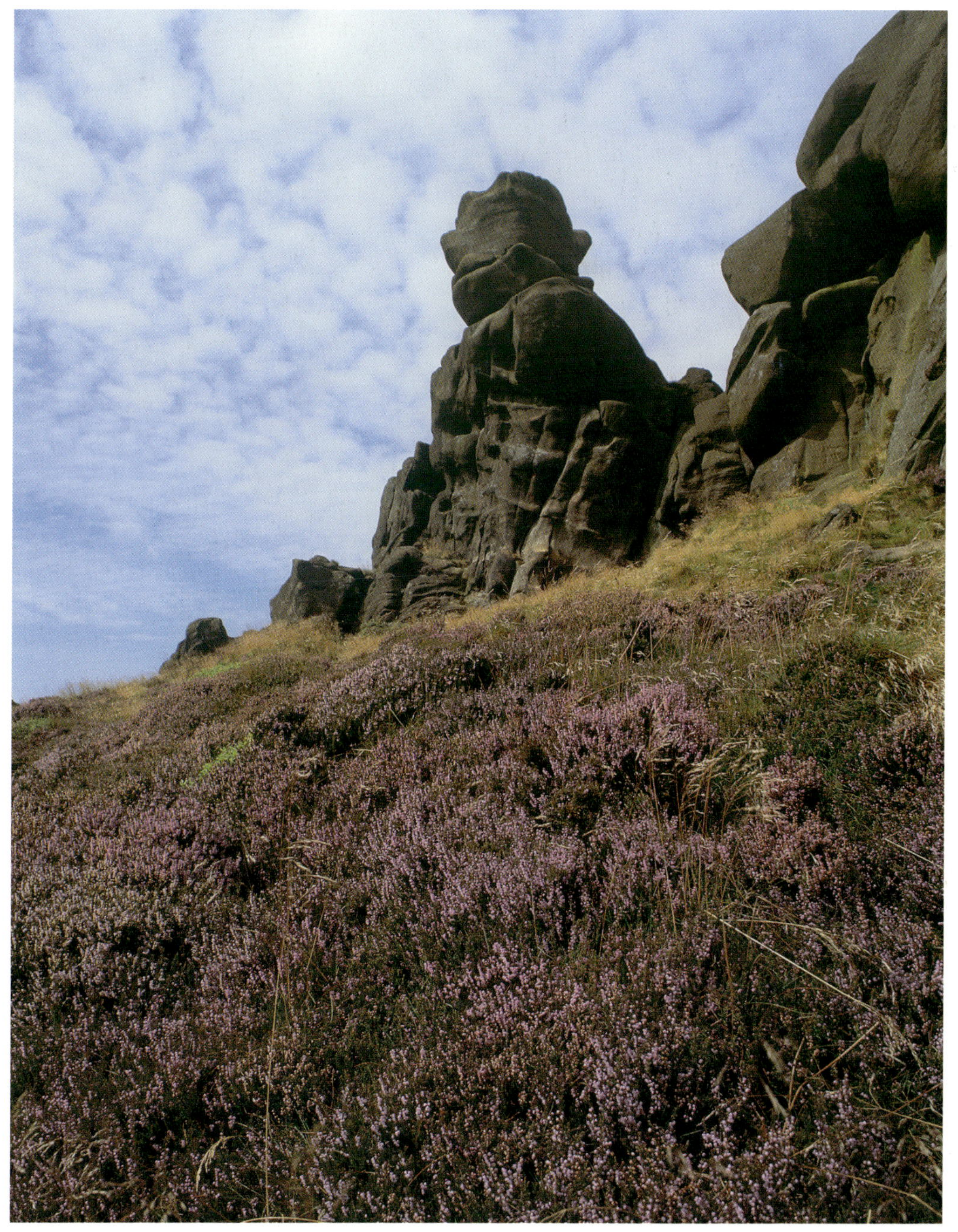

Loaf and Cheese
An eroded gritstone pinnacle known as the Loaf and Cheese rears above the slopes of purple heather at Ramshaw Rocks.

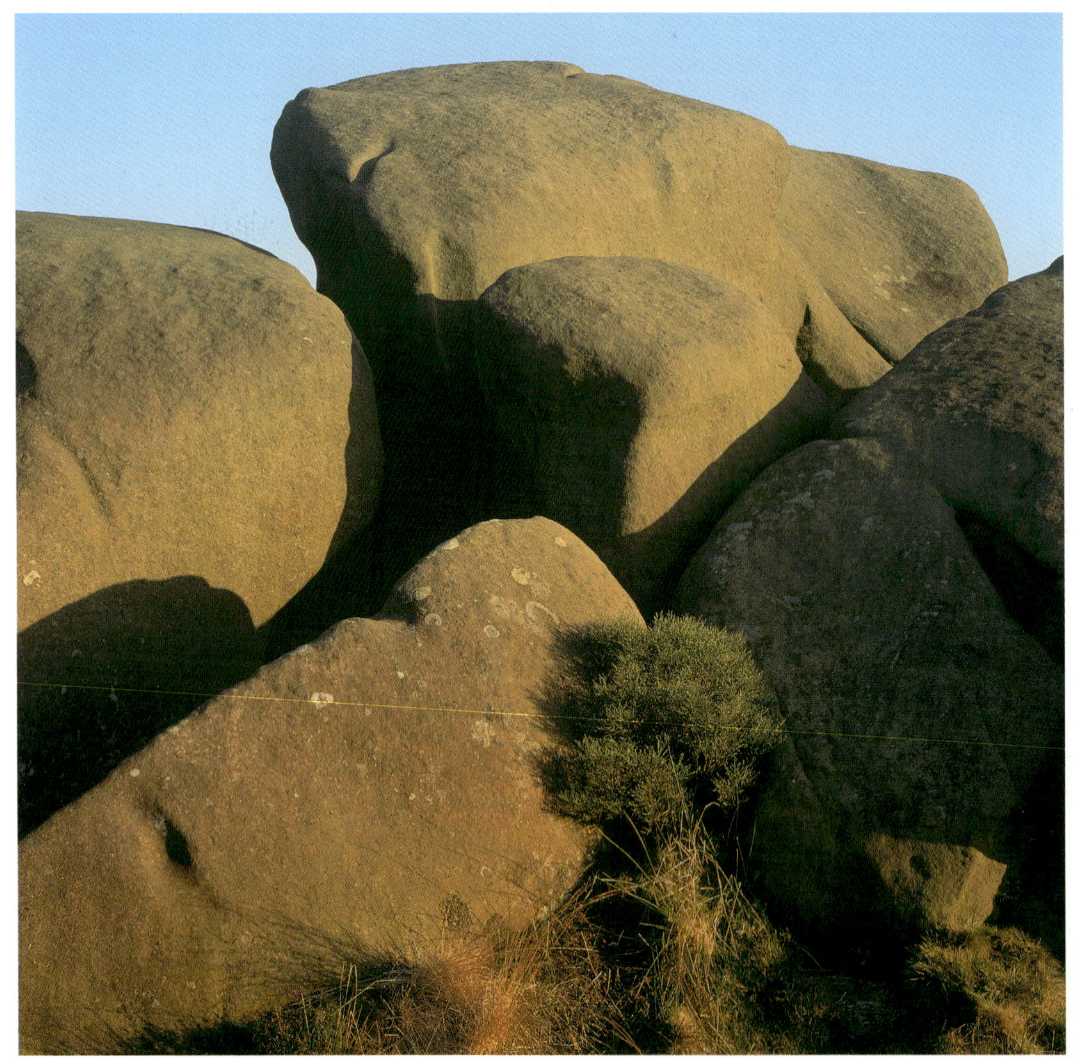

Rock art
Green vegetation enlivens a group of eroded gritstone boulders.

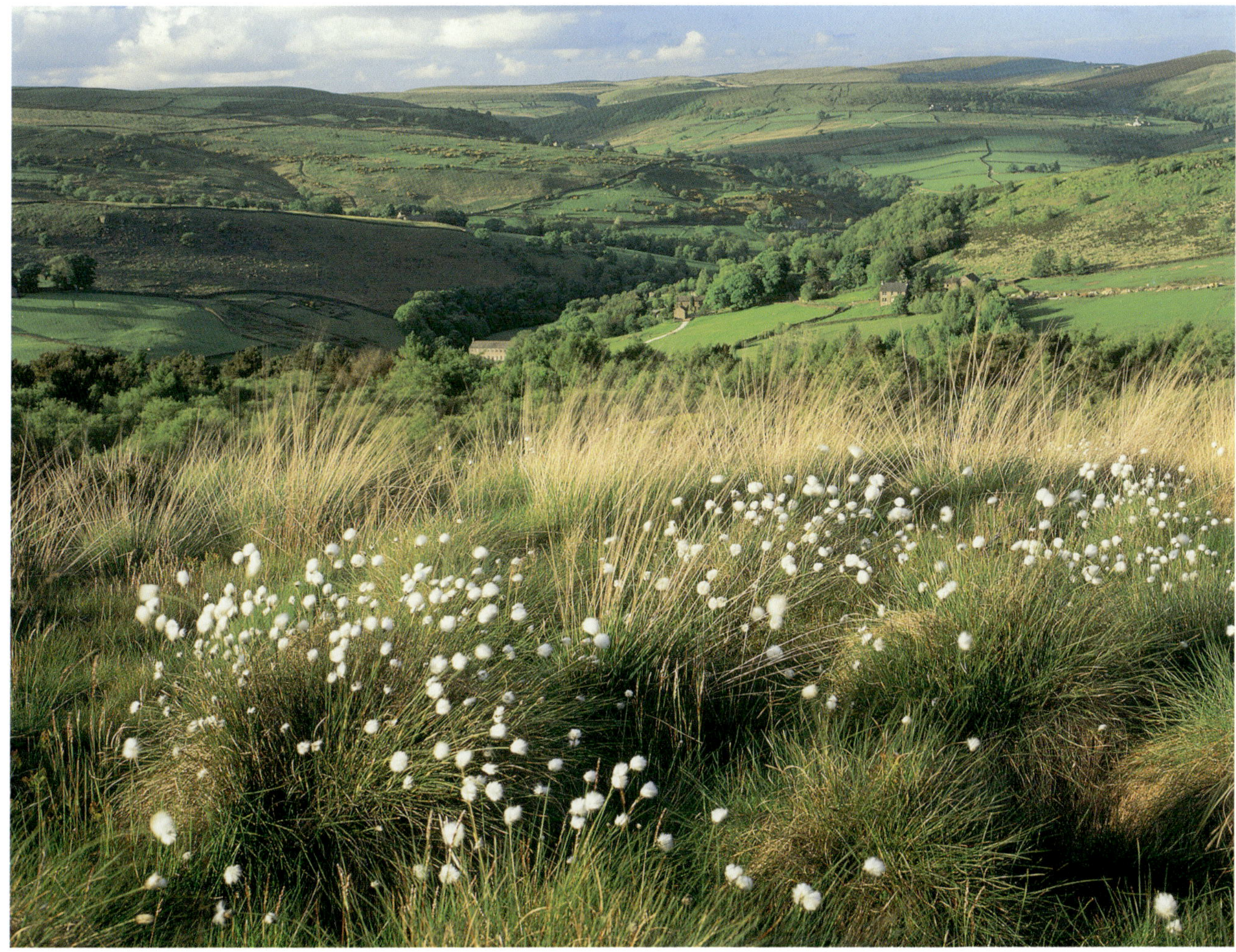

Cotton grass
Fluffy white heads of cotton grass add lightness and movement to this moorland view across Gradbach to Three Shire Heads.

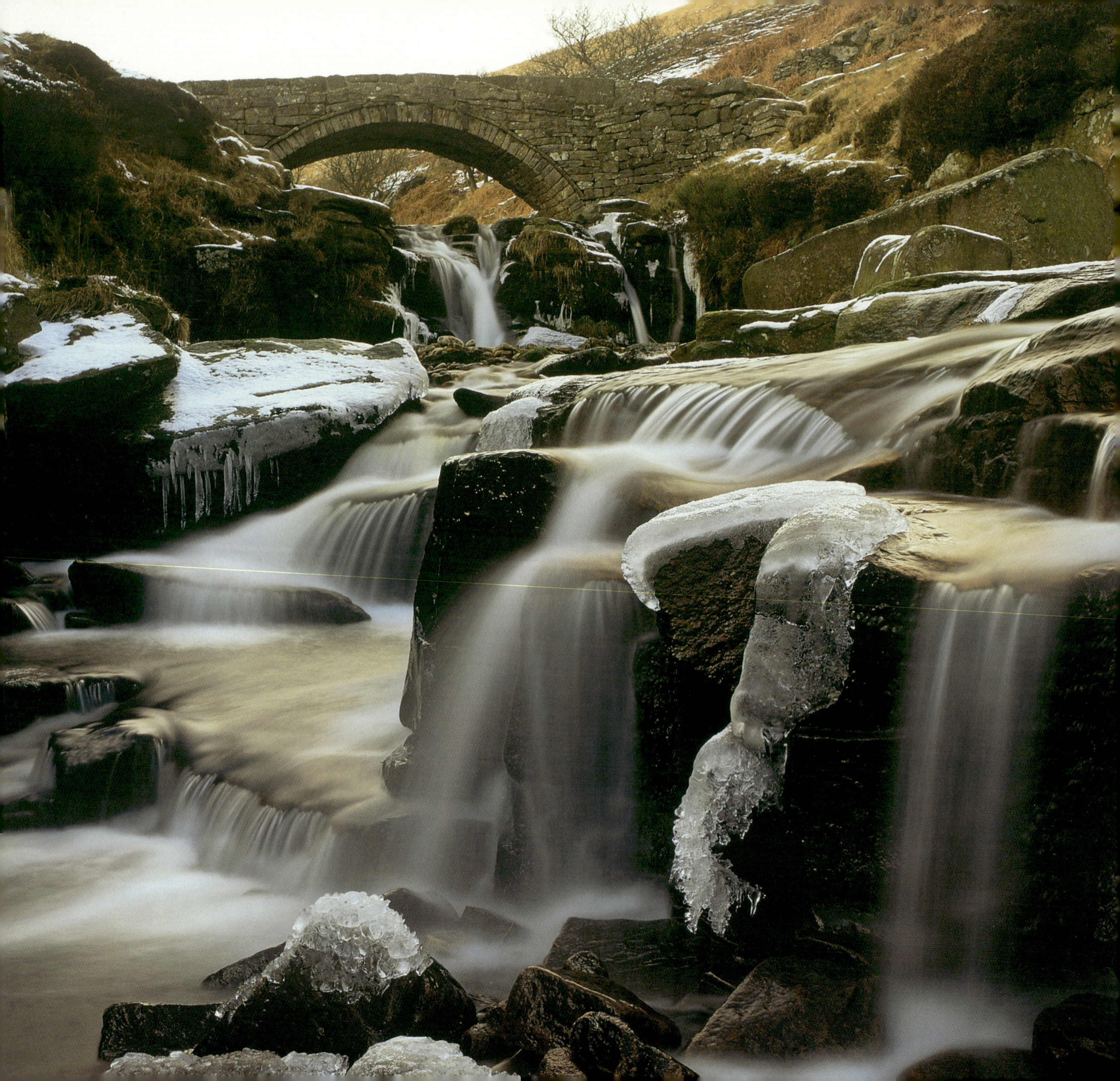

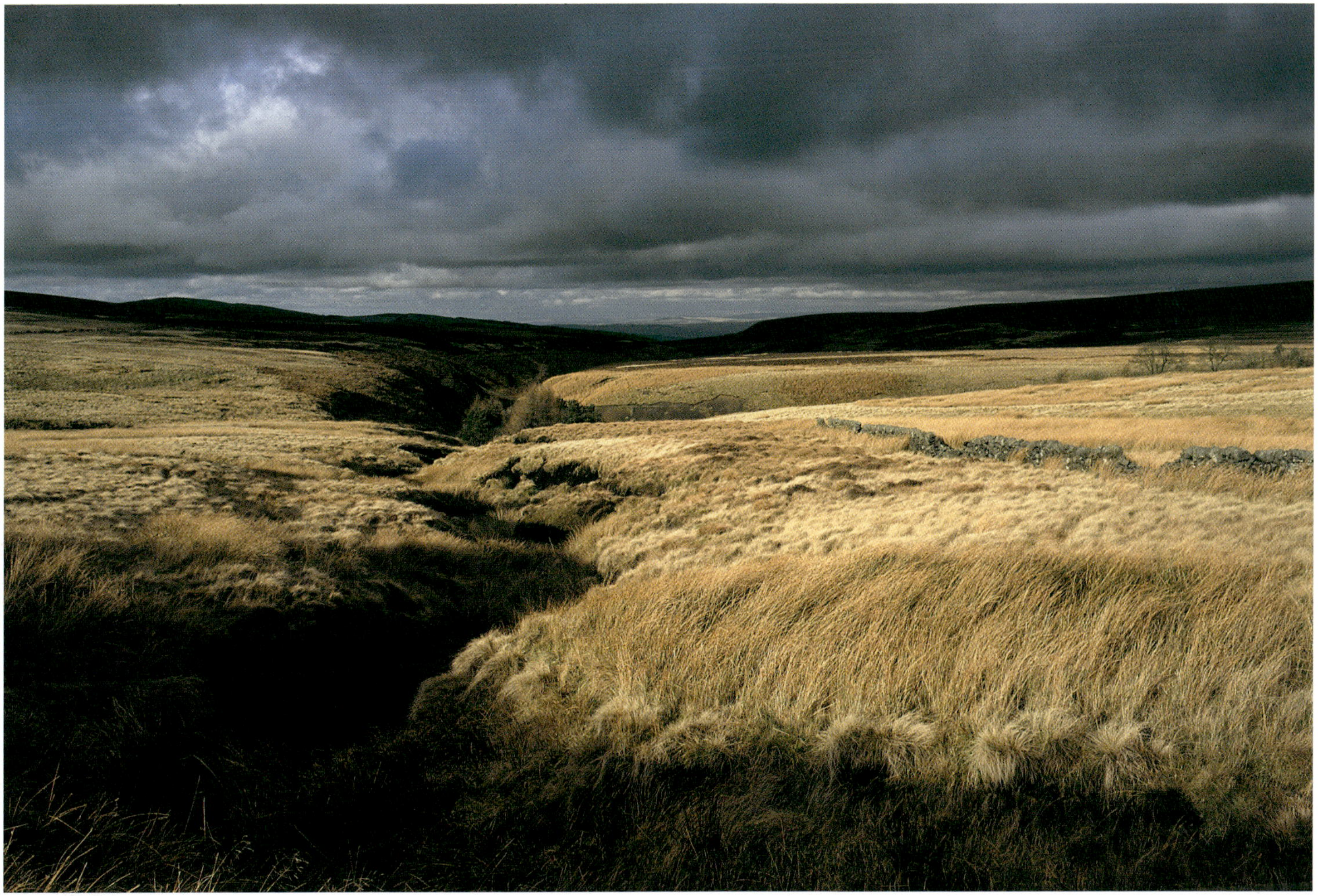

Moorland storm
A storm approaches the upper reaches of the Goyt Valley on the moors west of Buxton.

Left: **Three Shire Heads**
An icy River Dane flows under the old packhorse bridge where the three counties of Staffordshire, Cheshire and Derbyshire meet.

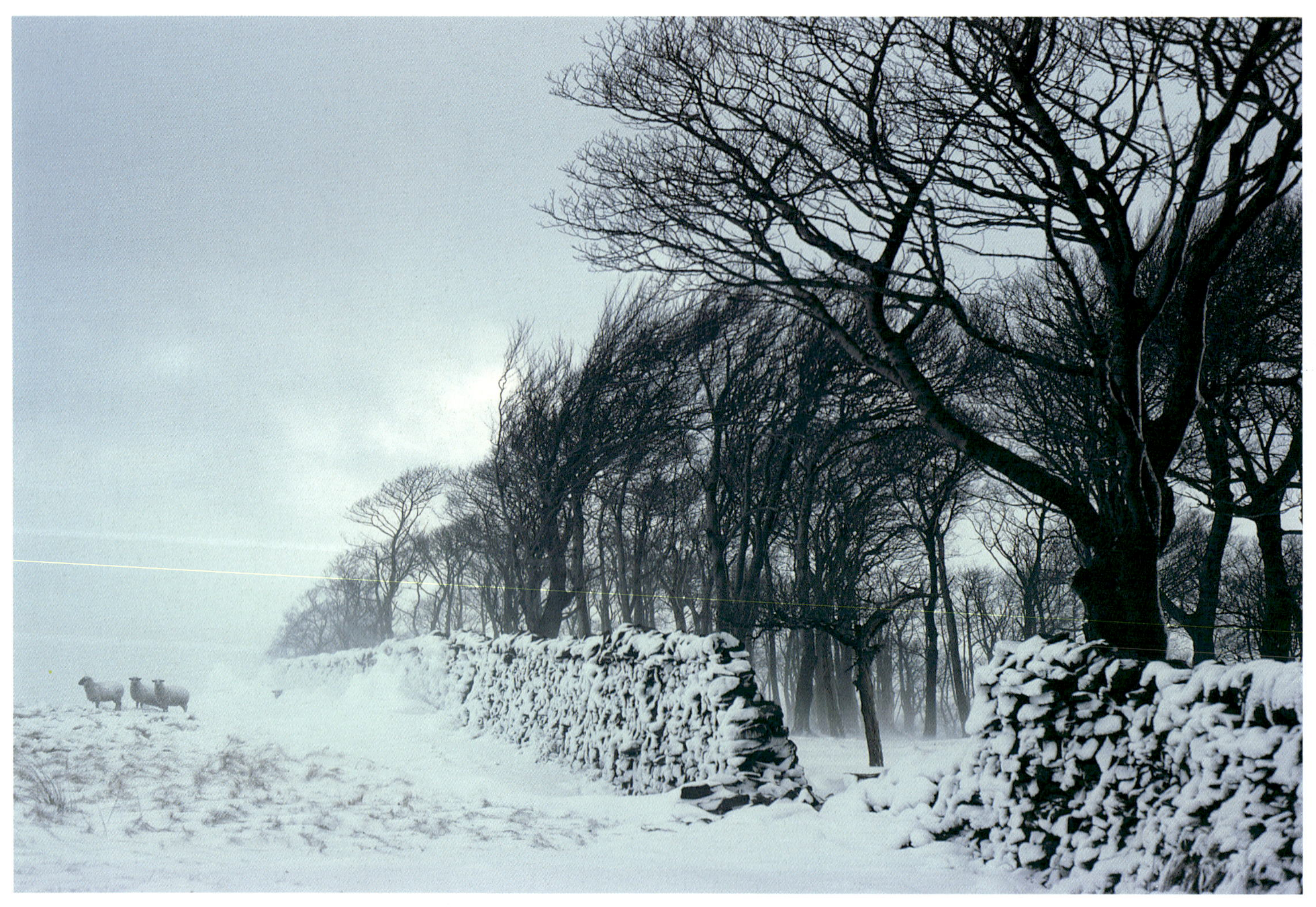

Monochrome snowscape
Sheep add movement to a bleak, monochrome snowscape on Burbage Edge above Buxton.

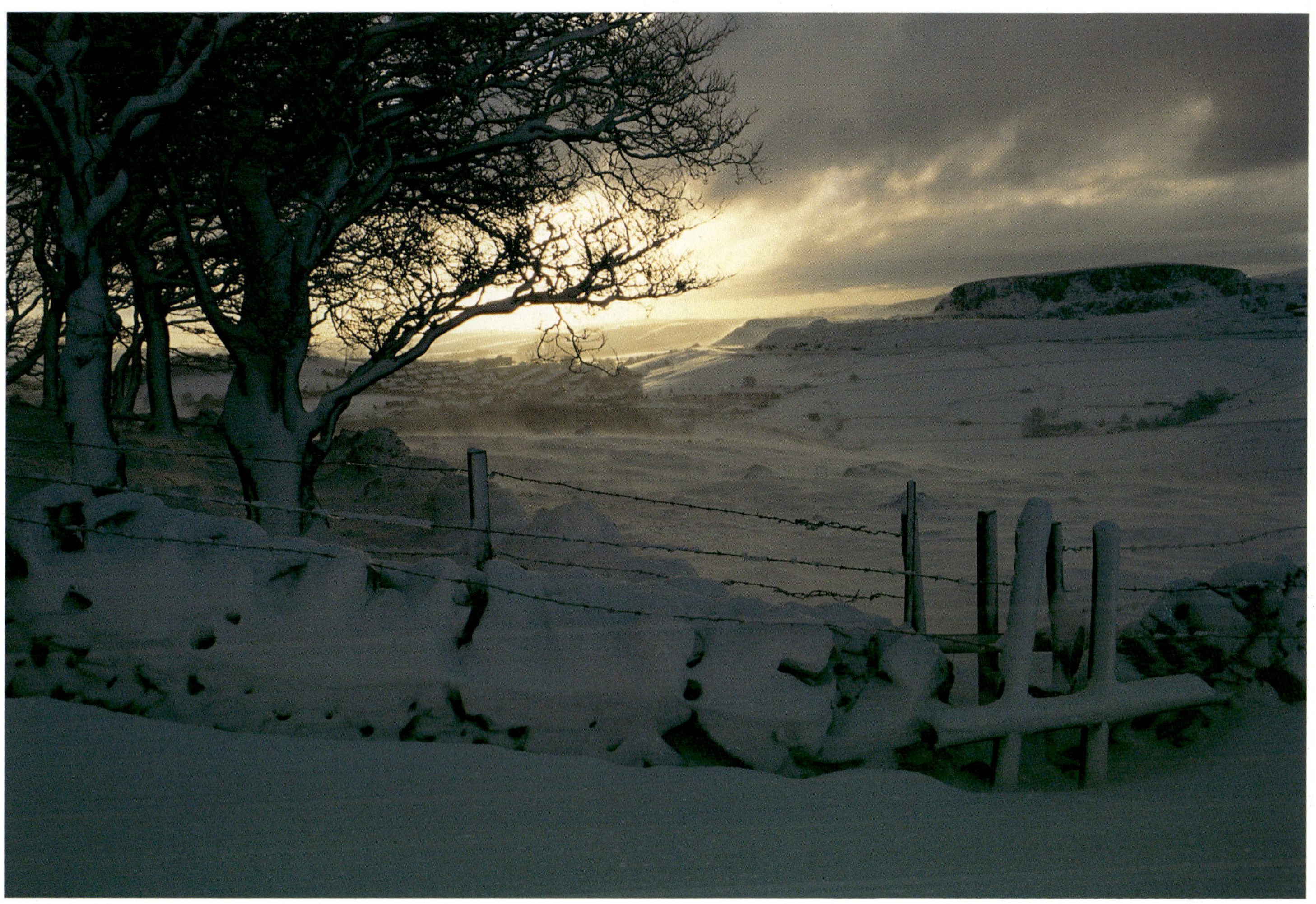

Snowy dawn
The rising winter sun peeps through clouds to illuminate this snow-covered landscape on Grin Low south of Buxton.

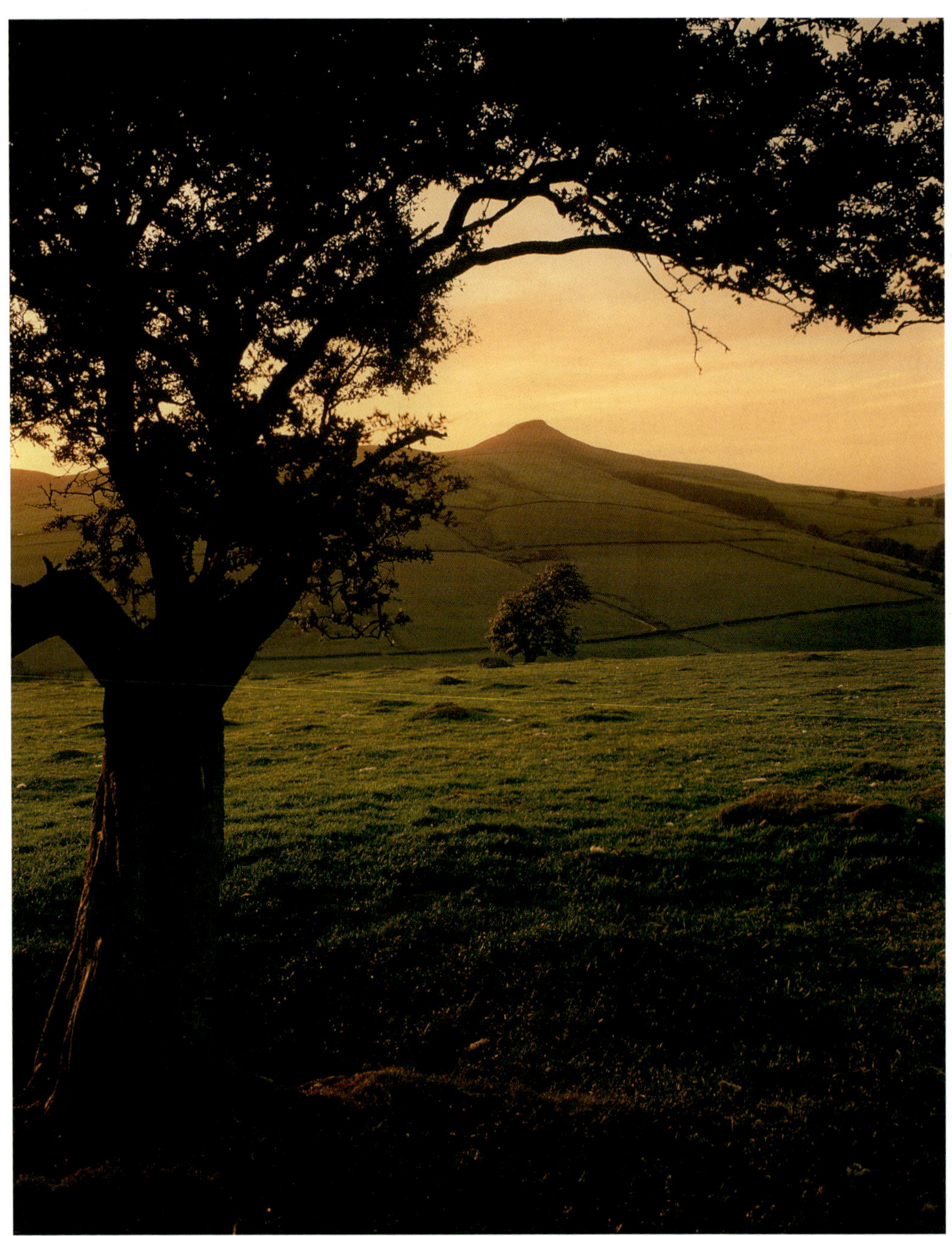

Shutlingsloe
The low evening sunlight gives warmth to this view of Shutlingsloe seen across the deep valley of Wildboarclough, with its scattered farms and leafy lanes.

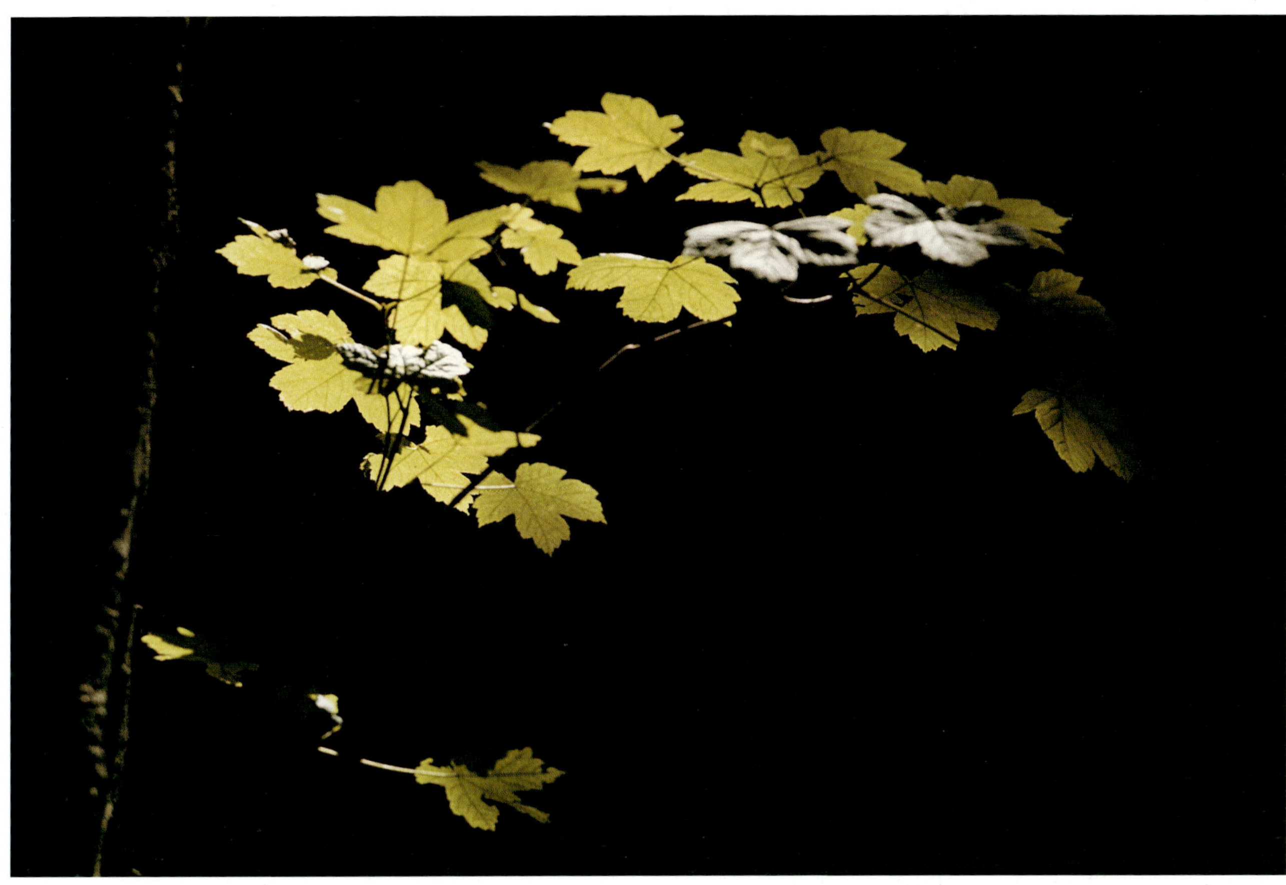

Sunlit leaves
The sun backlights sycamore leaves deep in Macclesfield Forest on the western flanks of Shutlingsloe.

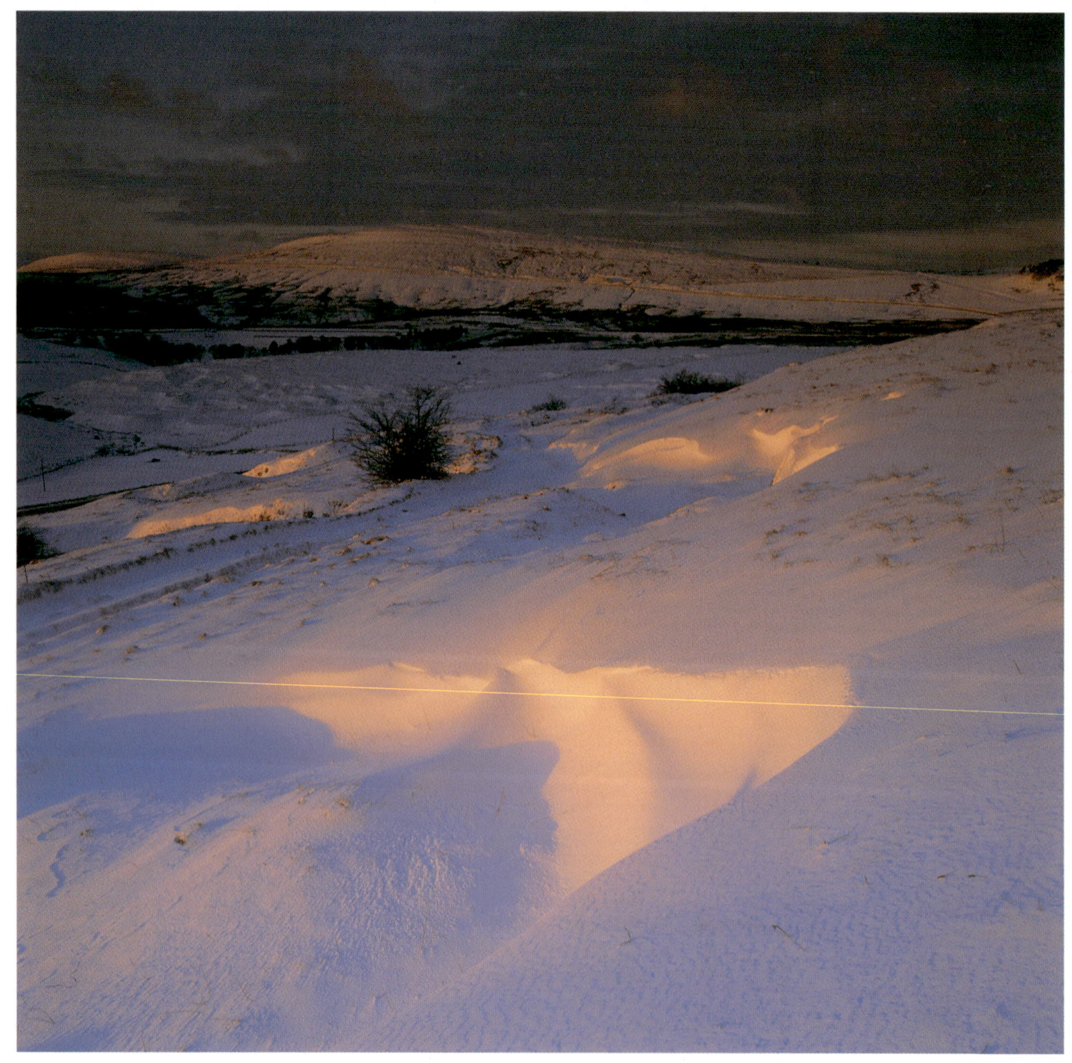

First light
The first light of a cold winter's dawn adds a rosy-pink hue to this snowy view across to Axe Edge Moor.

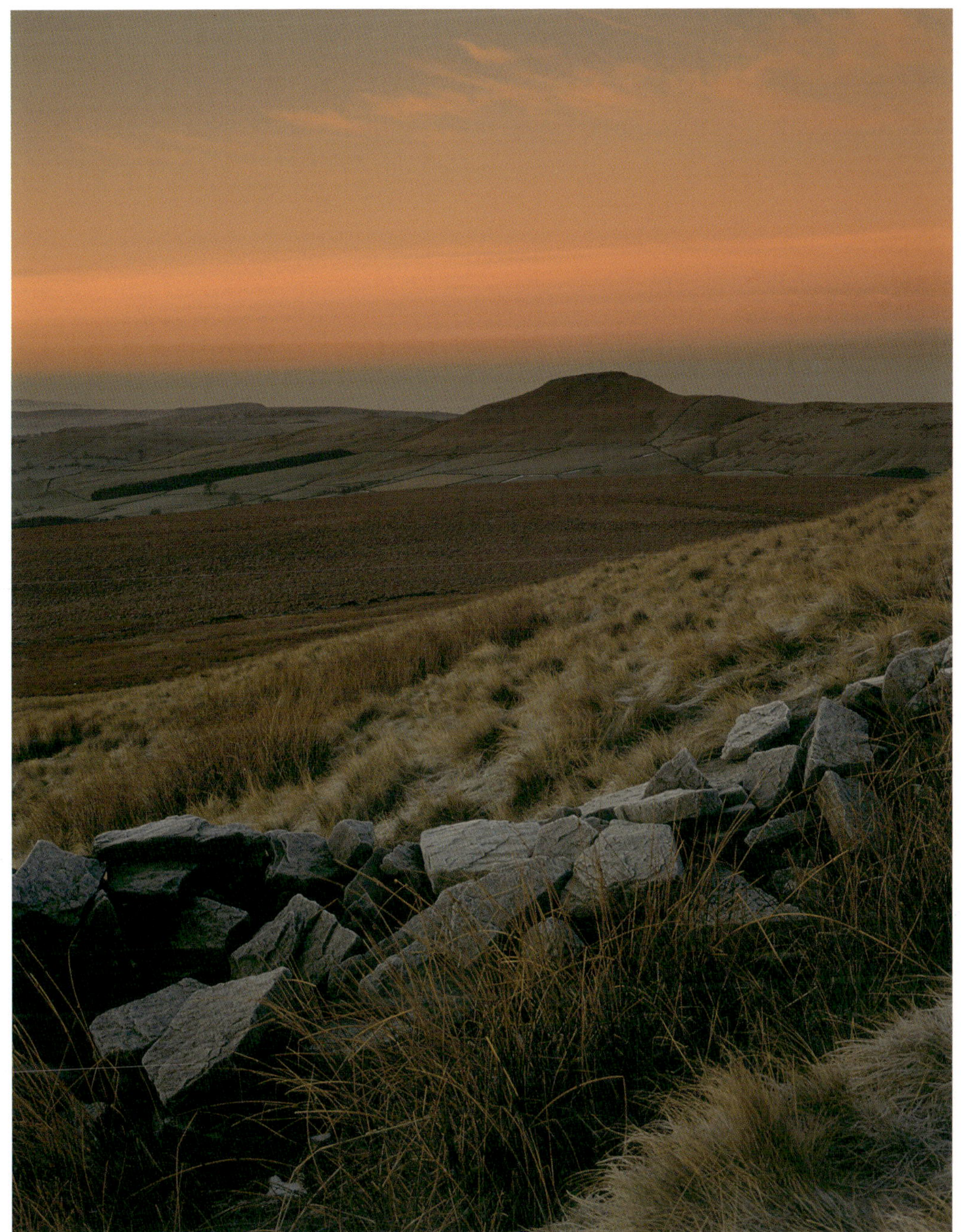

Frosty dawn

A frost-covered wall acts as a foreground for this dawn view west to Shutlingsloe, from near the Cat and Fiddle Inn on the Buxton to Macclesfield road.

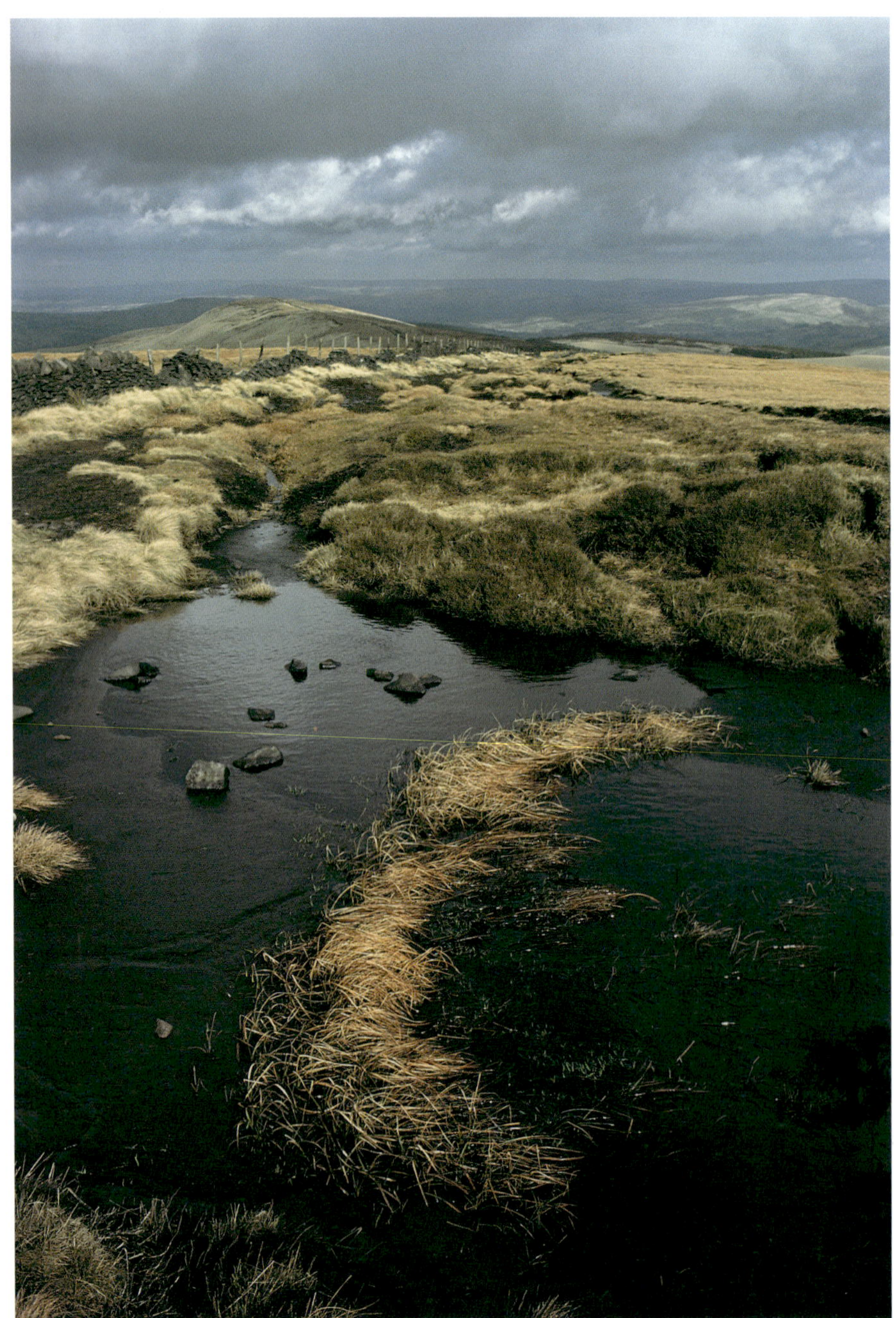

Shining Tor
A pool set among peat and heather at the summit of Shining Tor leads the eye northwards along the broad moorland ridge with the Goyt Valley on the right.

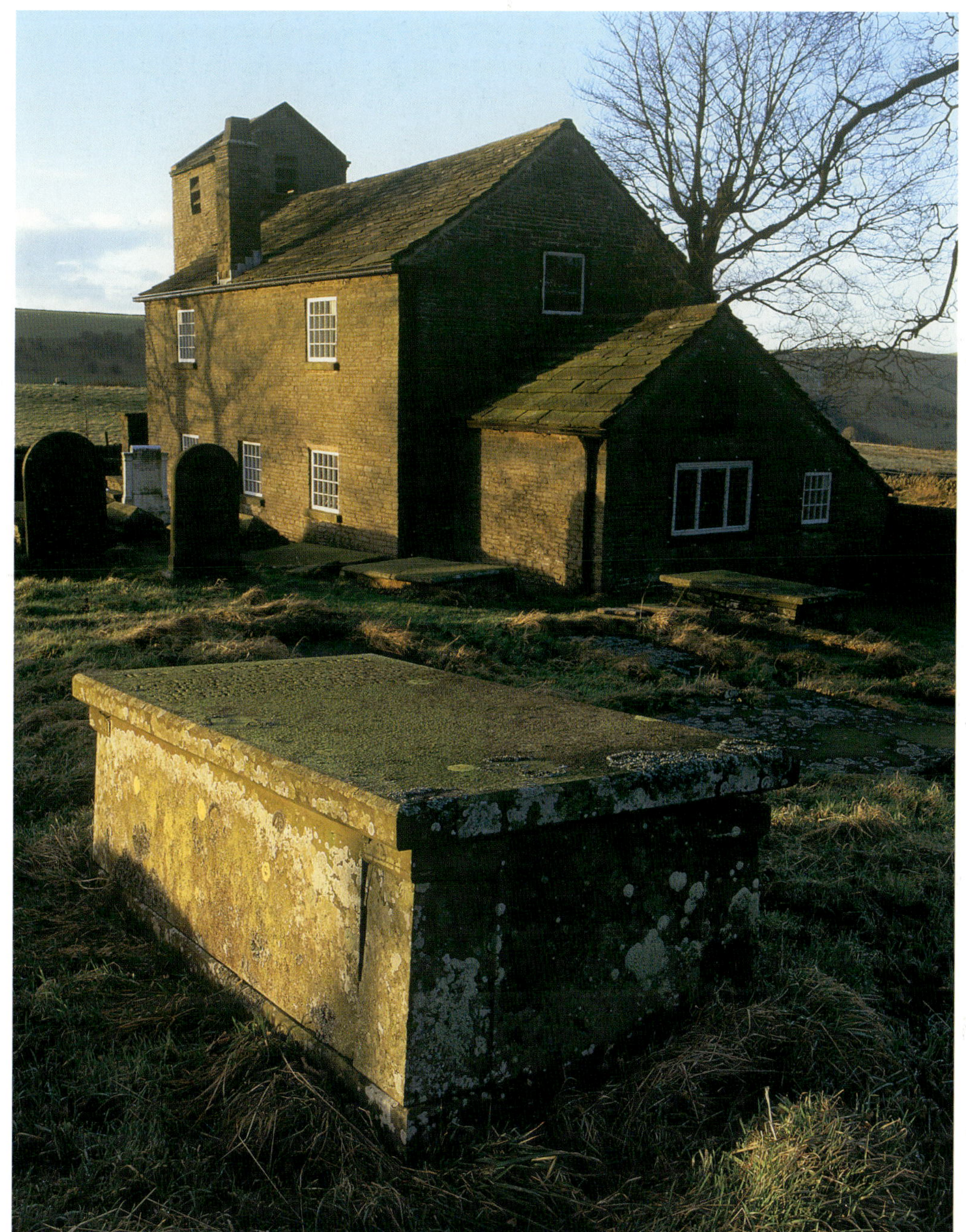

Jenkin Chapel
The isolated church of St John the Baptist, Saltersford on the moors east of Rainow is known as Jenkin Chapel. The chapel is situated at the crossroads on an old saltway.

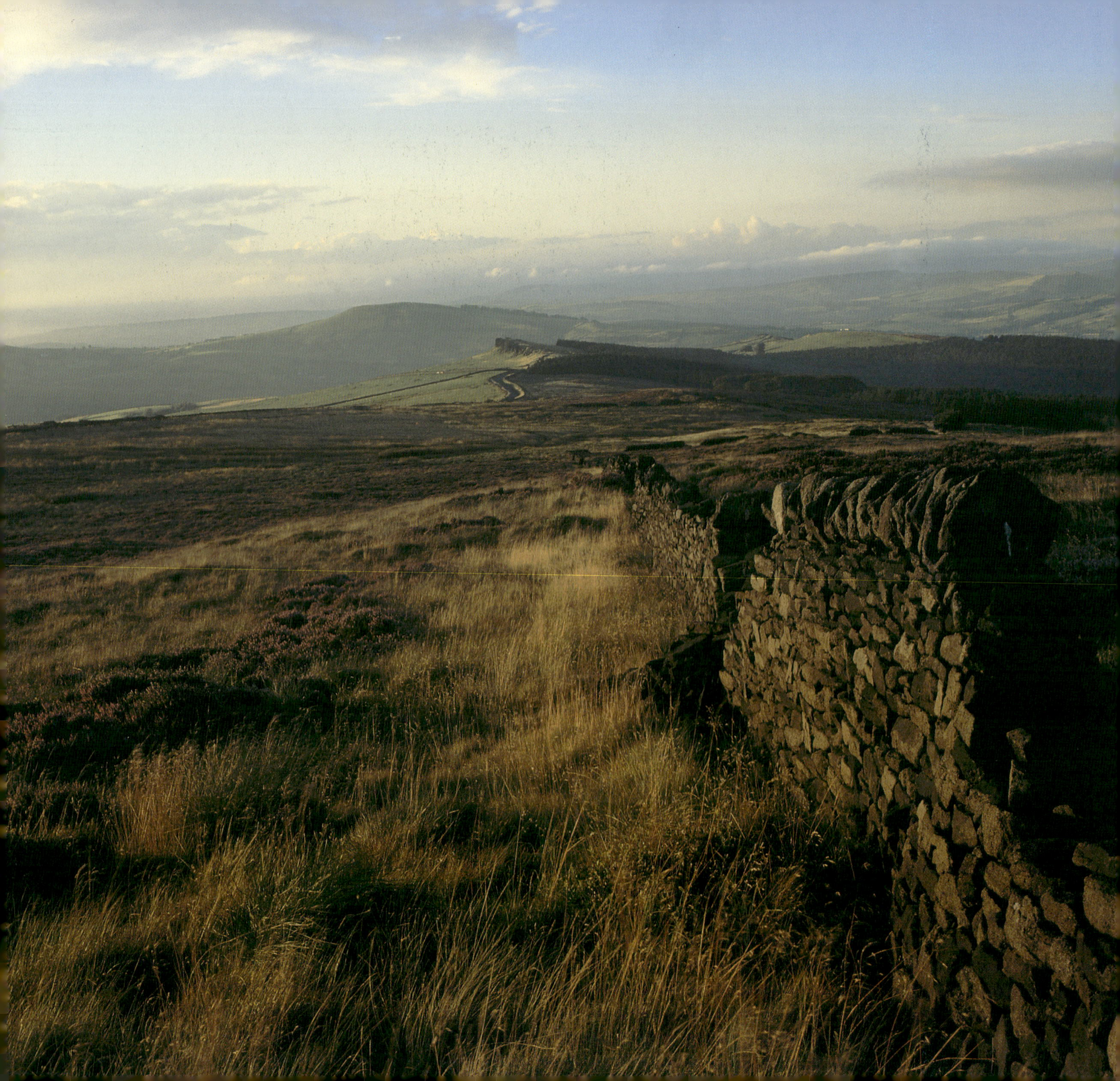

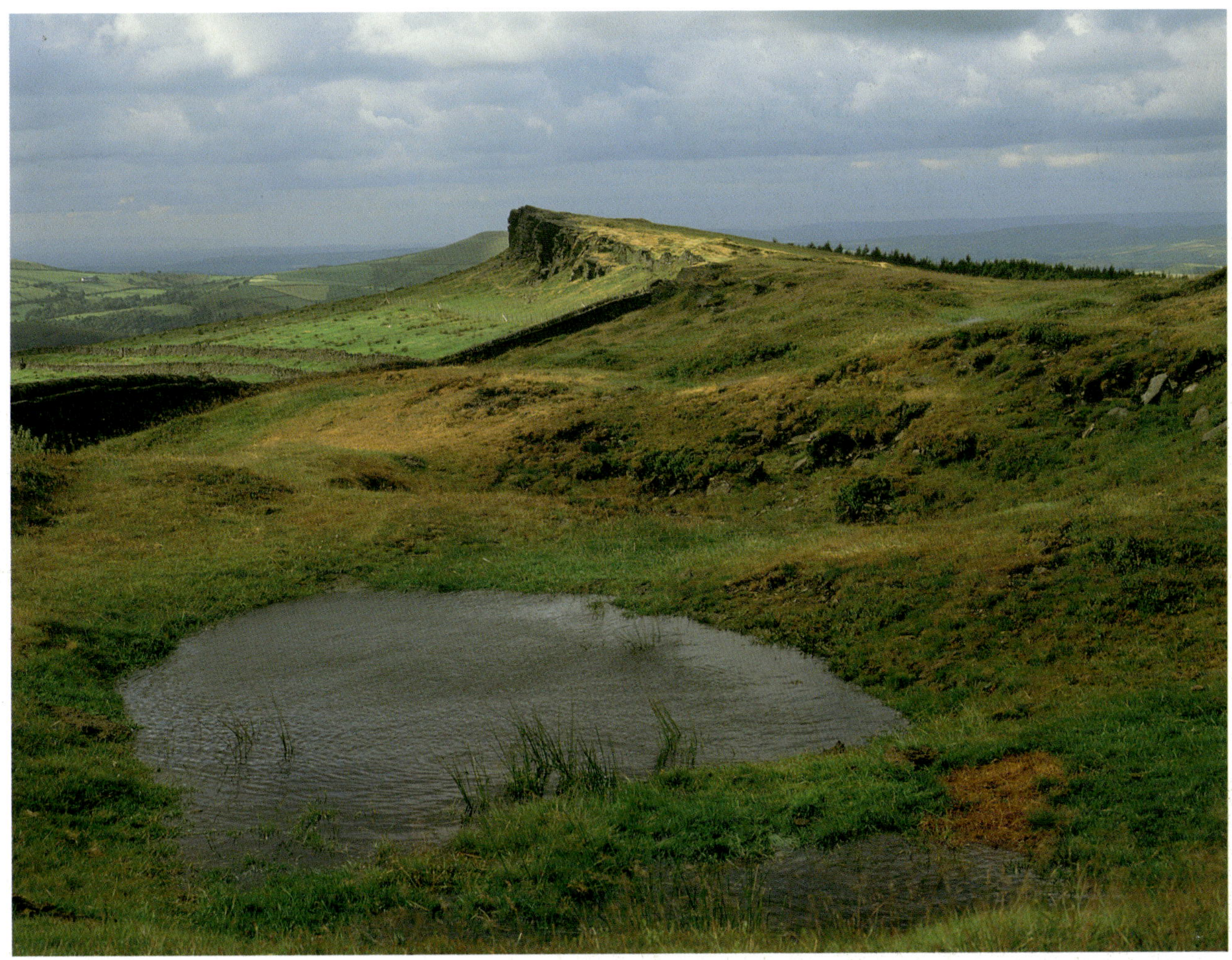

Windy ridge
The aptly-named Windgather Rocks on the open ridge above the village of Kettleshulme.

Left: **Pym Chair**
A late evening view north from Pym Chair, the high point of The Street, a Roman road that crossed the Goyt Valley. In the distance is Black Hill and Stockport.

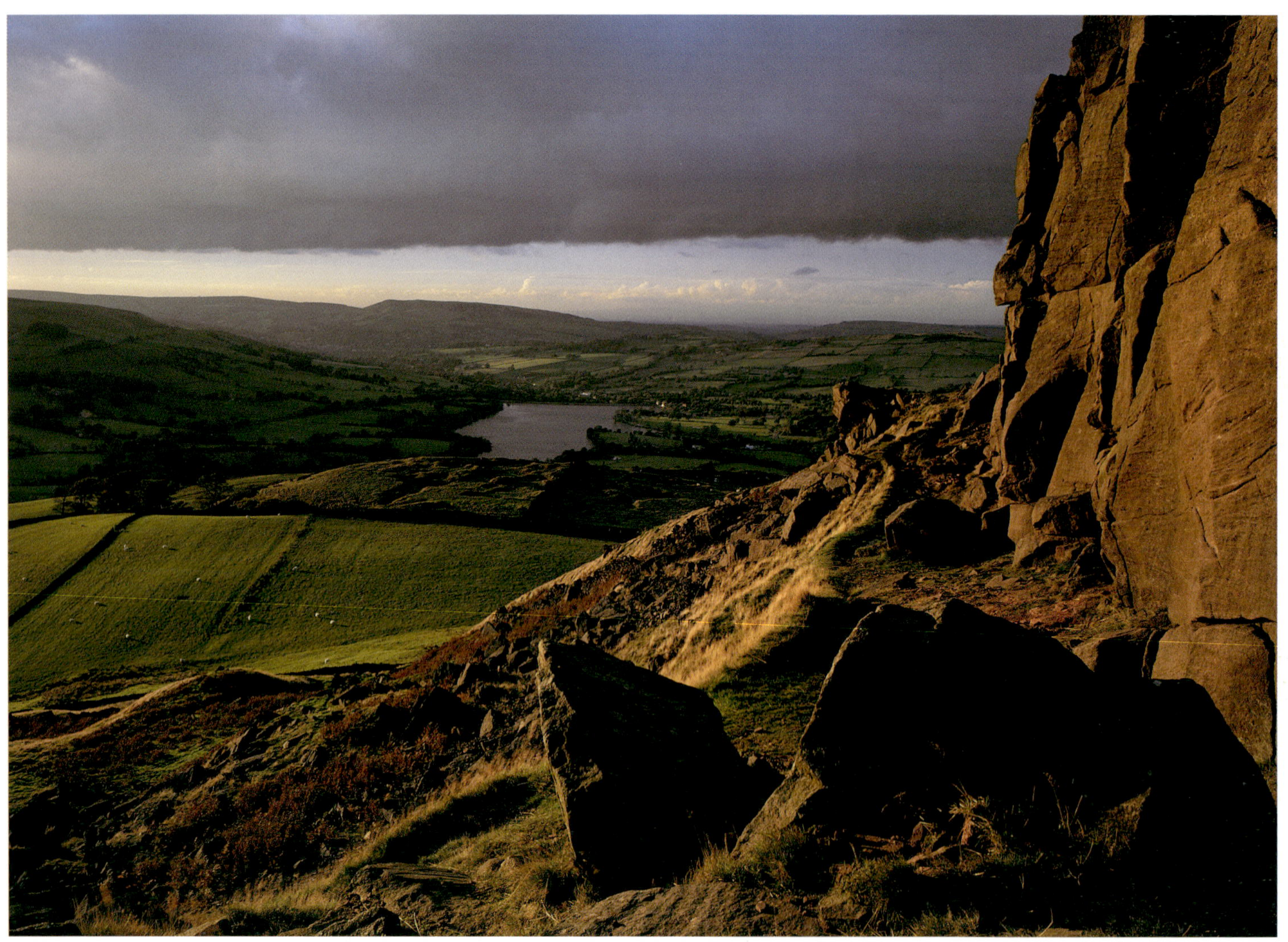

Castle Naze

The setting sun highlights the gritstone rocks of Castle Naze, the site of an Iron Age hillfort, overlooking the distant Combs Reservoir near Chapel-en-le-Frith.

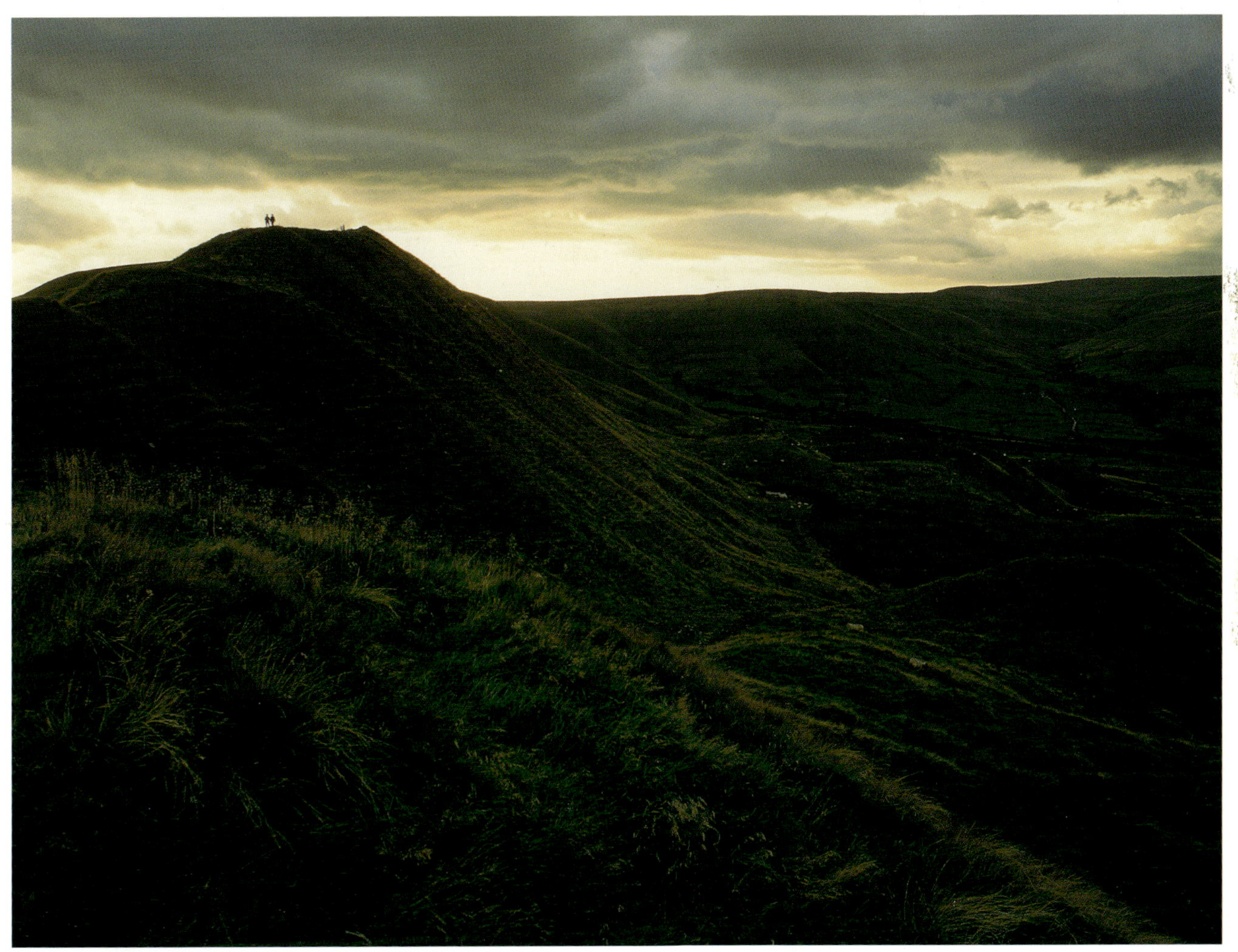

Rushup Edge

Rushup Edge and Lord's Seat, site of an ancient burial mound. Huge landslips after the last Ice Age caused the hummocks on the slopes on the right, which overlook the Edale Valley.

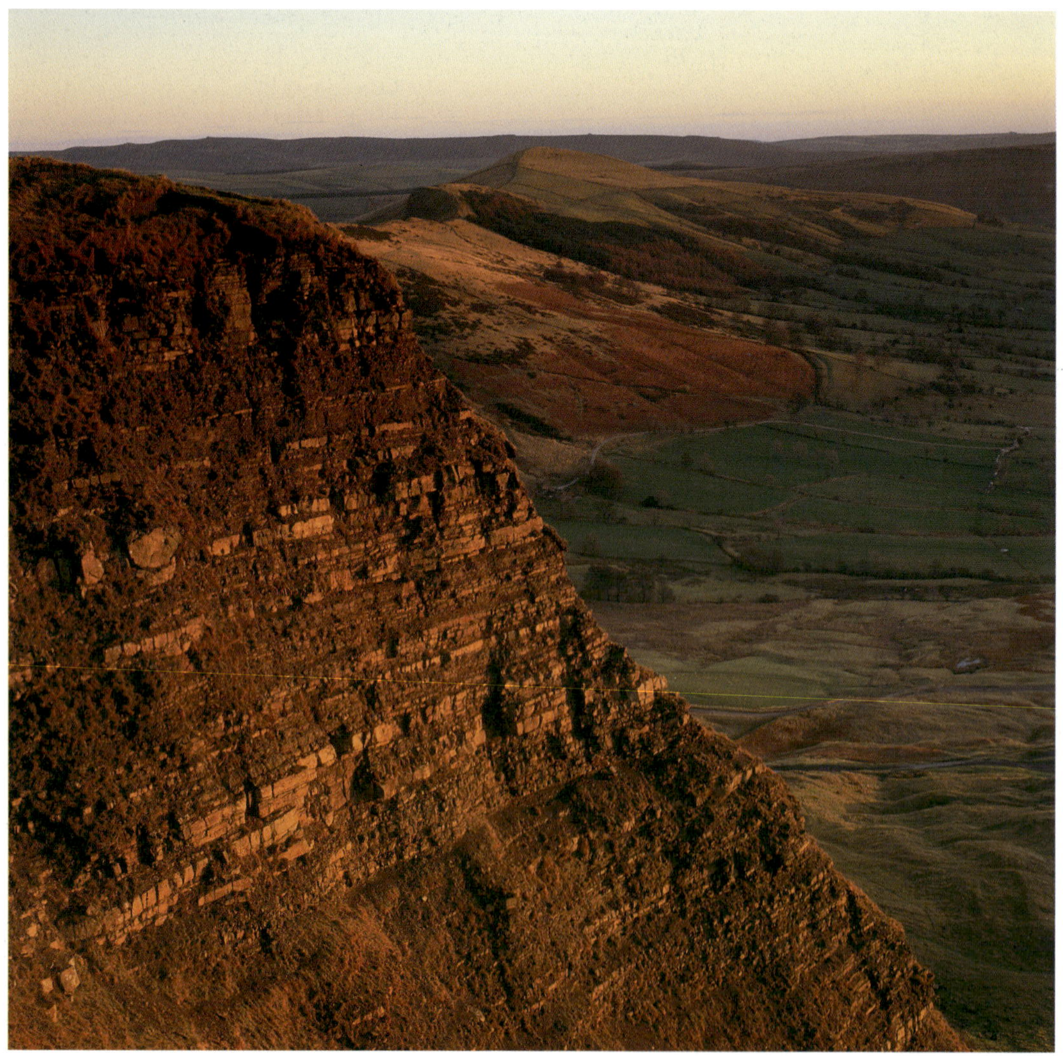

Shivering Mountain

Mam Tor, site of an Iron Age hillfort and now owned by the National Trust, dominates the head of the Hope Valley. The crumbling nature of Mam Tor's east face gives rise to the name 'Shivering Mountain.'

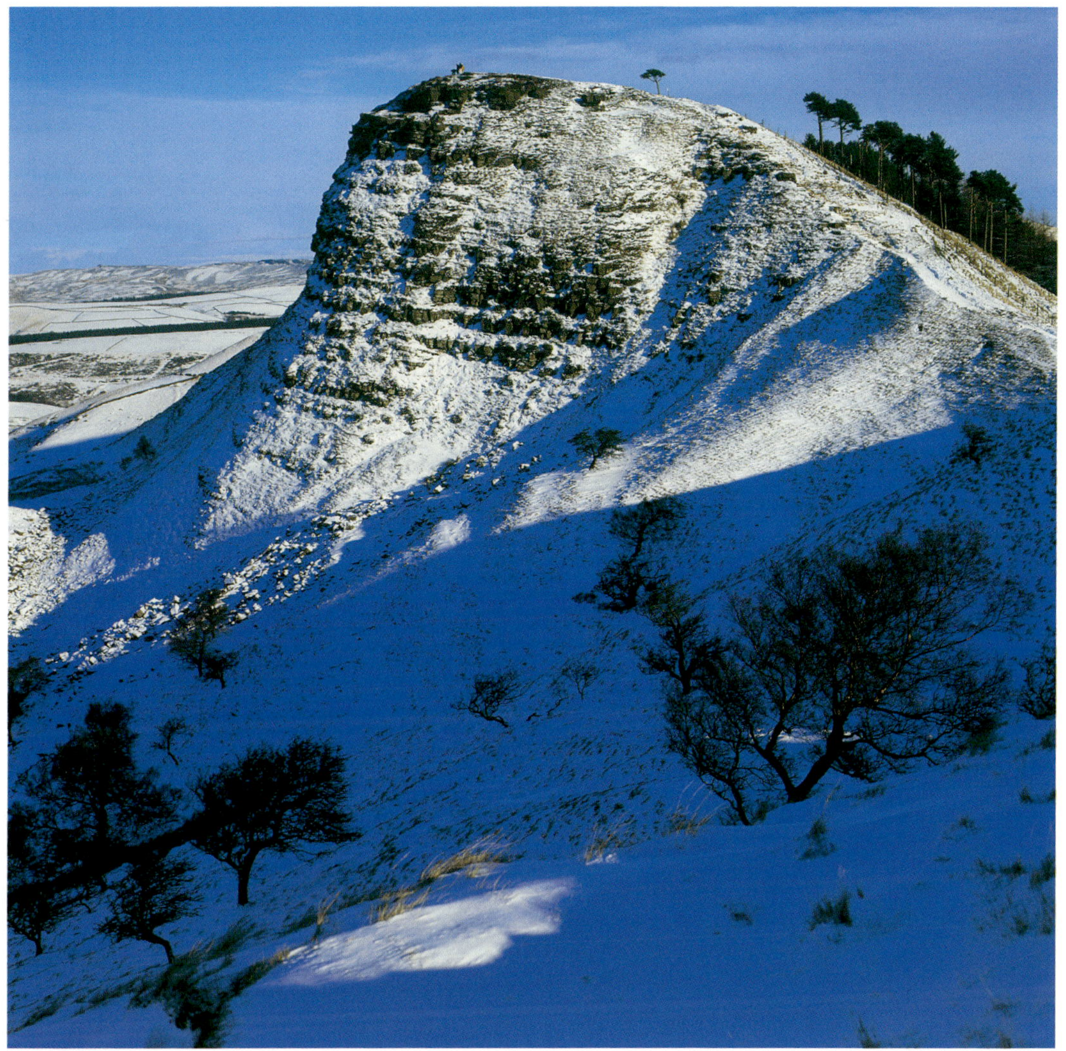

Winter mantle

Dressed in an icy mantle, the craggy Back Tor lies on the ridge linking Mam Tor and Lose Hill. The ridge separates the dark Kinder grits and shales to the north from the white limestone landscape to the south.

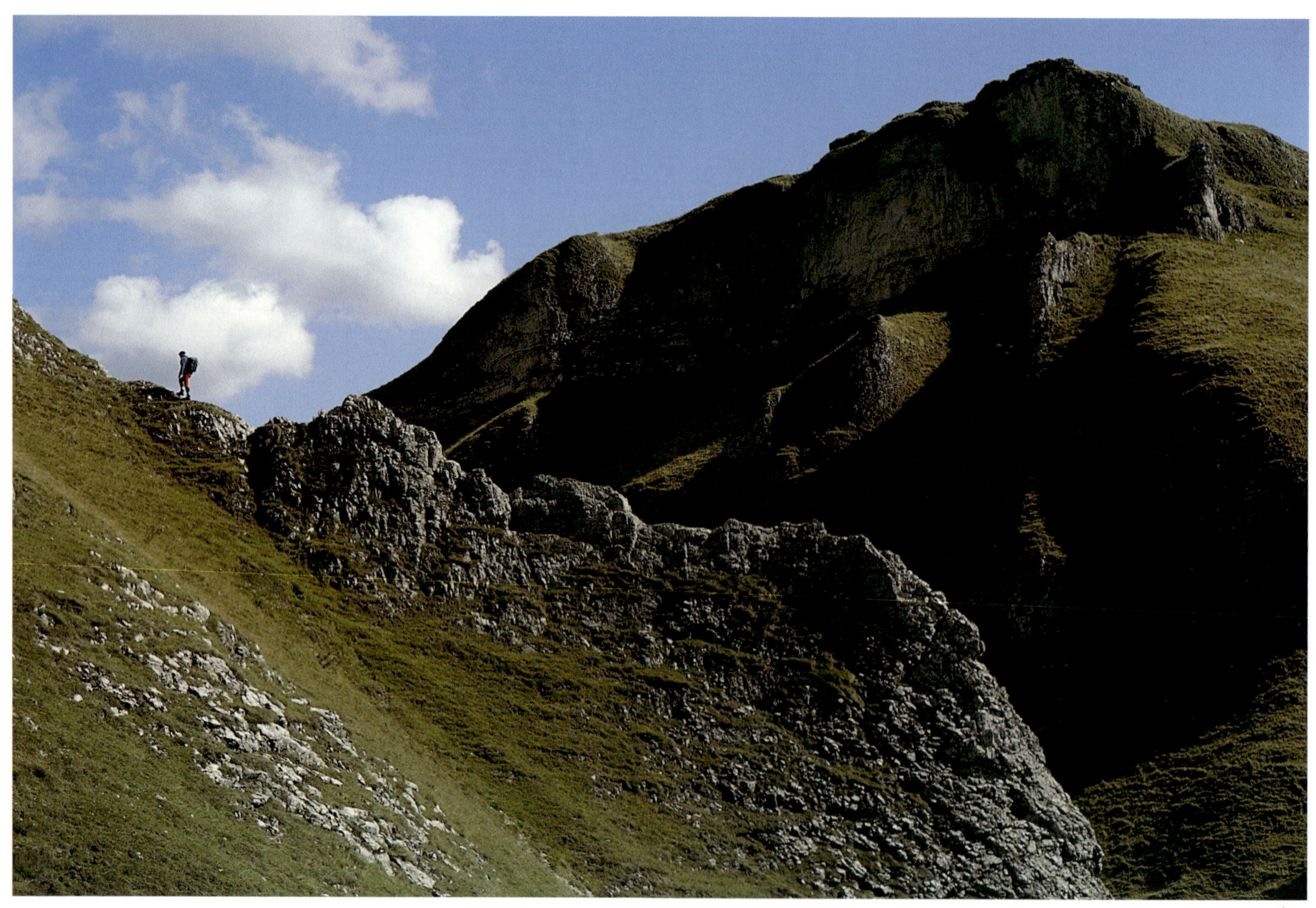

Winnats Pass

The spectacular limestone gorge of Winnats Pass near Castleton was formed under a tropical sea 350 million years ago.

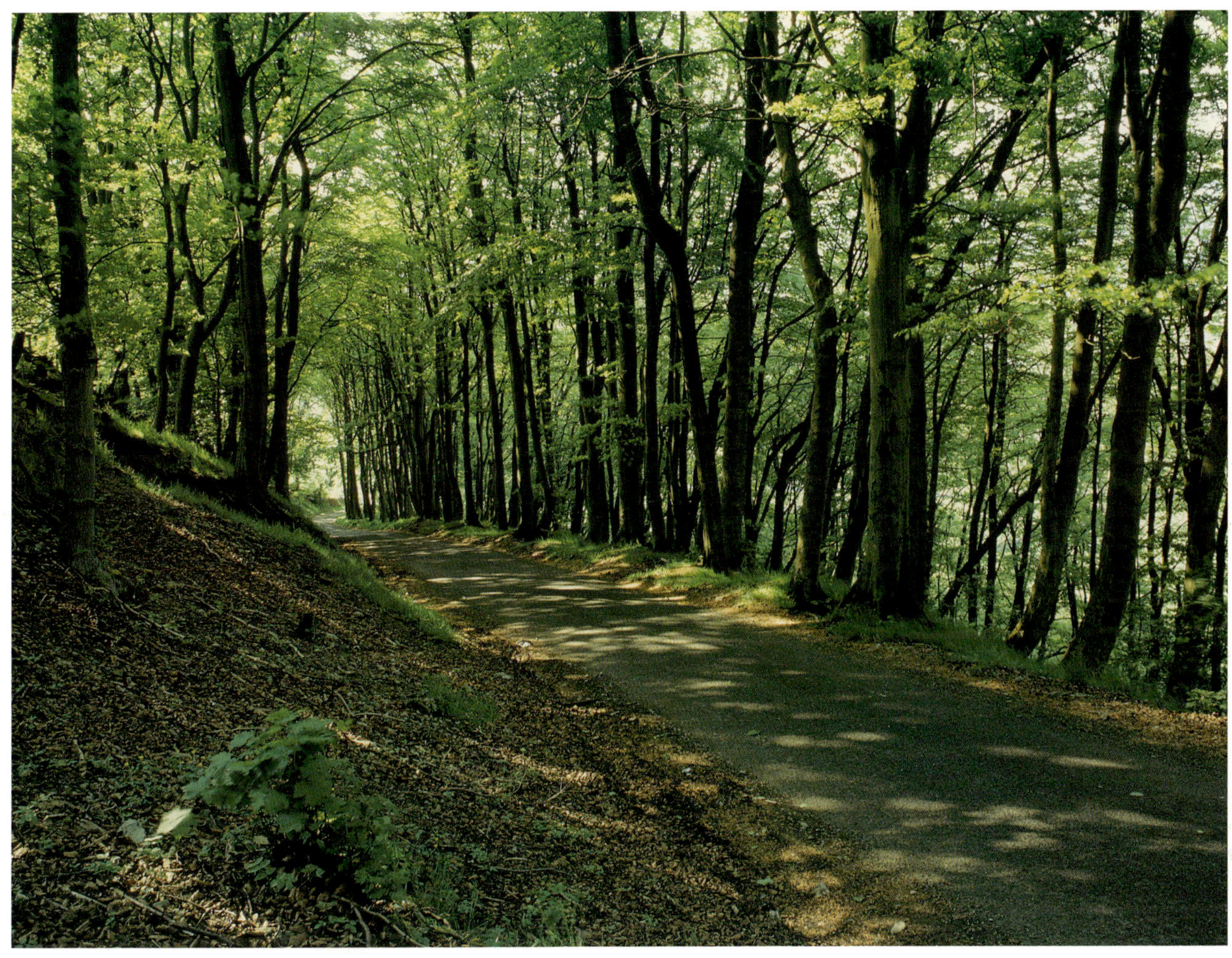

Avenue of trees
Trees form a natural avenue along this quiet country road known as Siggate ('side gate'), leading down into the village of Castleton.

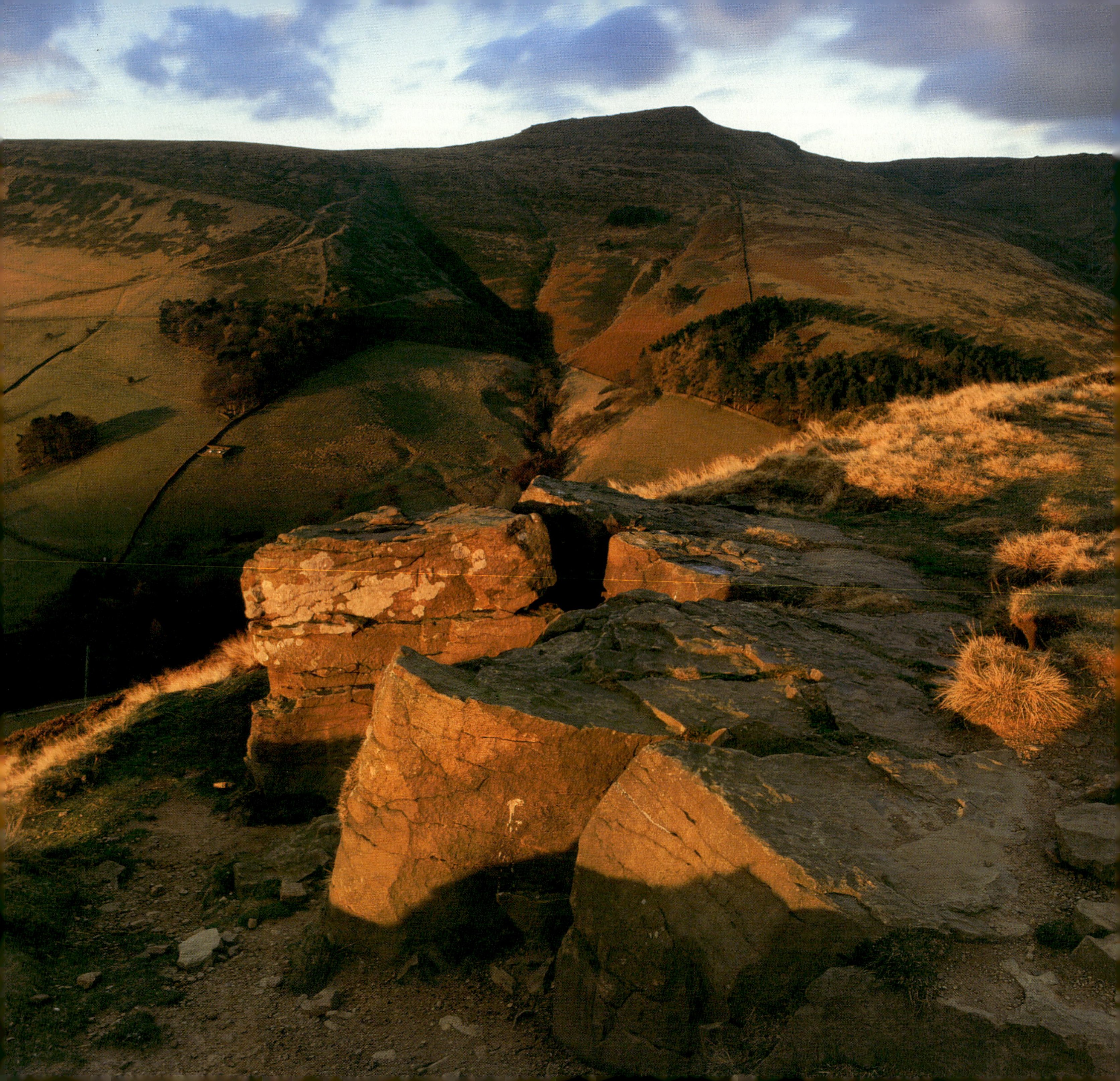

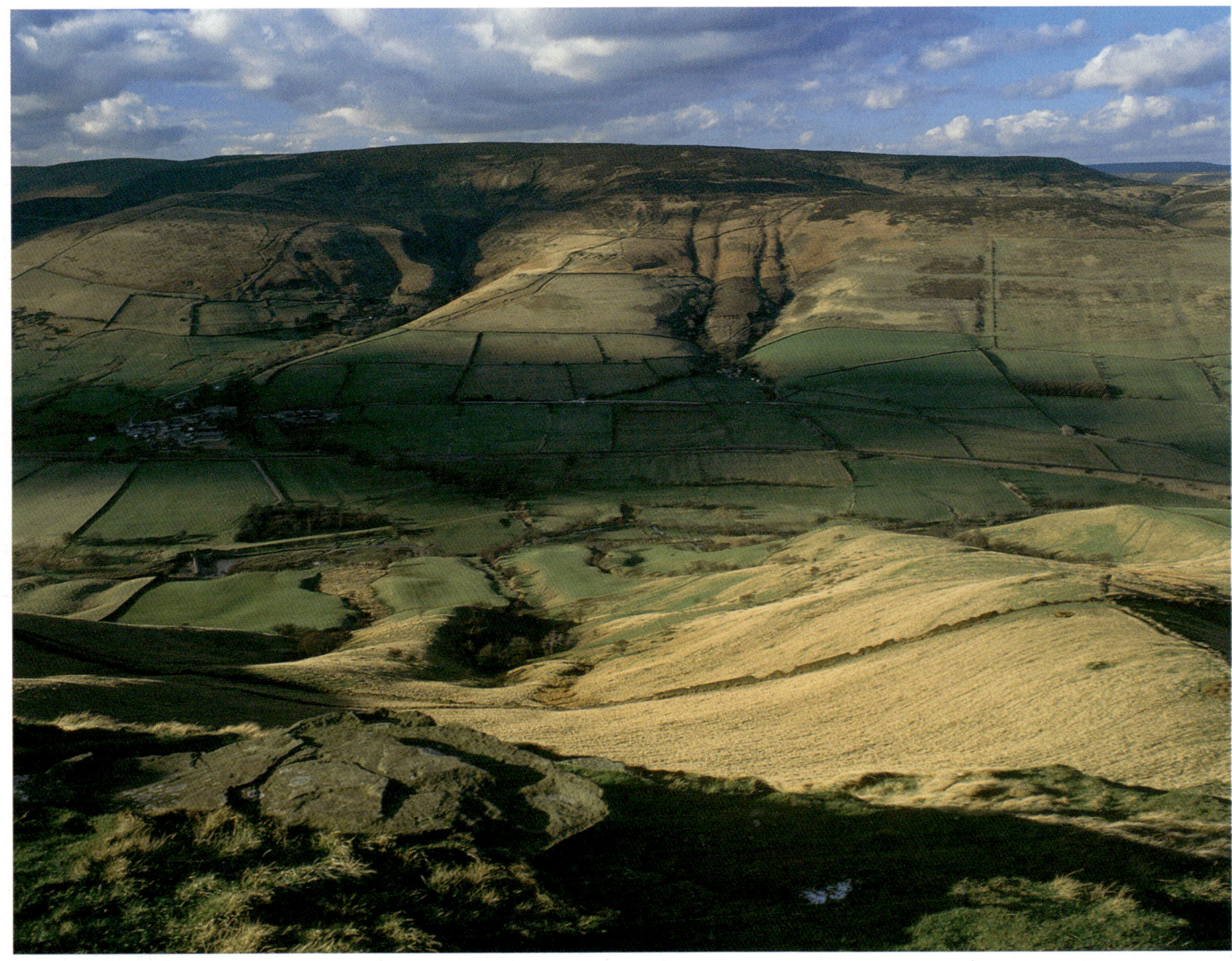

Vale of Edale
Light and shadow create patterns across the Vale of Edale in this view from Lose Hill.

Left: **The Nab**
Dawn light paints the rocks on The Nab, in this view across Grindsbrook to Grindslow Knoll, Kinder Scout.

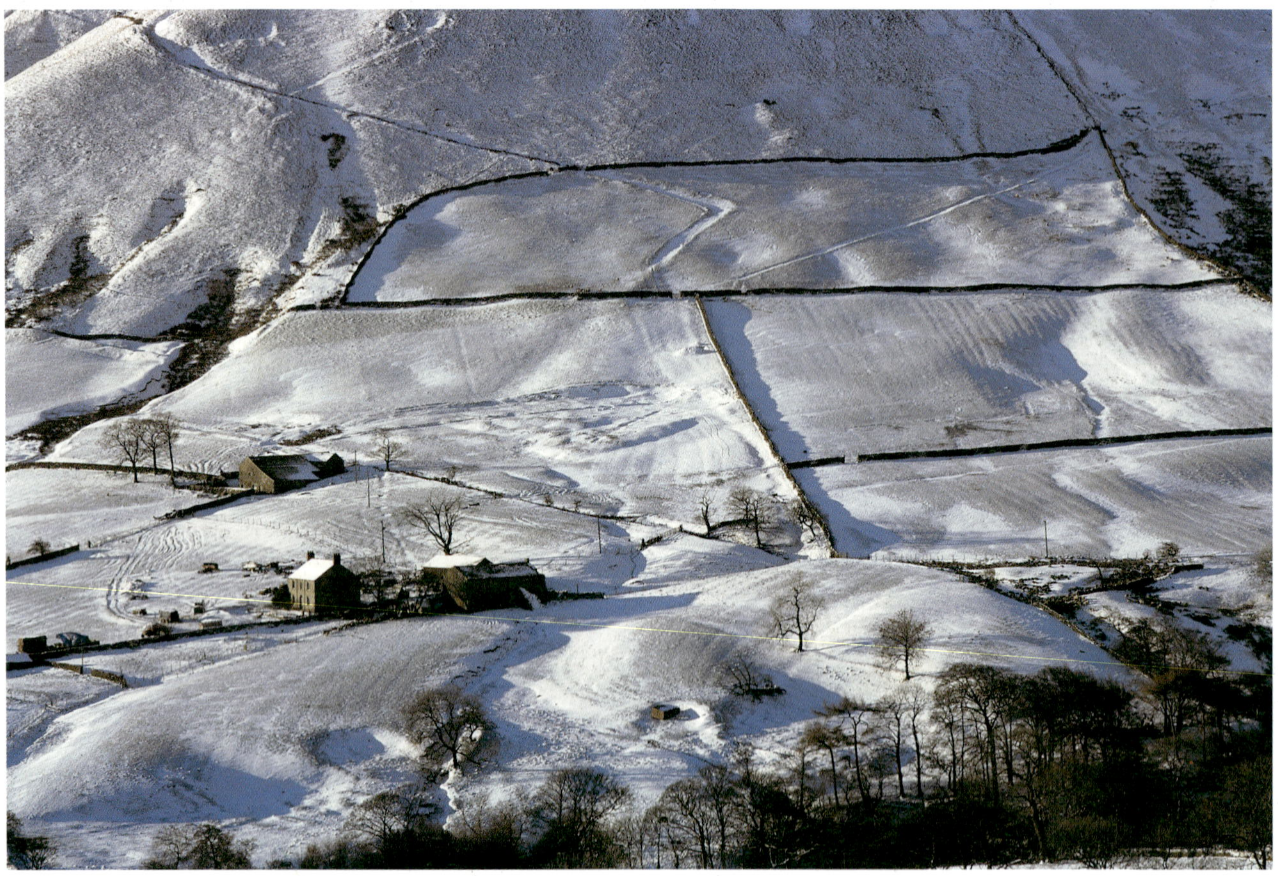

Bleak midwinter
A farm at the head of the Edale Valley near Upper Booth. Note the patterns of medieval ridge and furrow cultivation outlined by the snow.

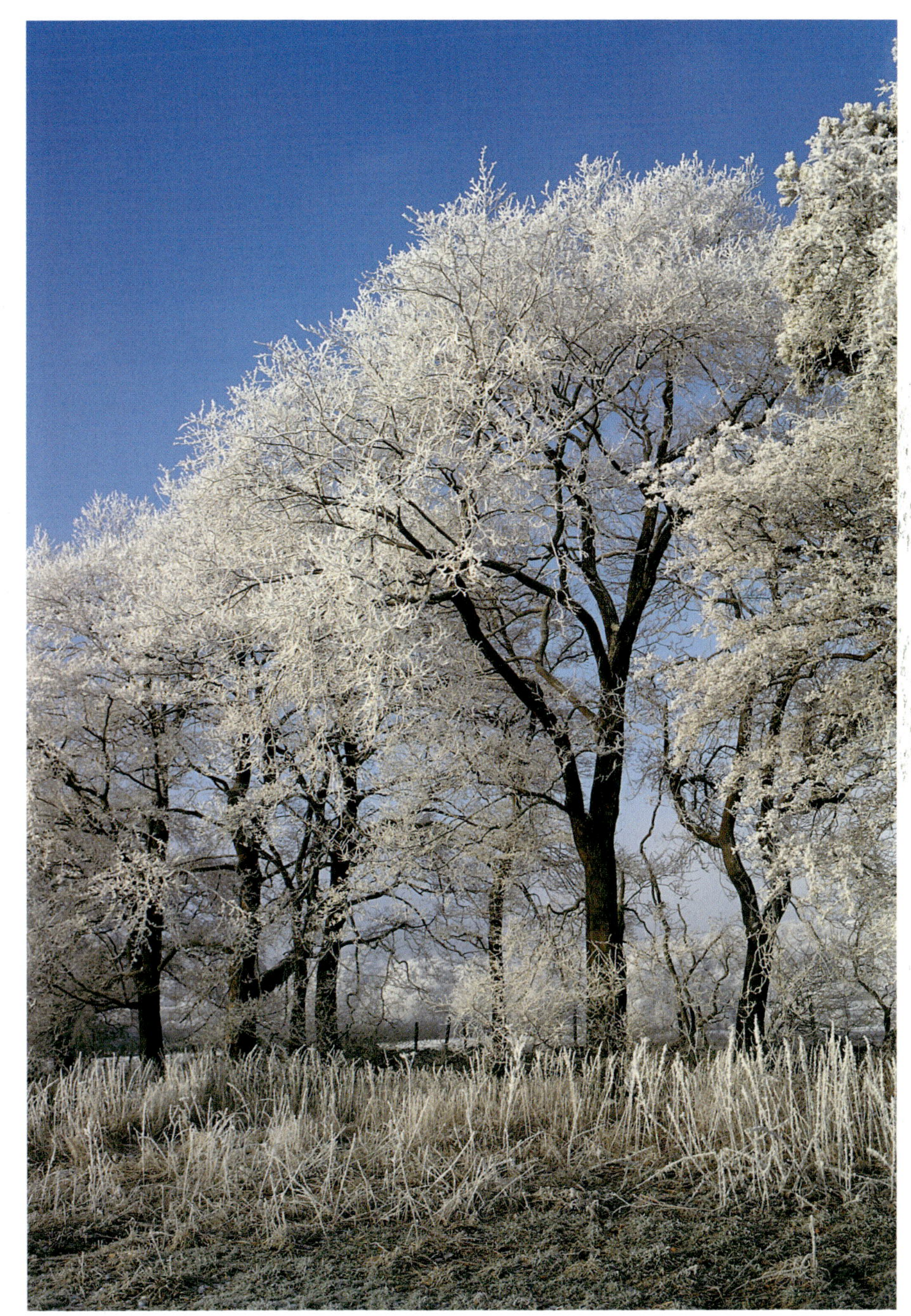

Frosty trees
Layers of hoar frost crystals cloak a row of trees.

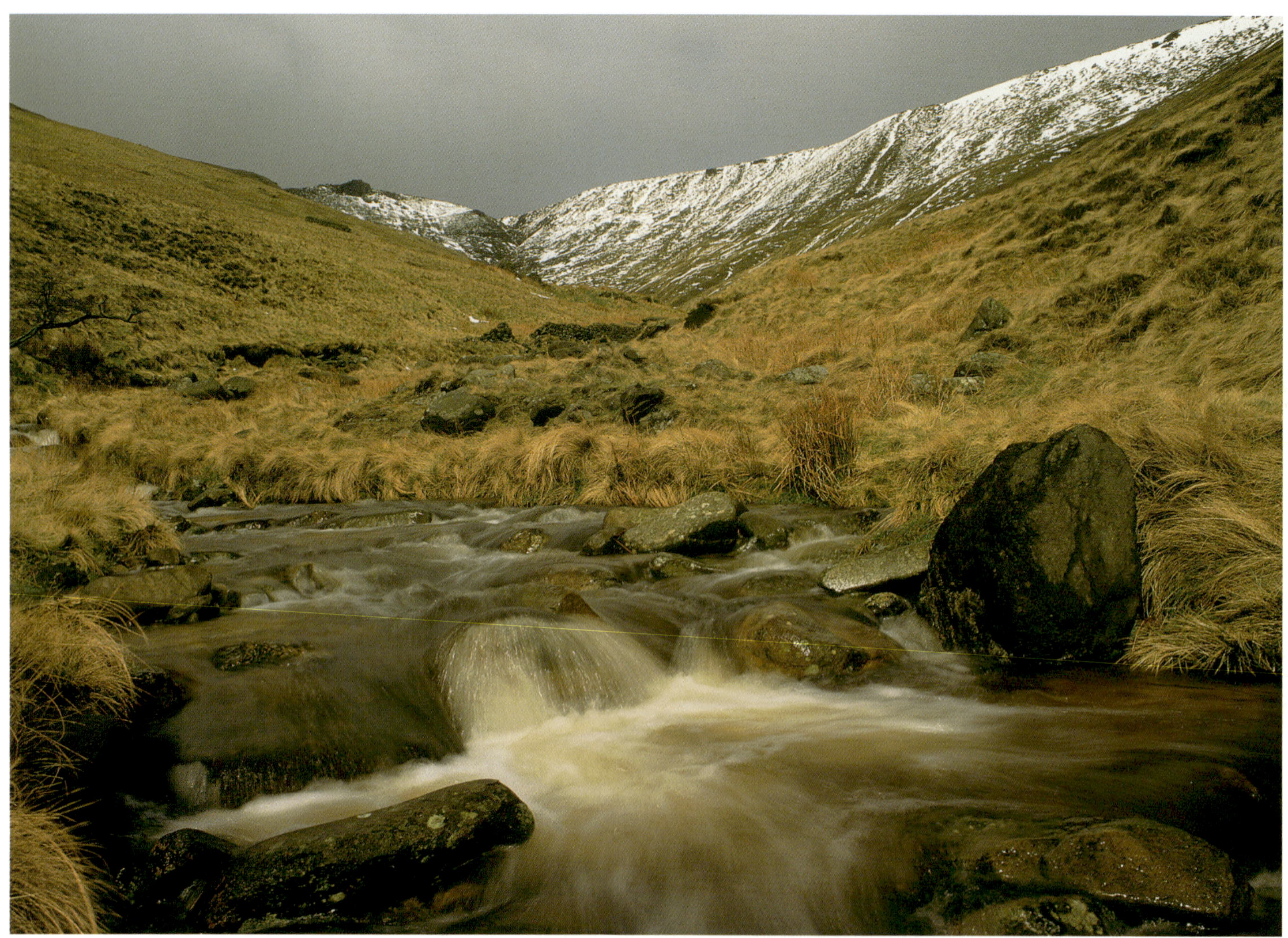

Winter skyline
The last snows of winter on the skyline above Crowden Clough, one of the finest approaches to the Kinder Scout plateau.

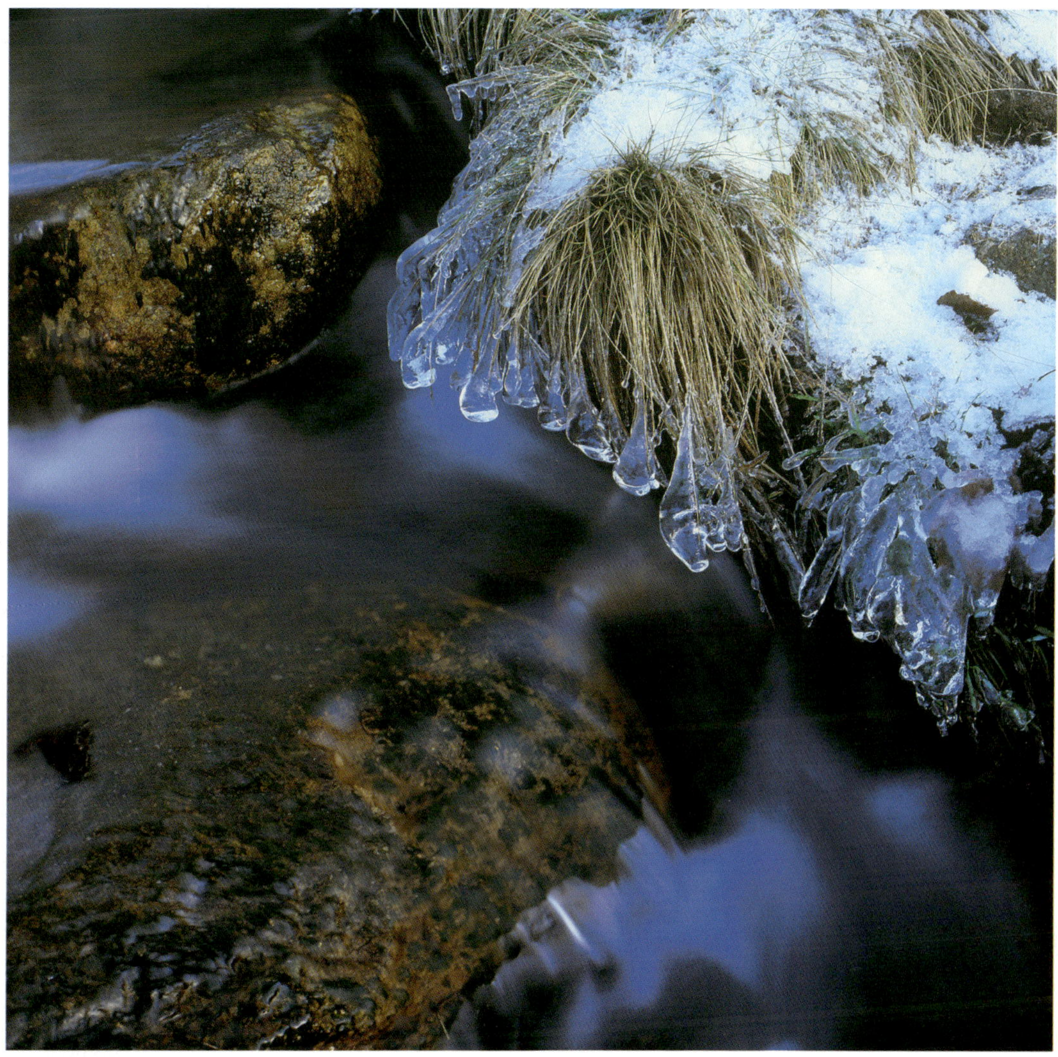

Fast flowing brook
Crowden Brook rushes down from the peaty slopes of Kinder Scout, sweeping its way around and over smooth boulders overhung by frozen grasses.

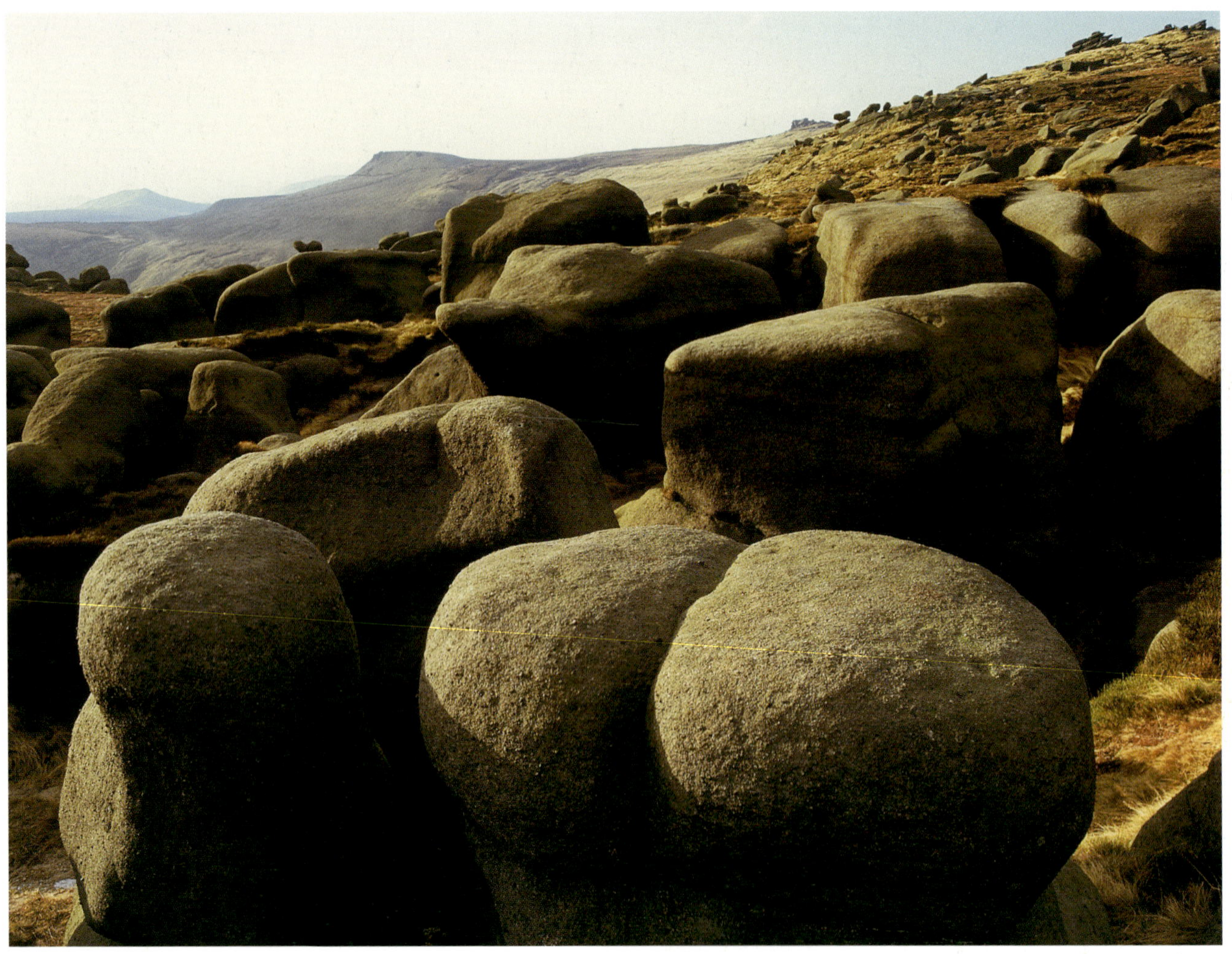

Eroded rocks
The weirdly eroded rocks known as the Wool Packs on the southern edge of the Kinder Scout plateau.

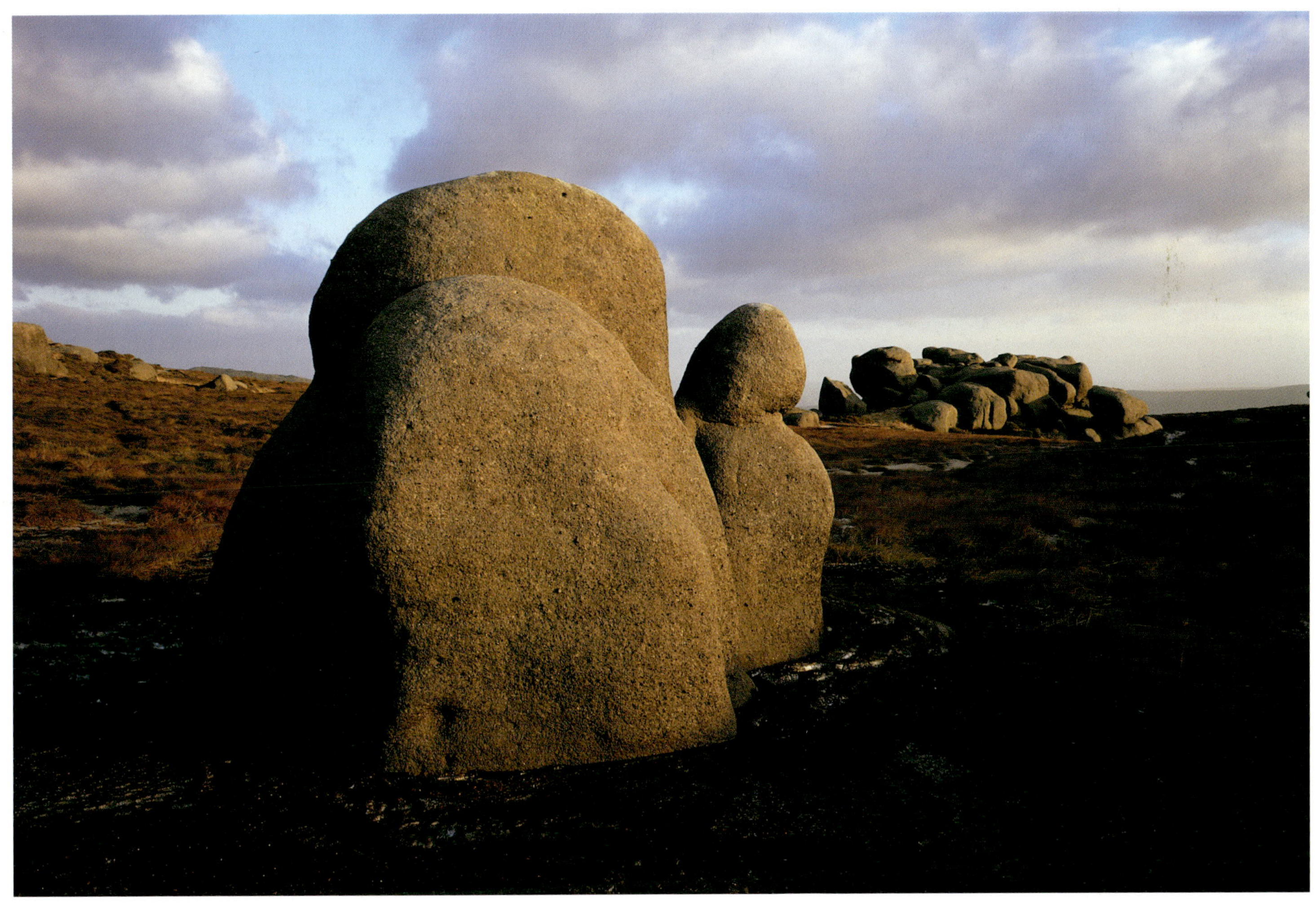

Gritstone sentinel
A lone gritstone boulder surrounded by peat among the Wool Packs on Kinder Scout.

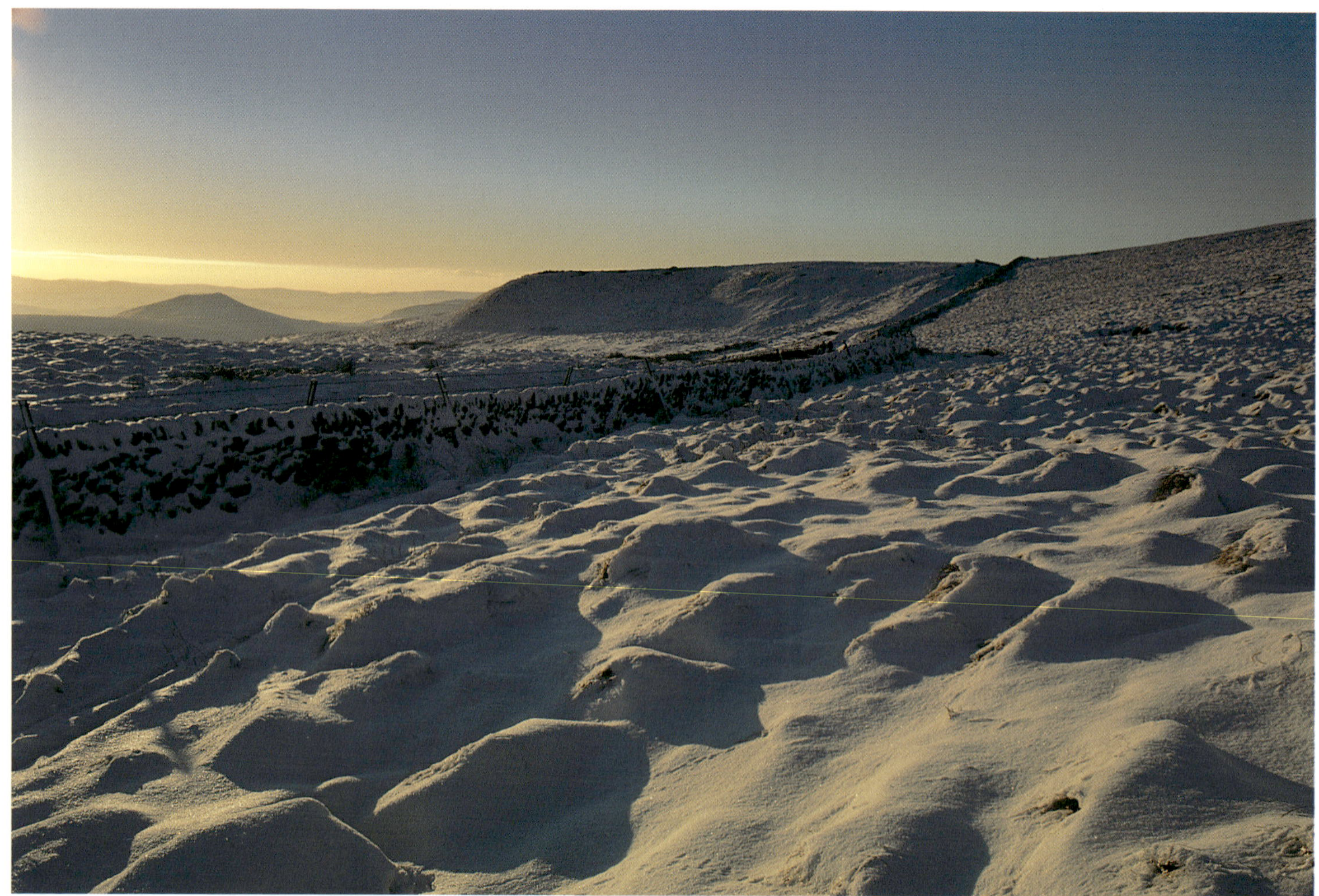

Winter glow
The setting sun casts yellow light across this snowy scene near Edale Cross, the high point on the old packhorse trail linking Edale with Hayfield.

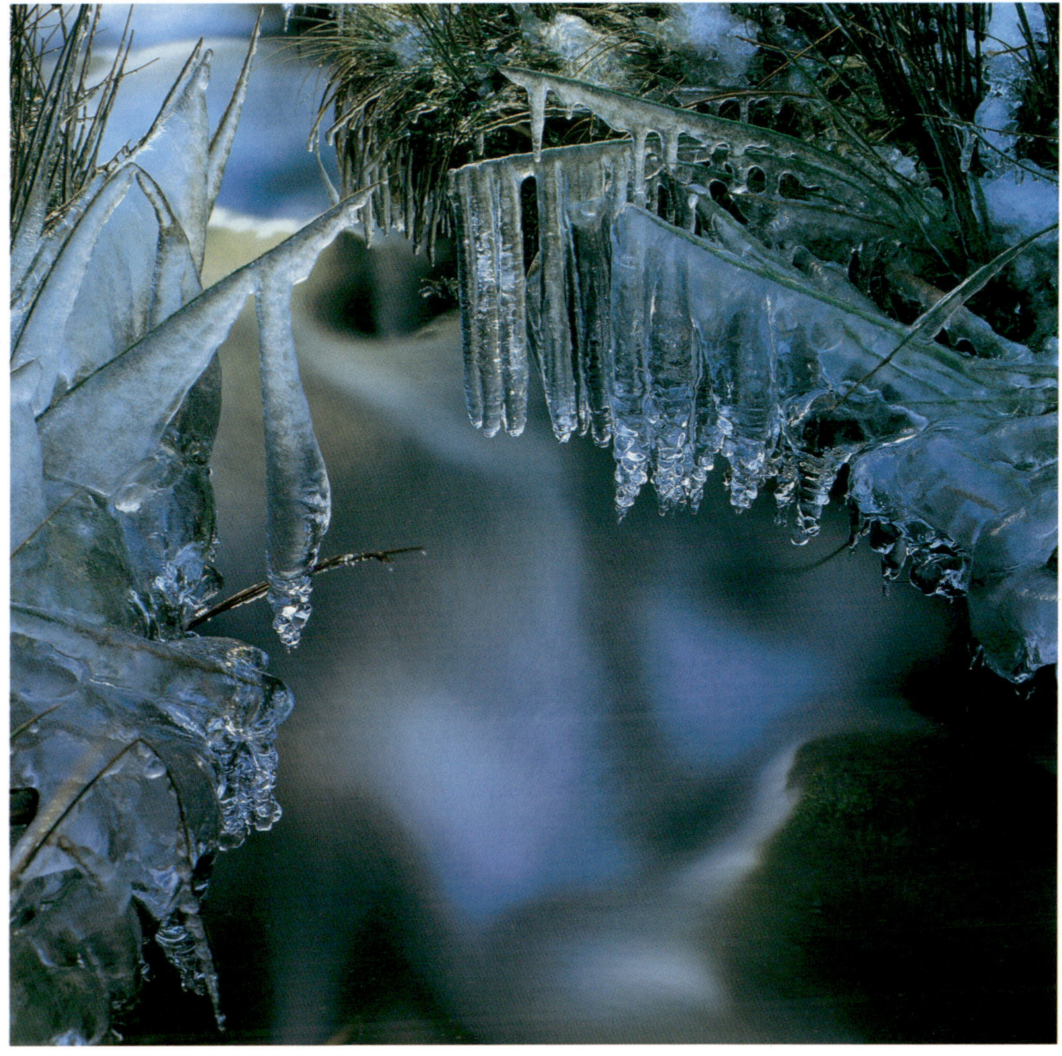

Iced grasses
Transparent ice coats stream-side grasses.

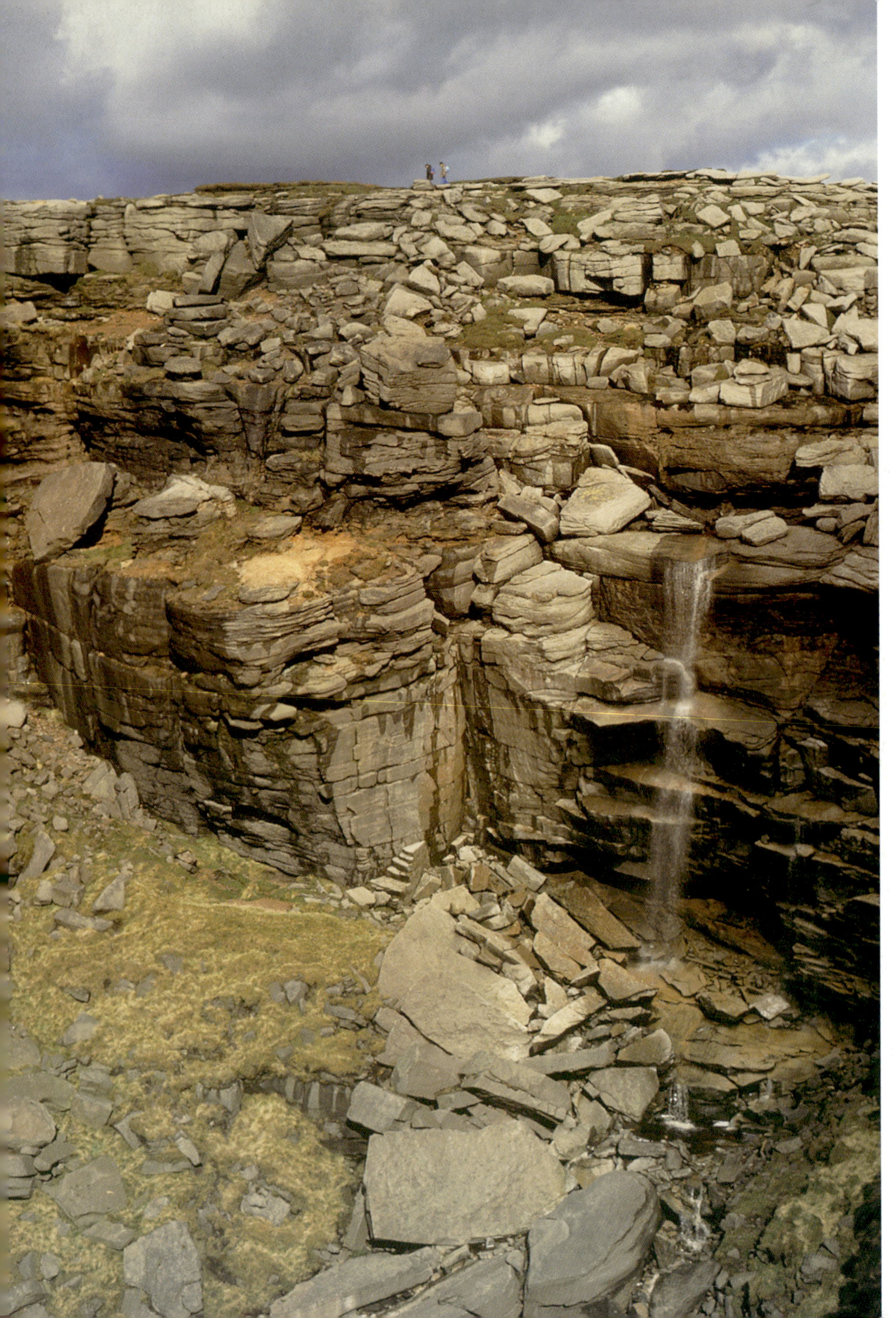

Kinder Downfall
Kinder Scout sheds much of its water over Kinder Downfall on the western edge of its plateau. At 100 feet high, this is the highest waterfall in the Peak District.

Icy curtain

Looking out through a curtain of translucent icicles, hanging like stalactites from the lip of an ice cave behind the frozen Kinder Downfall.

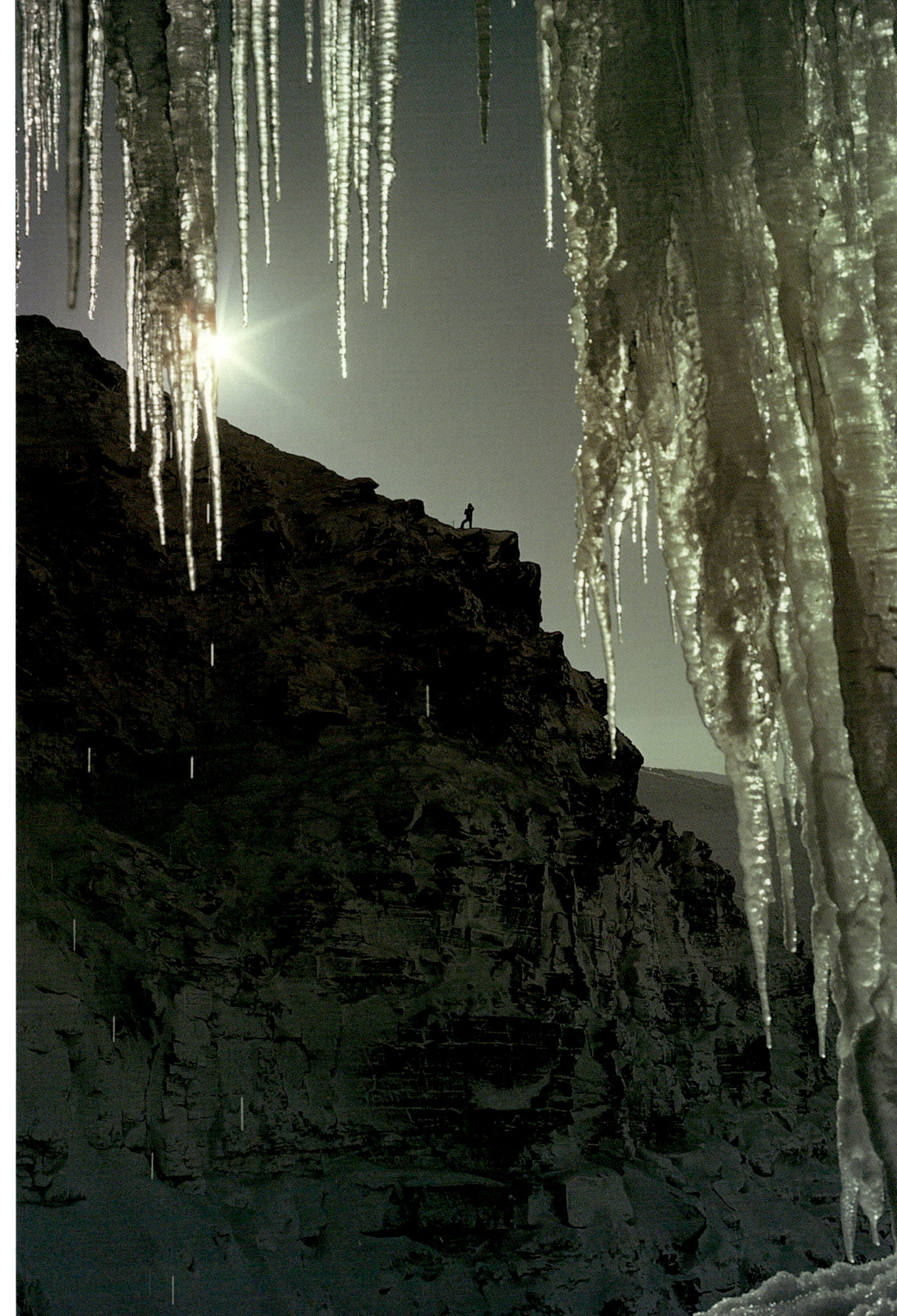

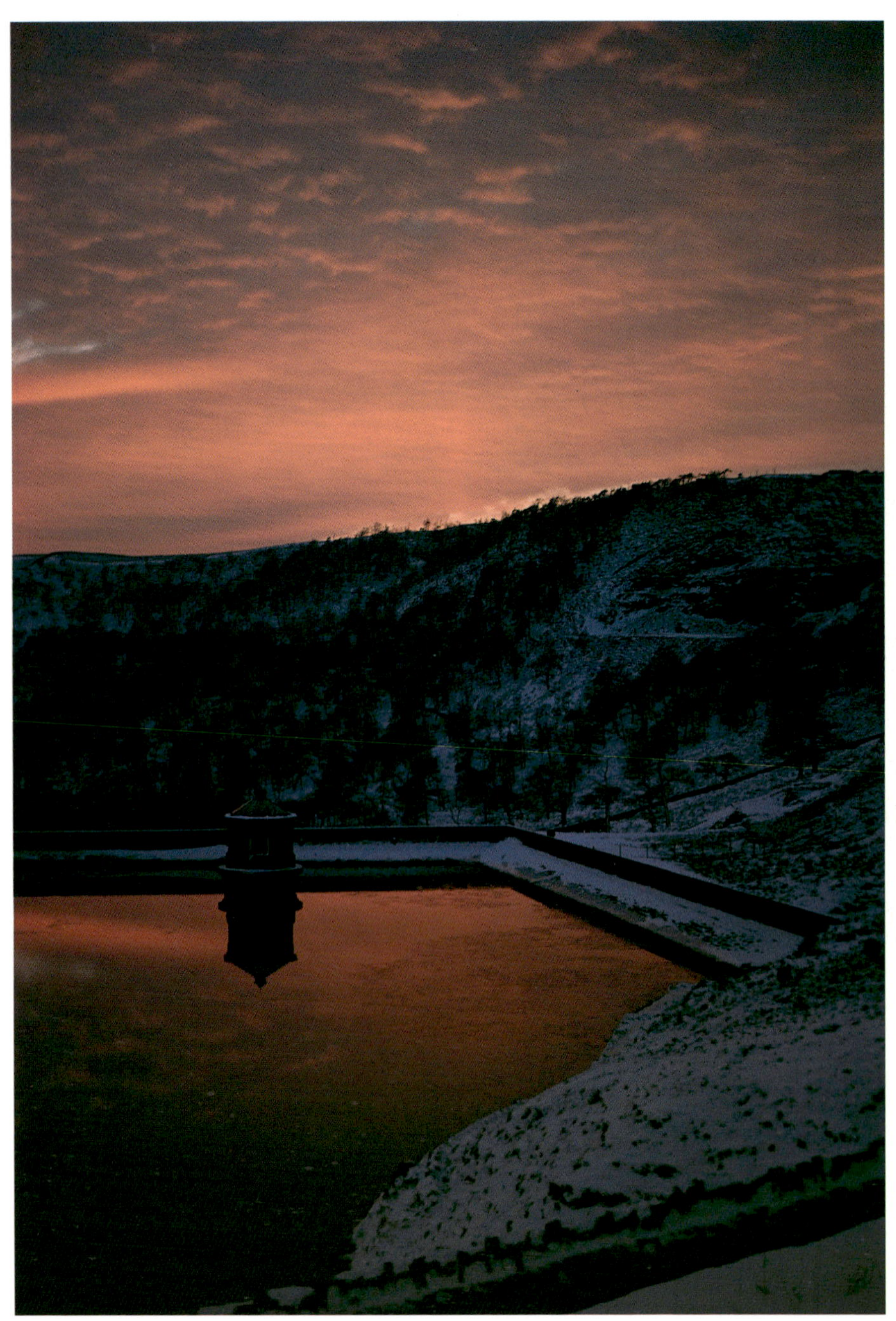

Kinder Reservoir
A dramatic sunset reflected in the waters of Kinder Reservoir near Hayfield.

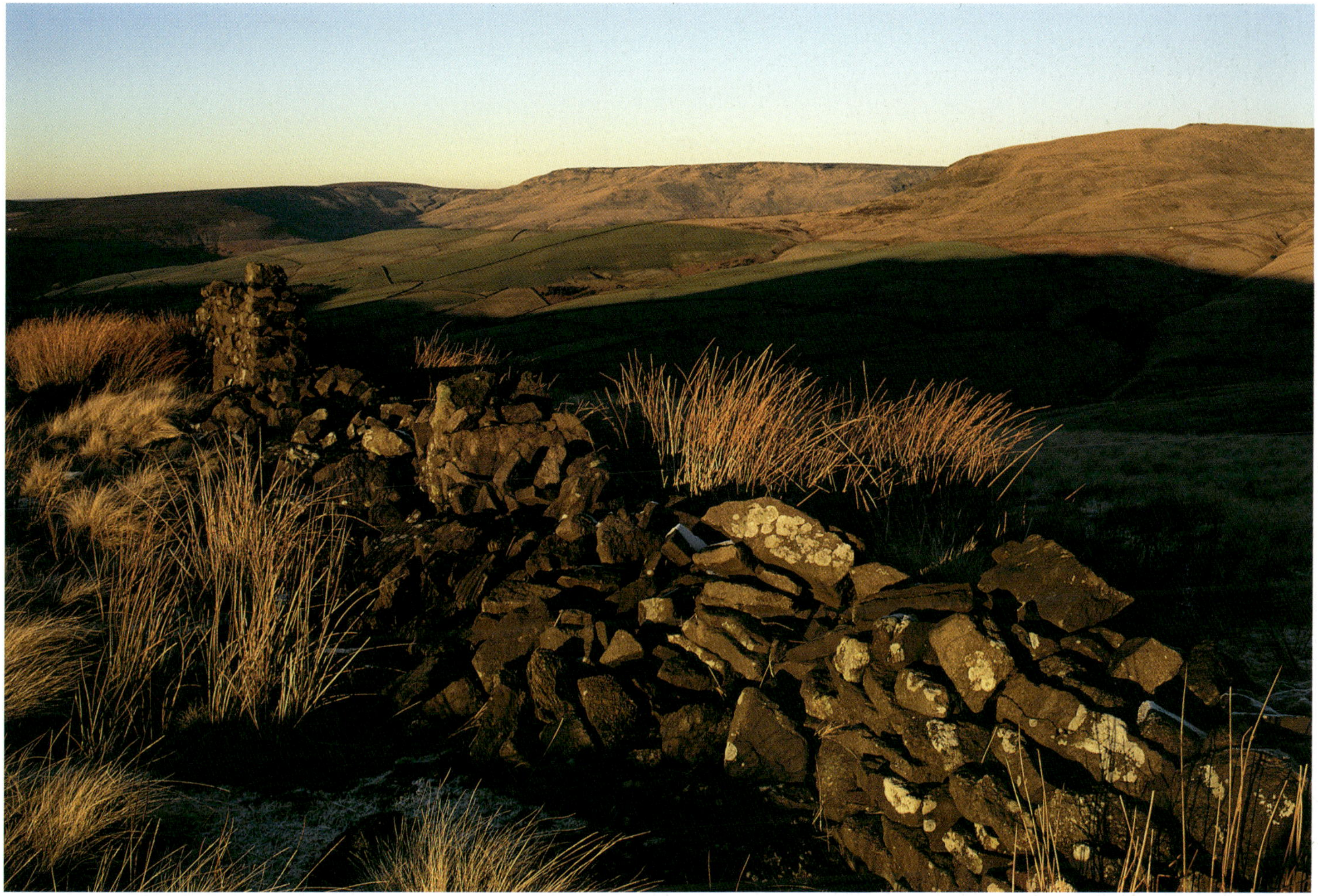

Sett Valley twilight
The last light of day picks out the western slopes of Kinder Low End seen across the valley of the River Sett near Hayfield.

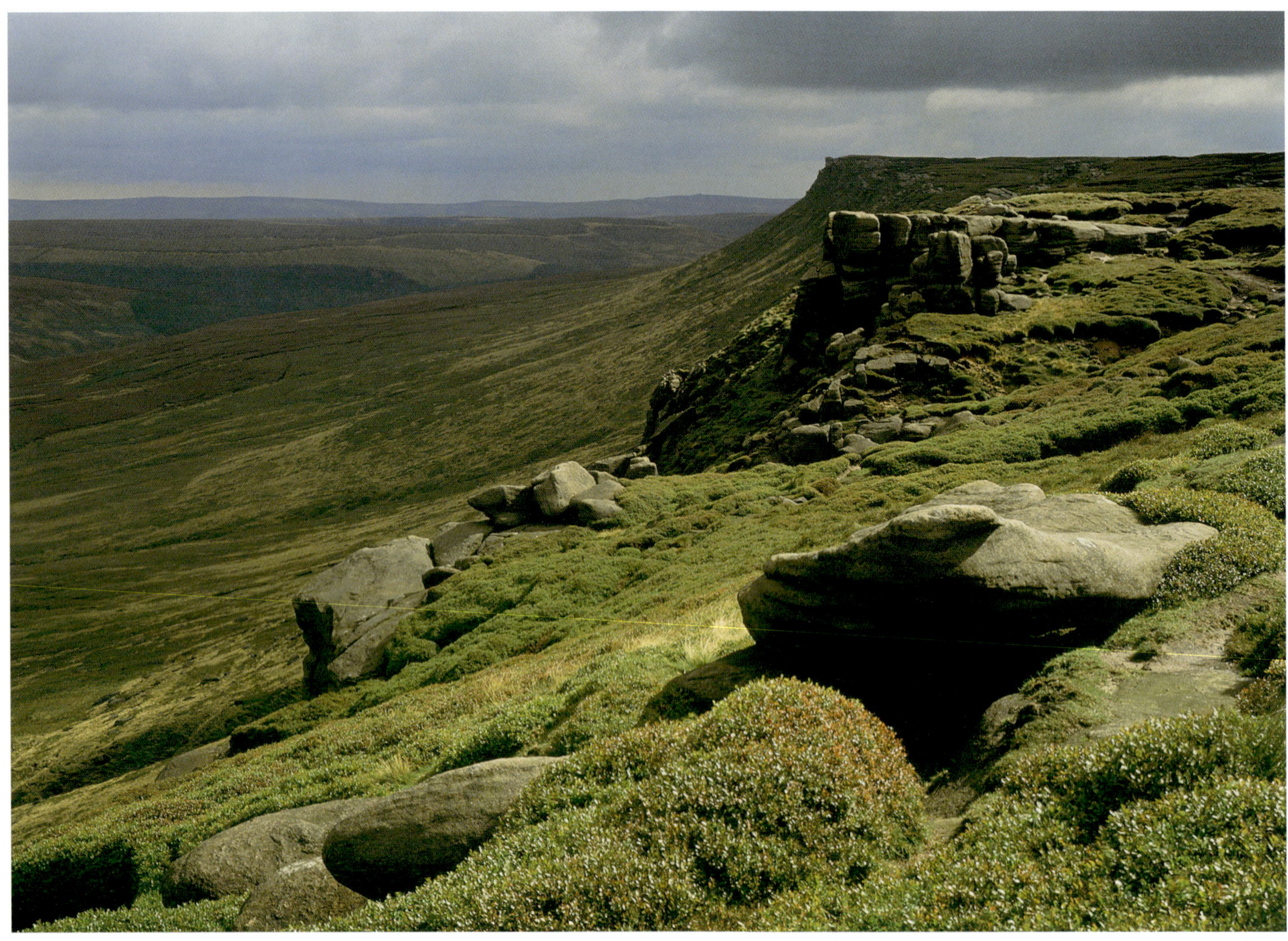

Bilberries and rocks
Clusters of bilberry dominate this view along the craggy skyline of Kinder Scout's northern edges.

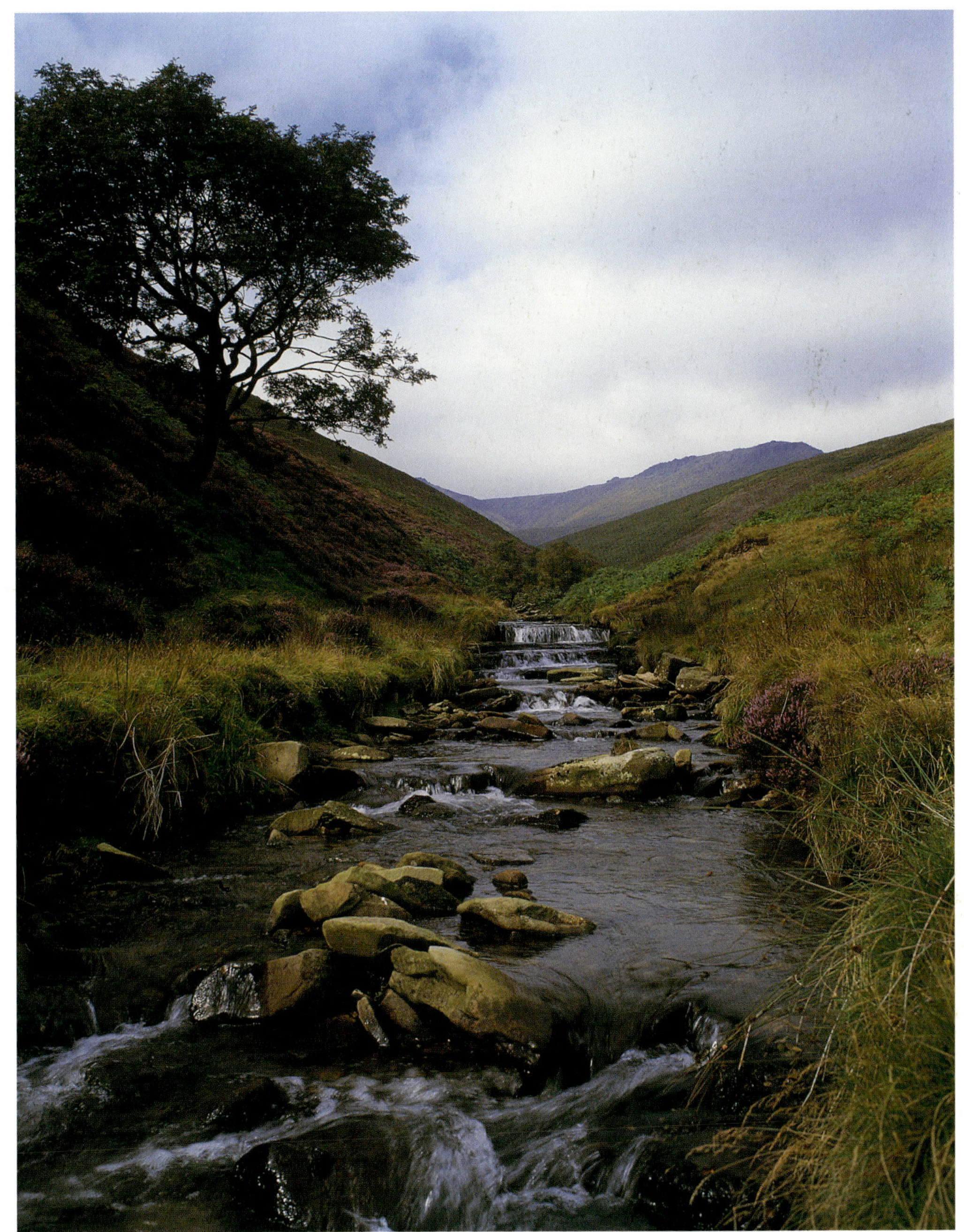

Fair Brook
The Fair Brook rushes down from Kinder Scout's northern flanks to join the River Ashop in the Woodlands Valley near the Snake Inn.

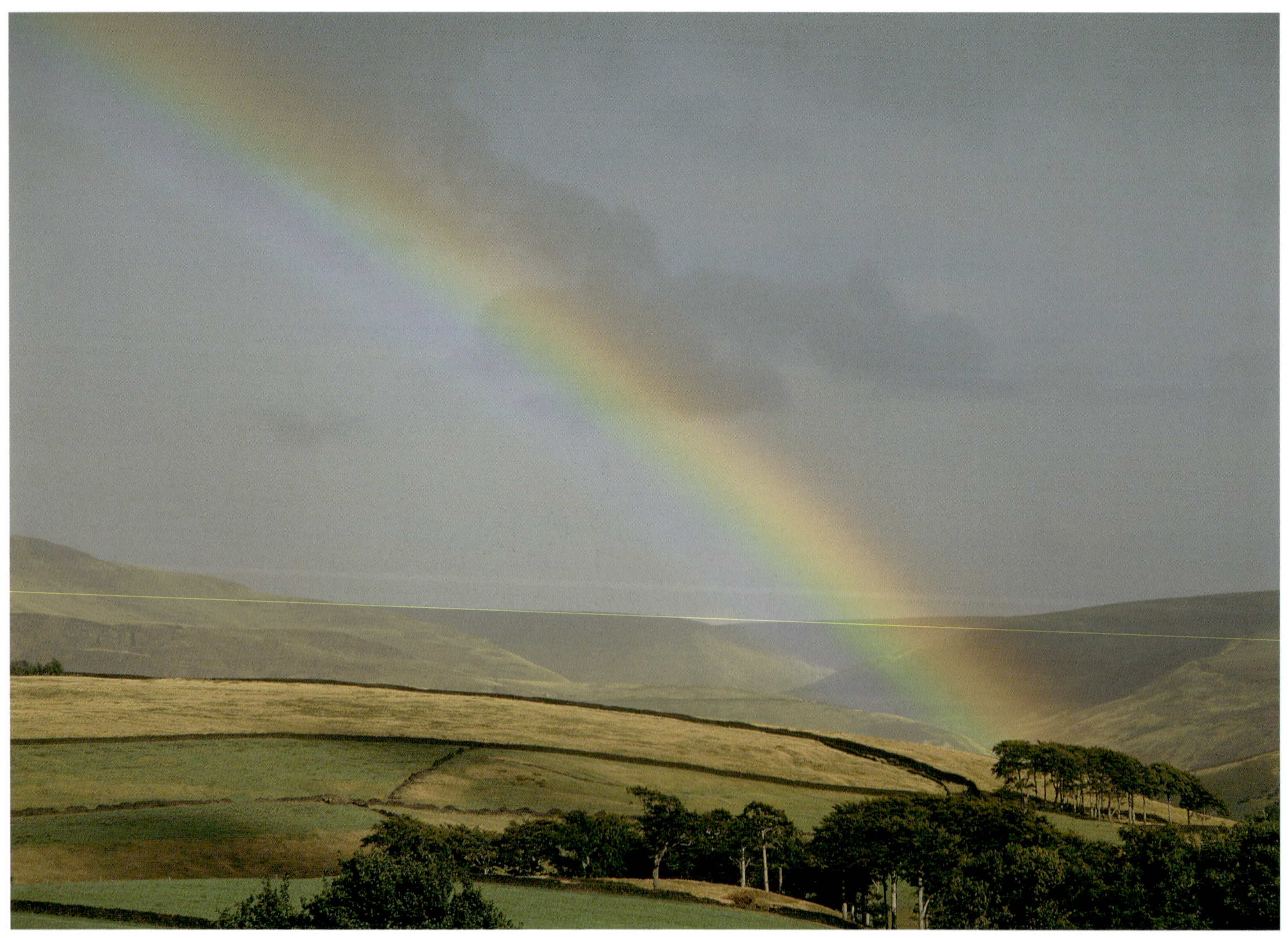

Stormy rainbow
A spectrum of colours contrasts with the dark, brooding storm clouds over Bleaklow.

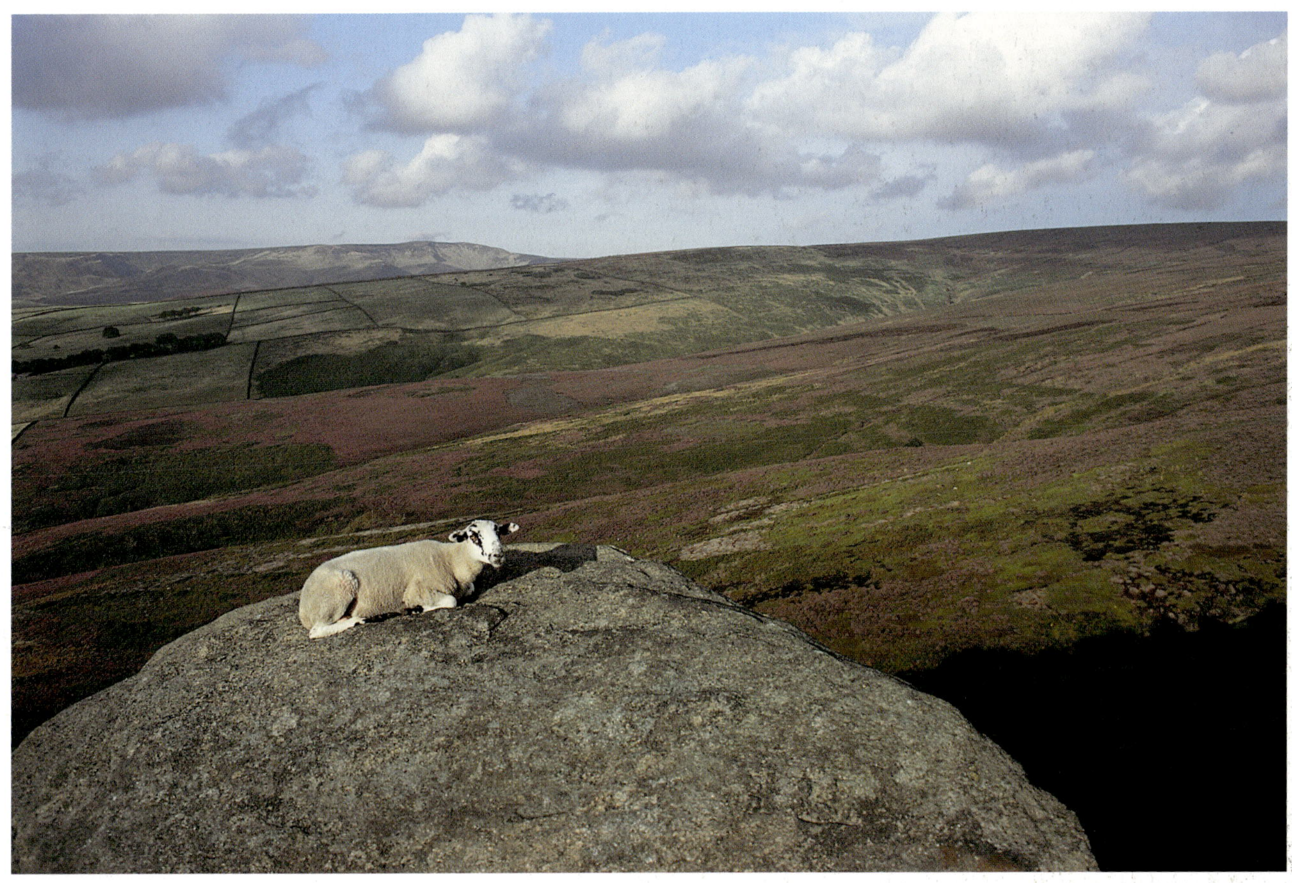

Just resting

A sheep soaks up the warm evening sunshine on Shaw Moor above Glossop. Grazing sheep have shaped much of this moorland landscape.

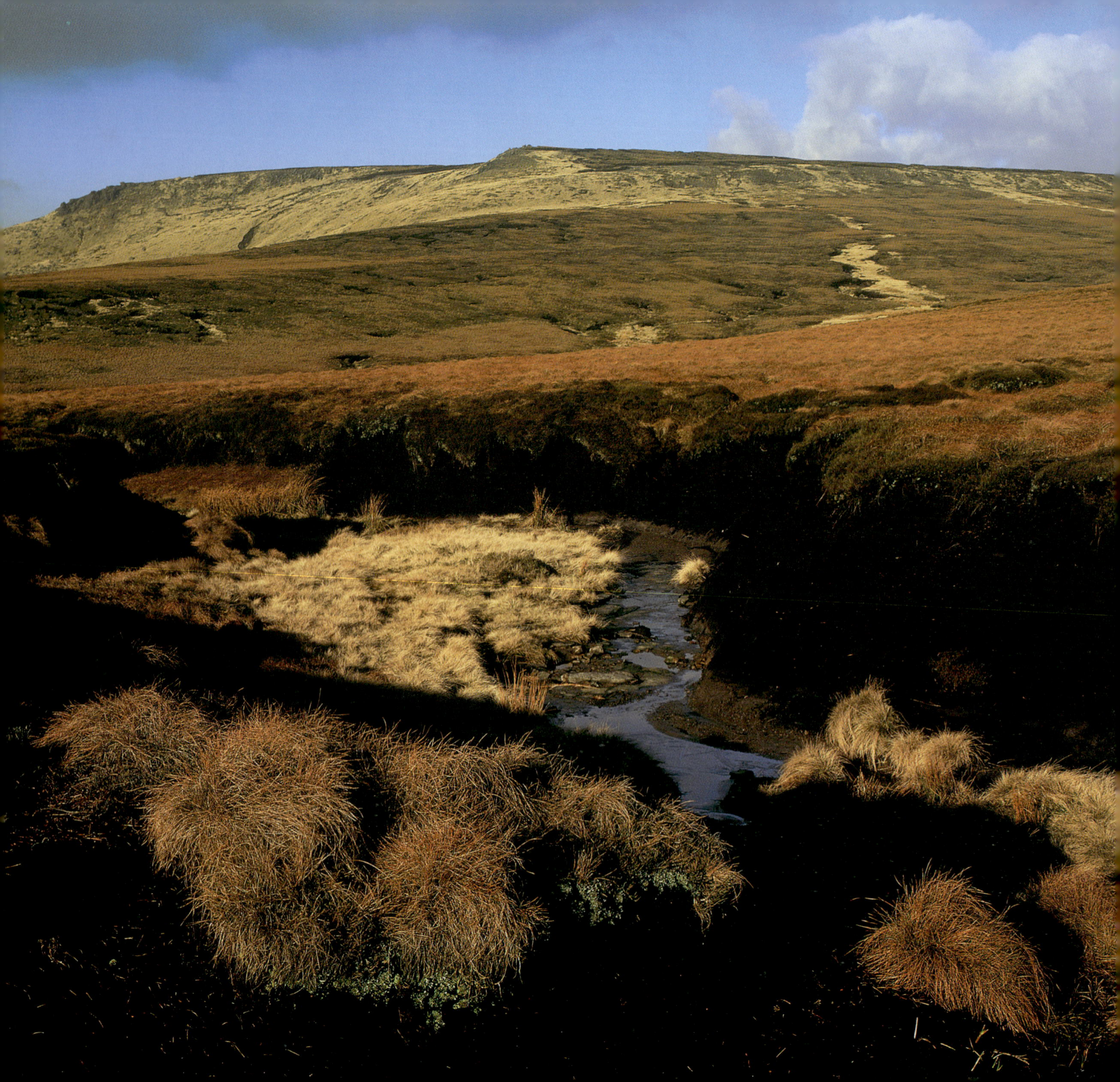

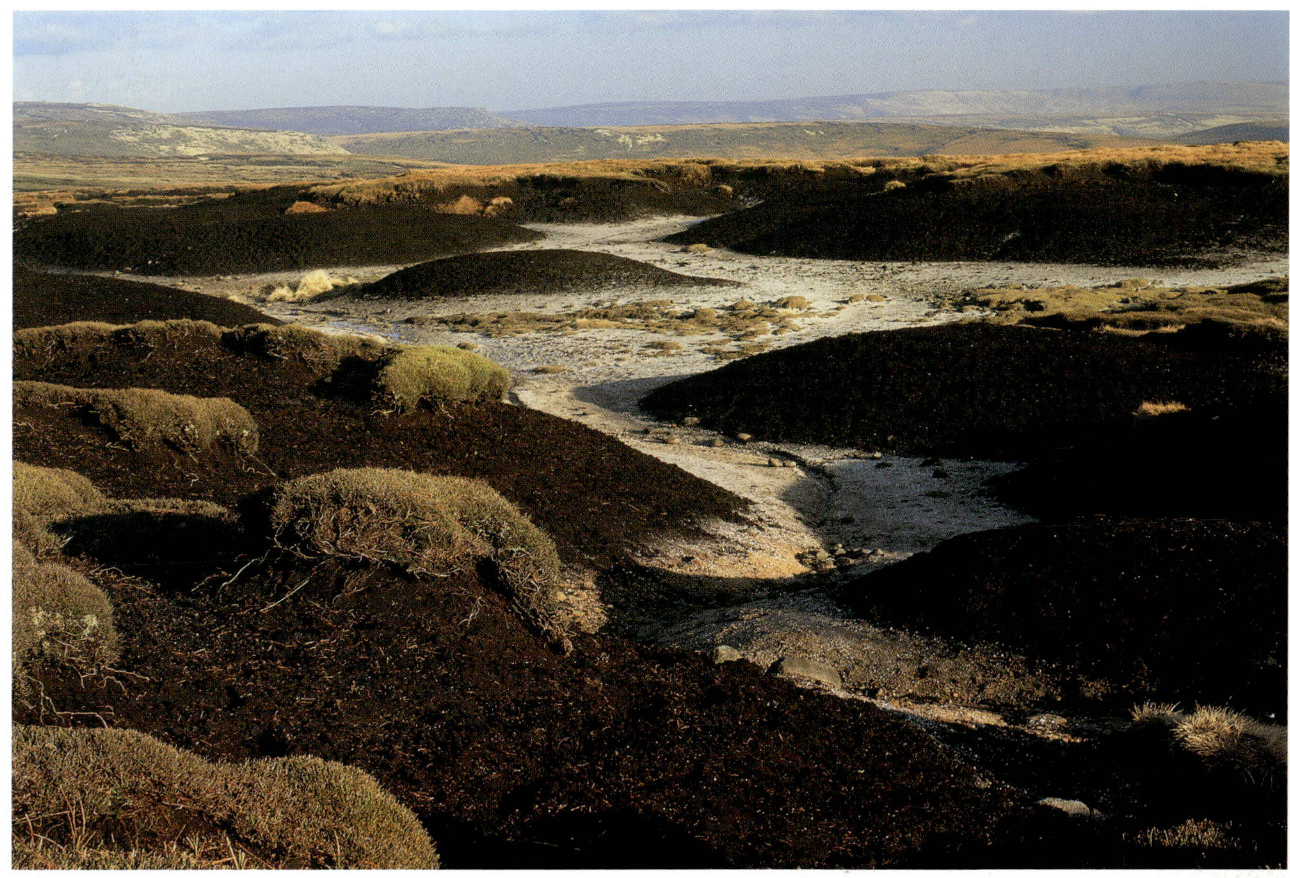

Moorland desert
The bare bones of the Bleaklow landscape.

Left: **A bleak landscape**
Grasses add a touch of colour to this bleak moorland landscape leading to Higher Shelf Stones and Bleaklow, seen from the Snake Pass.

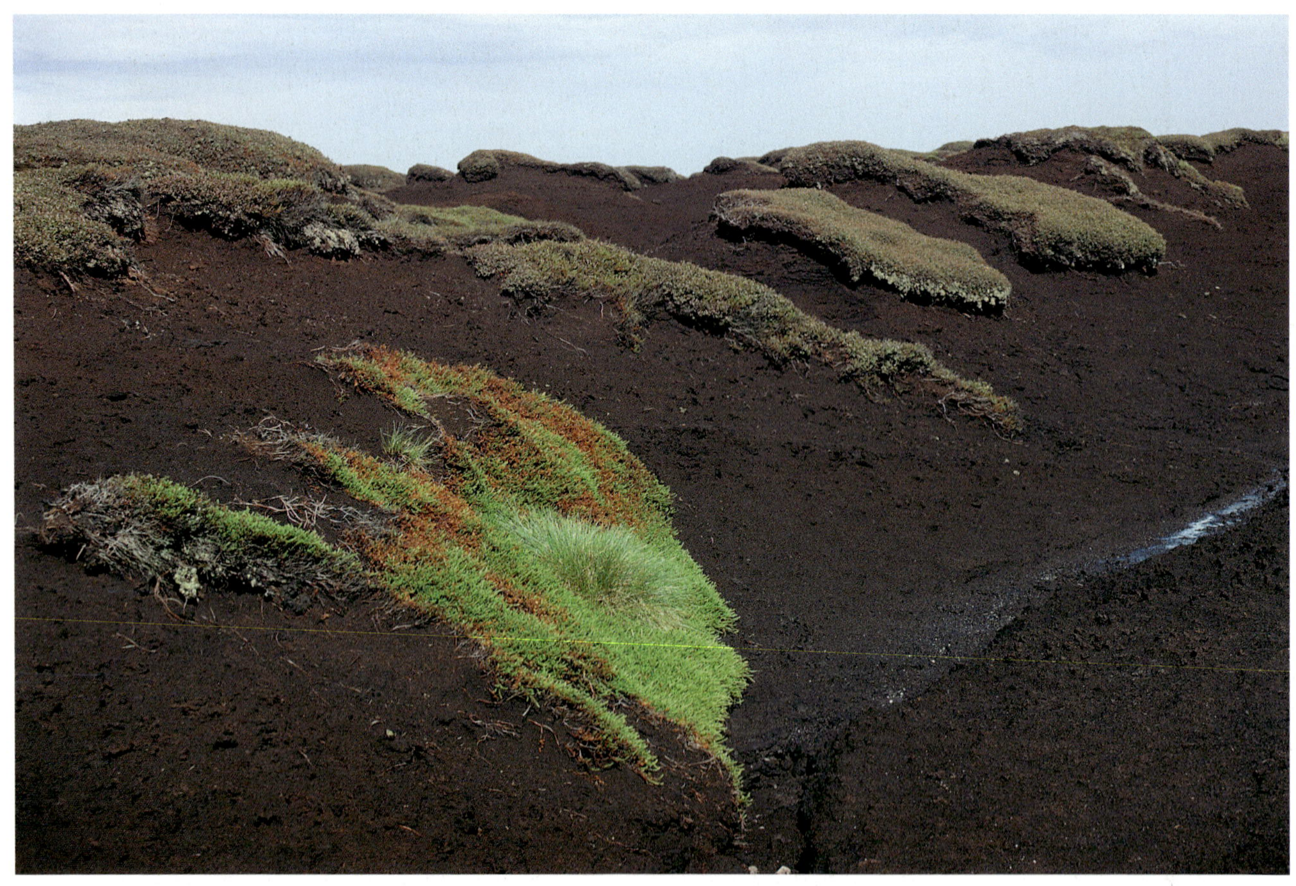

Hags and groughs
Bleaklow's dark and squelchy peaty wilderness is offset by the warm colour of grasses and bilberry clumps. This terrain has been described as 'land at the end of its tether.'

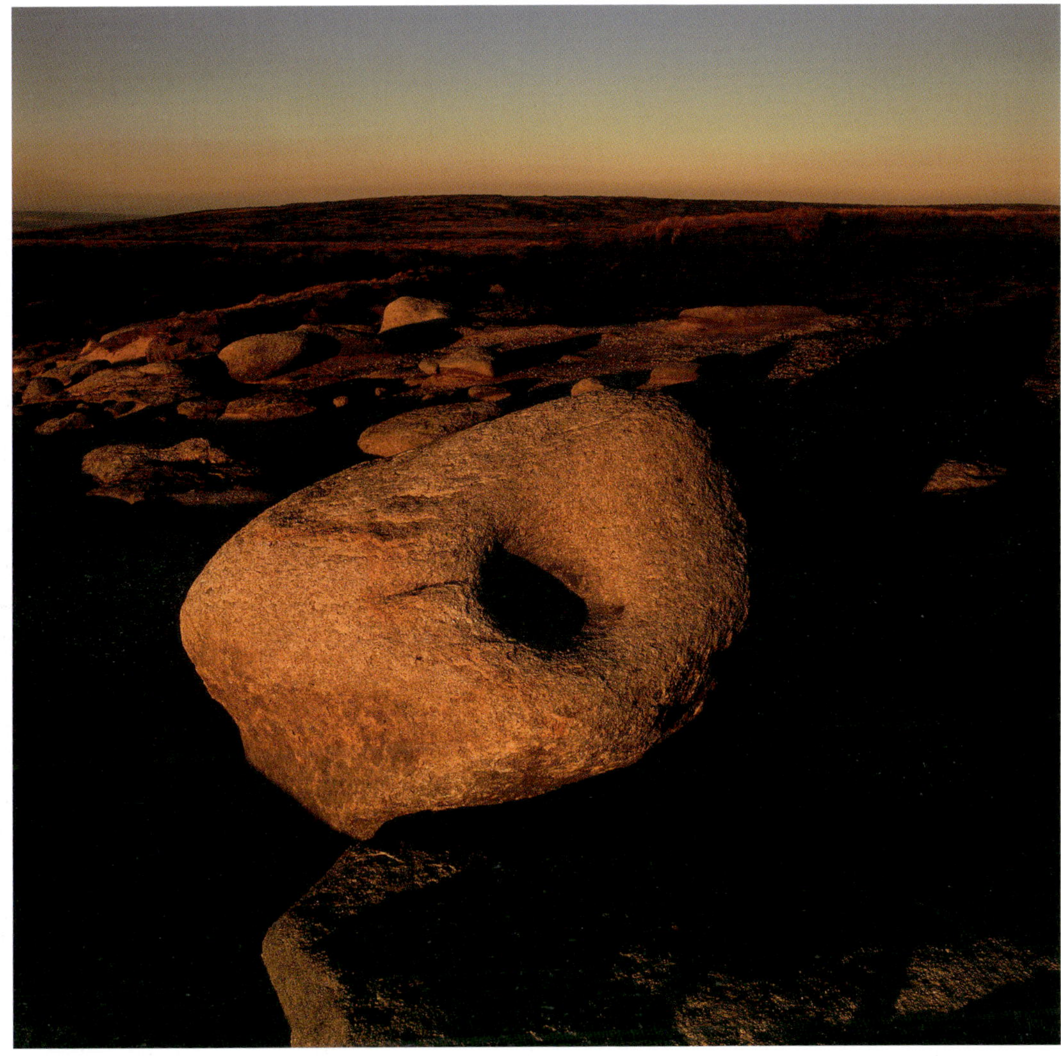

Burnished rocks
The last rays of winter sunshine cast a golden glow on eroded gritstone boulders, set in a desolate moorland landscape on the slopes of Bleaklow.

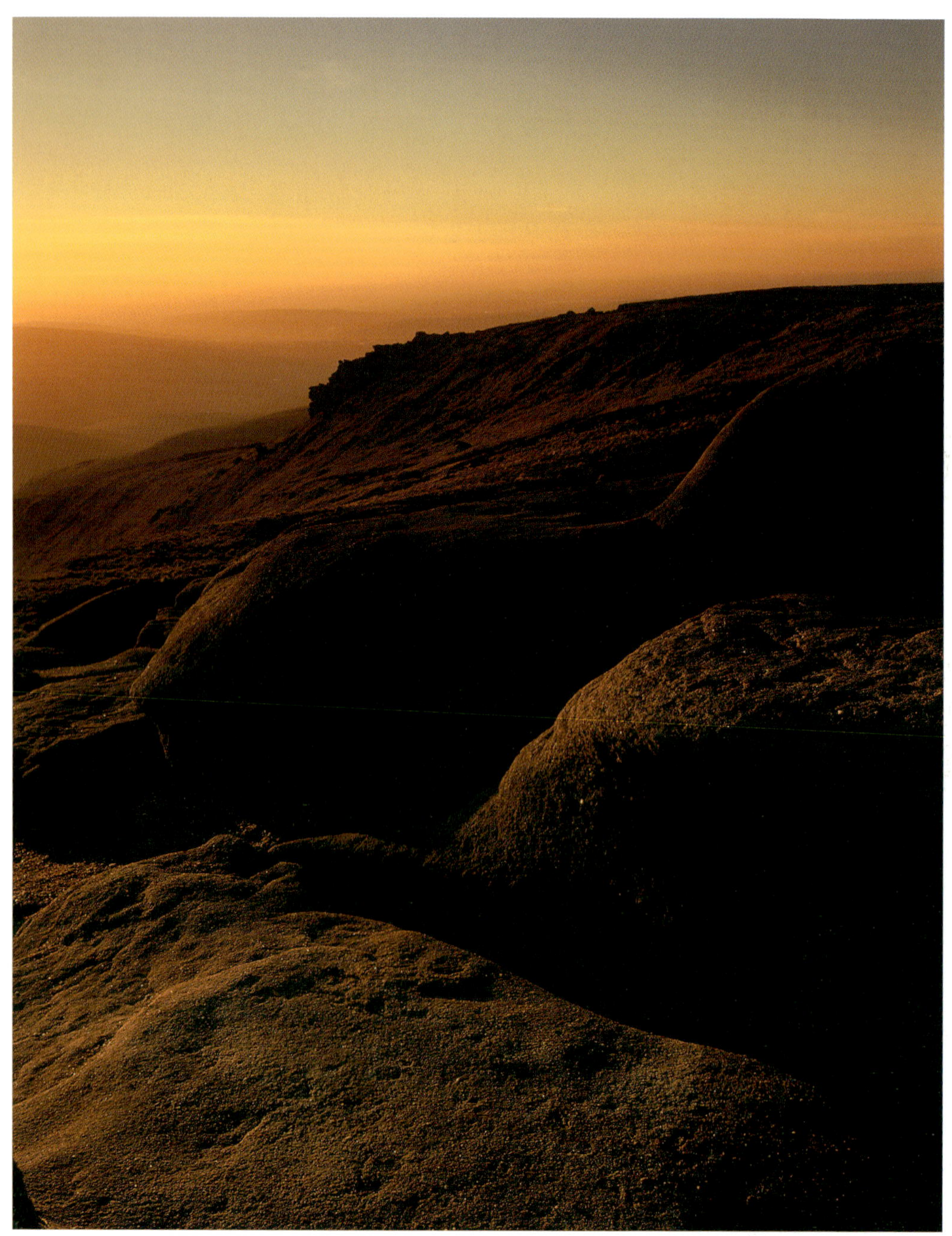

Light and shade
The setting sun casts shadows across the rocks at Higher Shelf Stones, above Glossop.

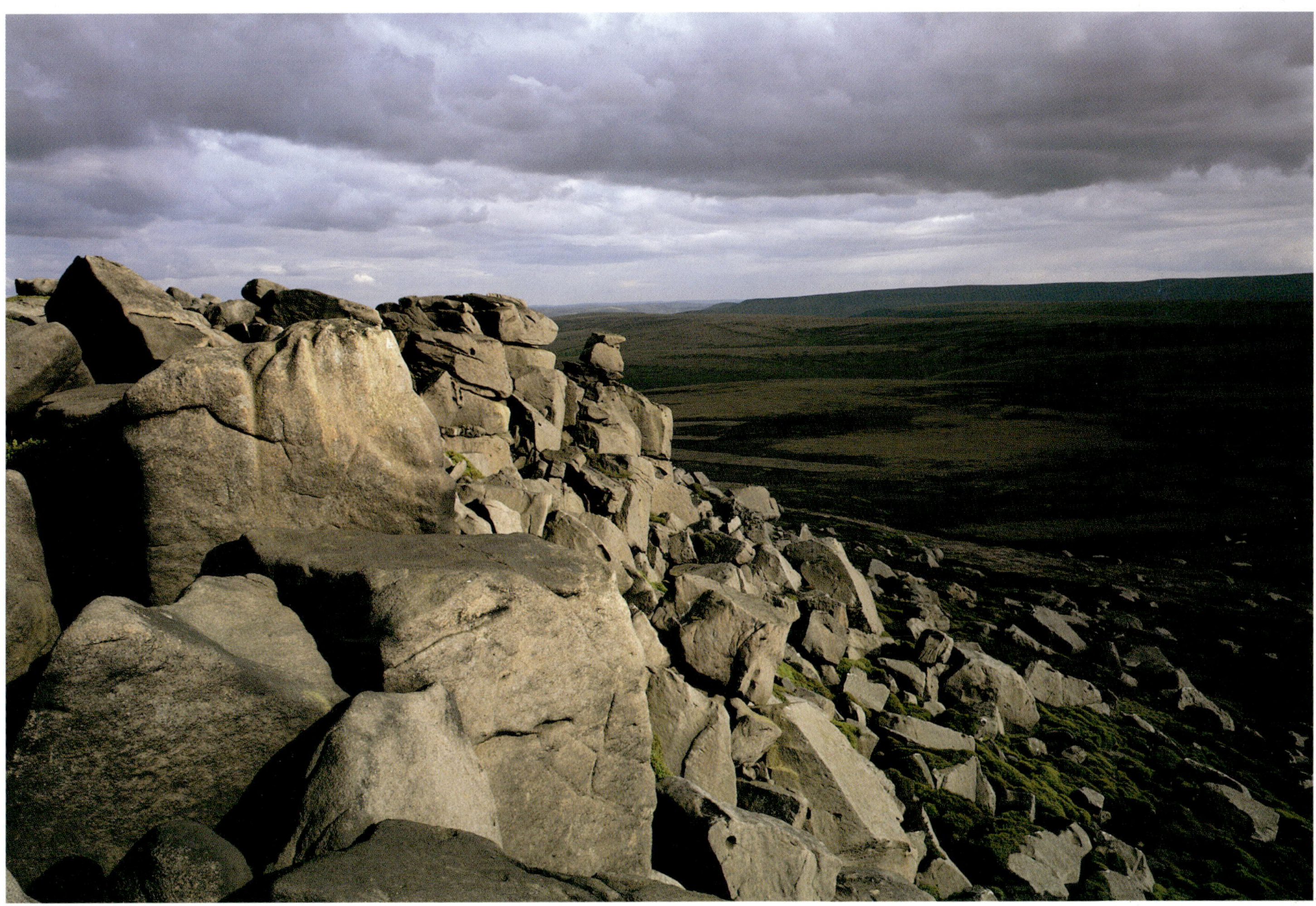

Grinah Stones
Looking east from the eroded rocks of the Grinah Stones high on the flanks of Bleaklow, as storm clouds sweep in across the moorland wilderness.

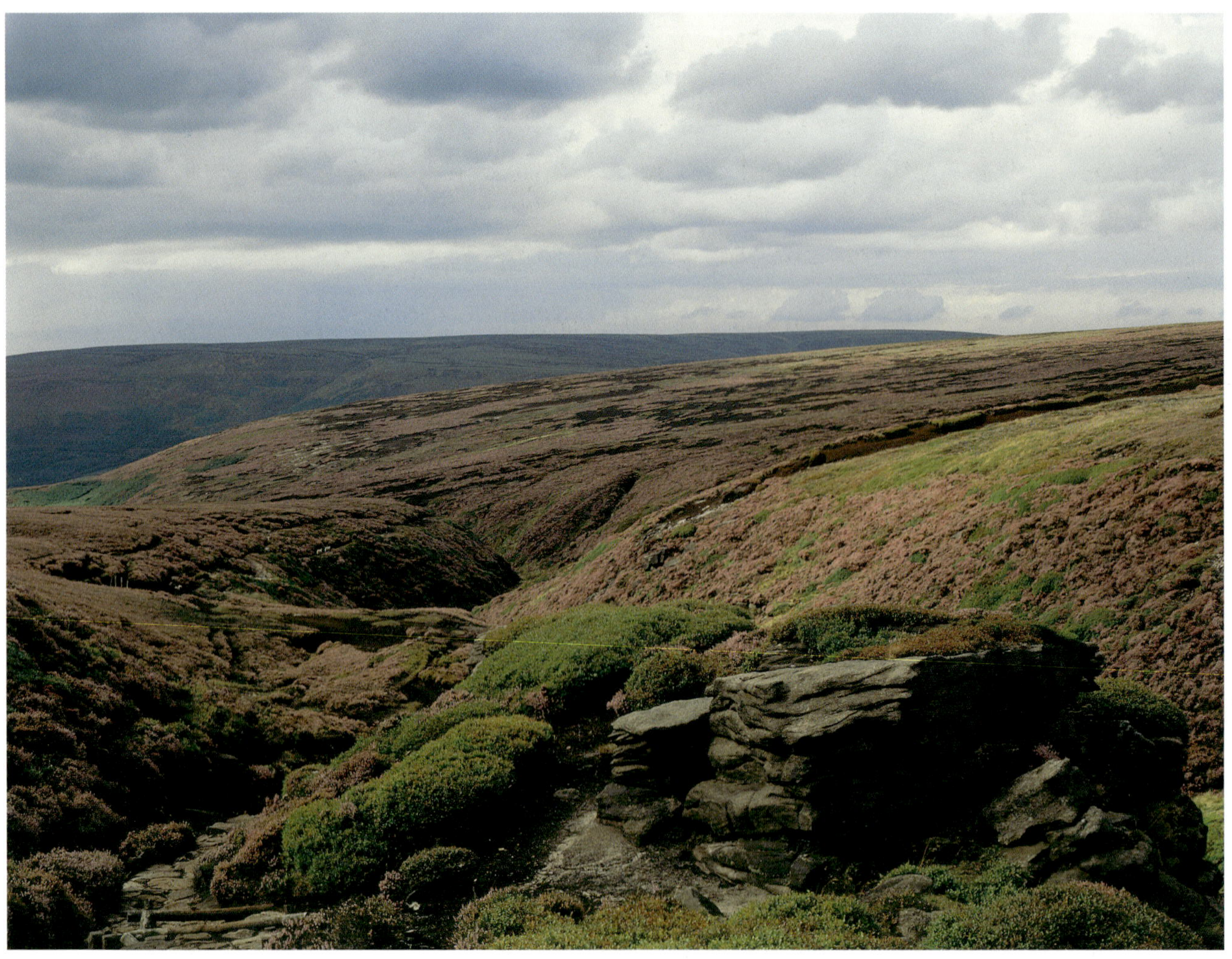

Purple carpet
Vibrant purple heather cloaks the slopes of Torside Clough on Bleaklow's northern flanks high above the Longdendale reservoirs.

Sunburst
A blaze of sunshine breaks through the storm clouds to illuminate the moors near Salter's Brook Bridge, on the Woodhead Pass.

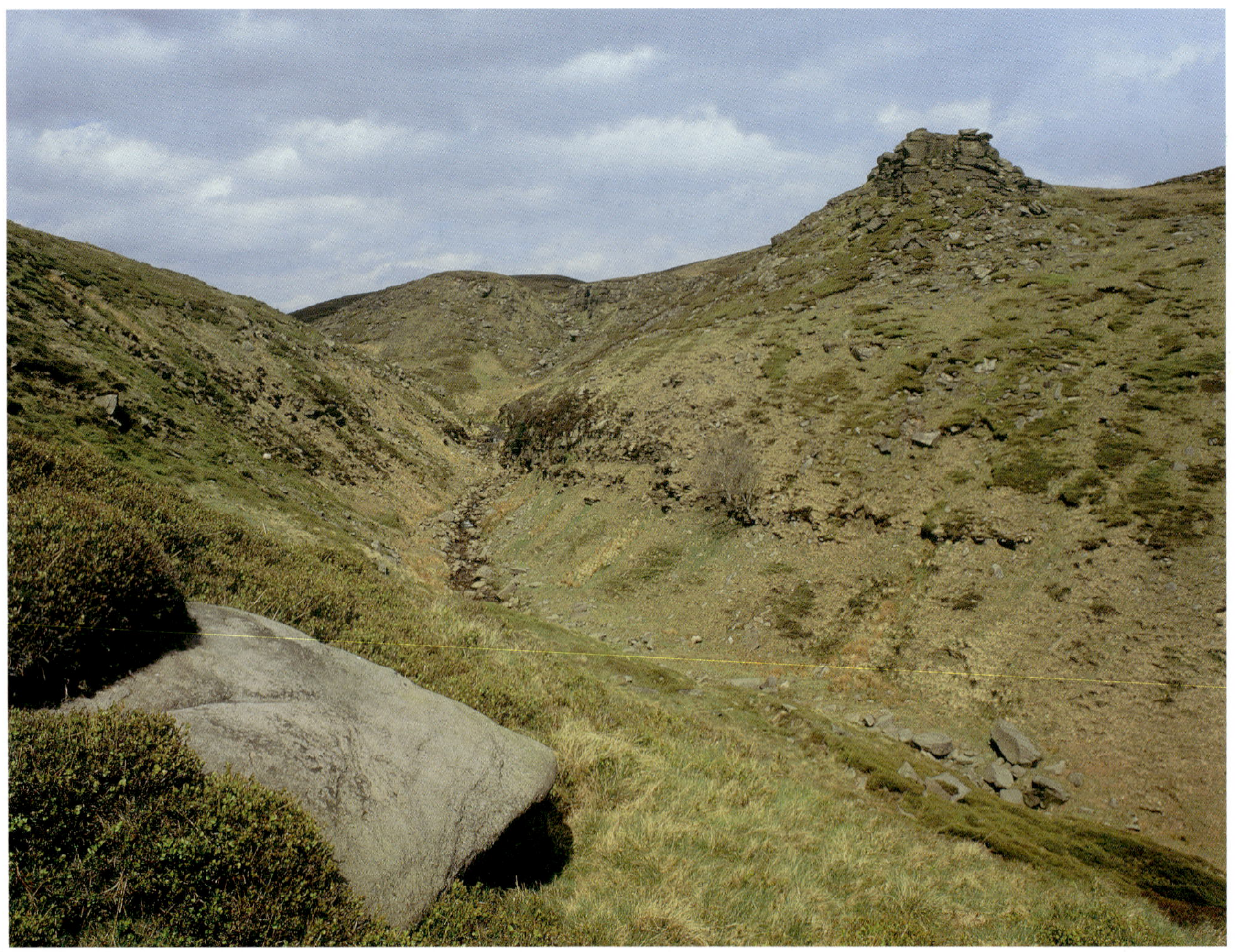

Crowden Great Brook
Crowden Great Brook etches deeply into the flanks of Black Hill. The gritstone buttresses of the Castles are visible on the skyline.

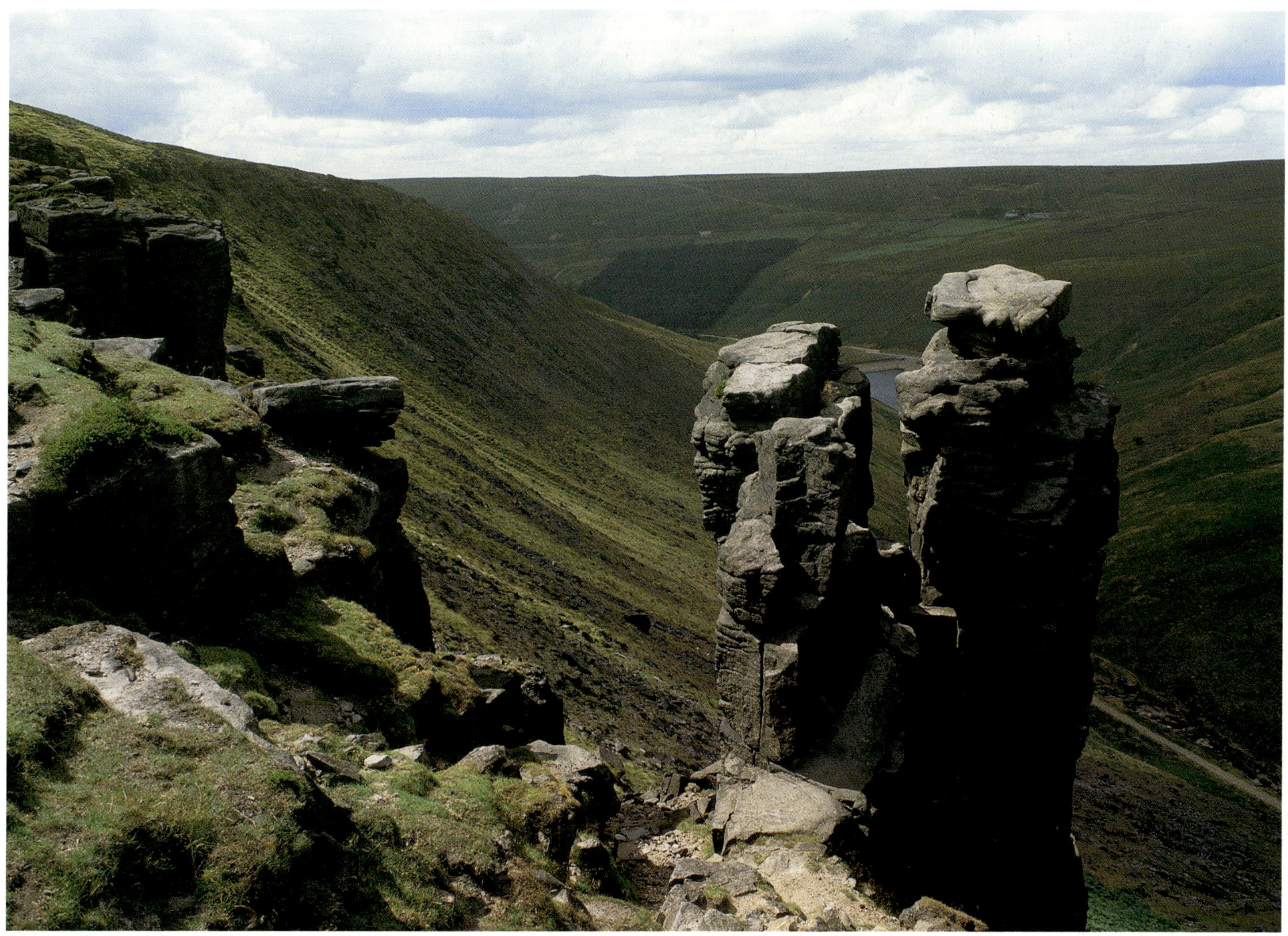

The Trinnacle

The isolated three-pronged gritstone pinnacle known as the Trinnacle at Ravenstones stands high above the scree slopes overlooking Greenfield Reservoir, on the western slopes of Black Hill.

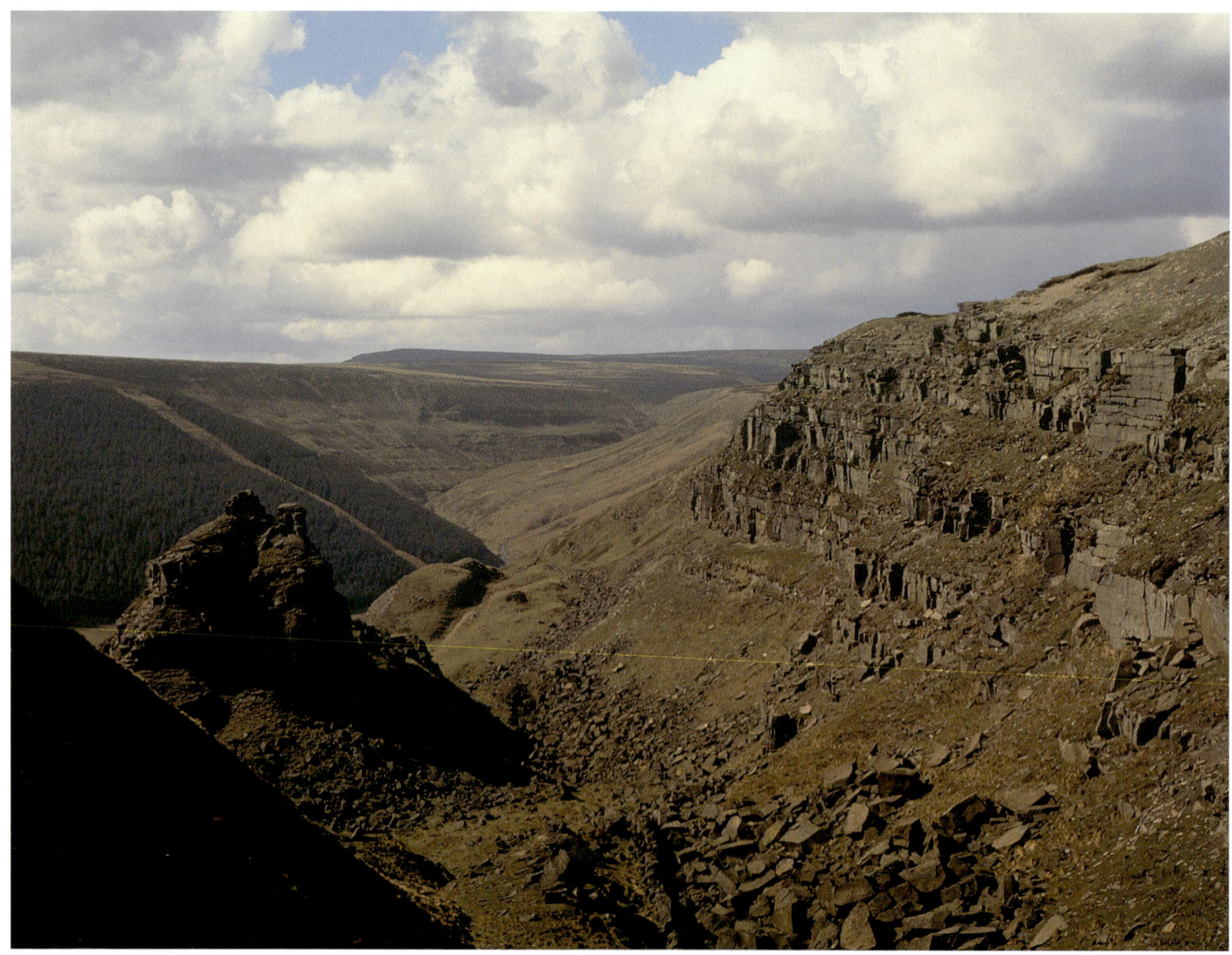

Rocky castles

Alport Castles just north of the Snake Road, is one of Britain's largest landslips. The detached block known as The Tower has slipped away below the cliff face and with its crenellated summit resembles a medieval castle.

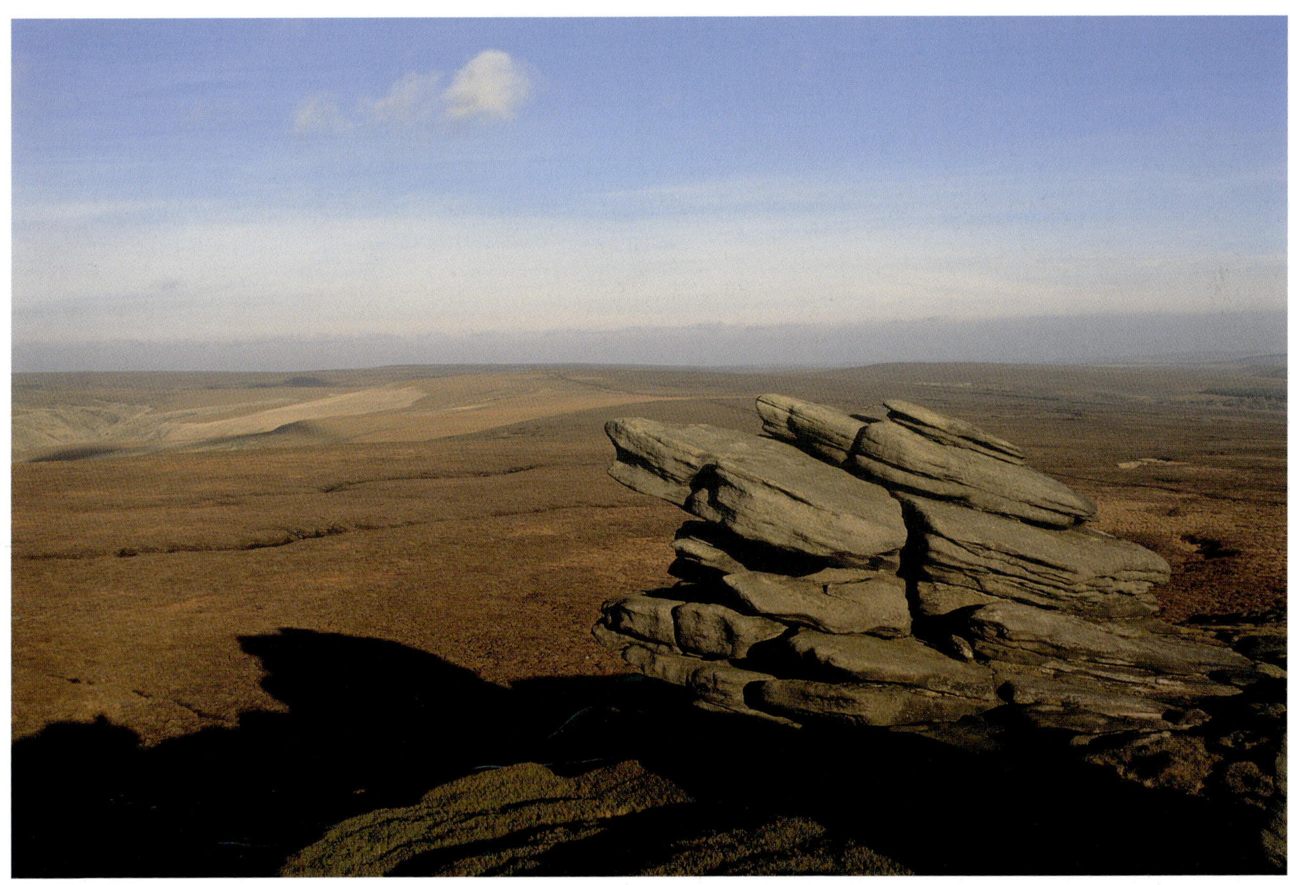

Eroded rocks
Erosion by wind, rain and frost has created this remarkable rocky tor on Derwent Edge.

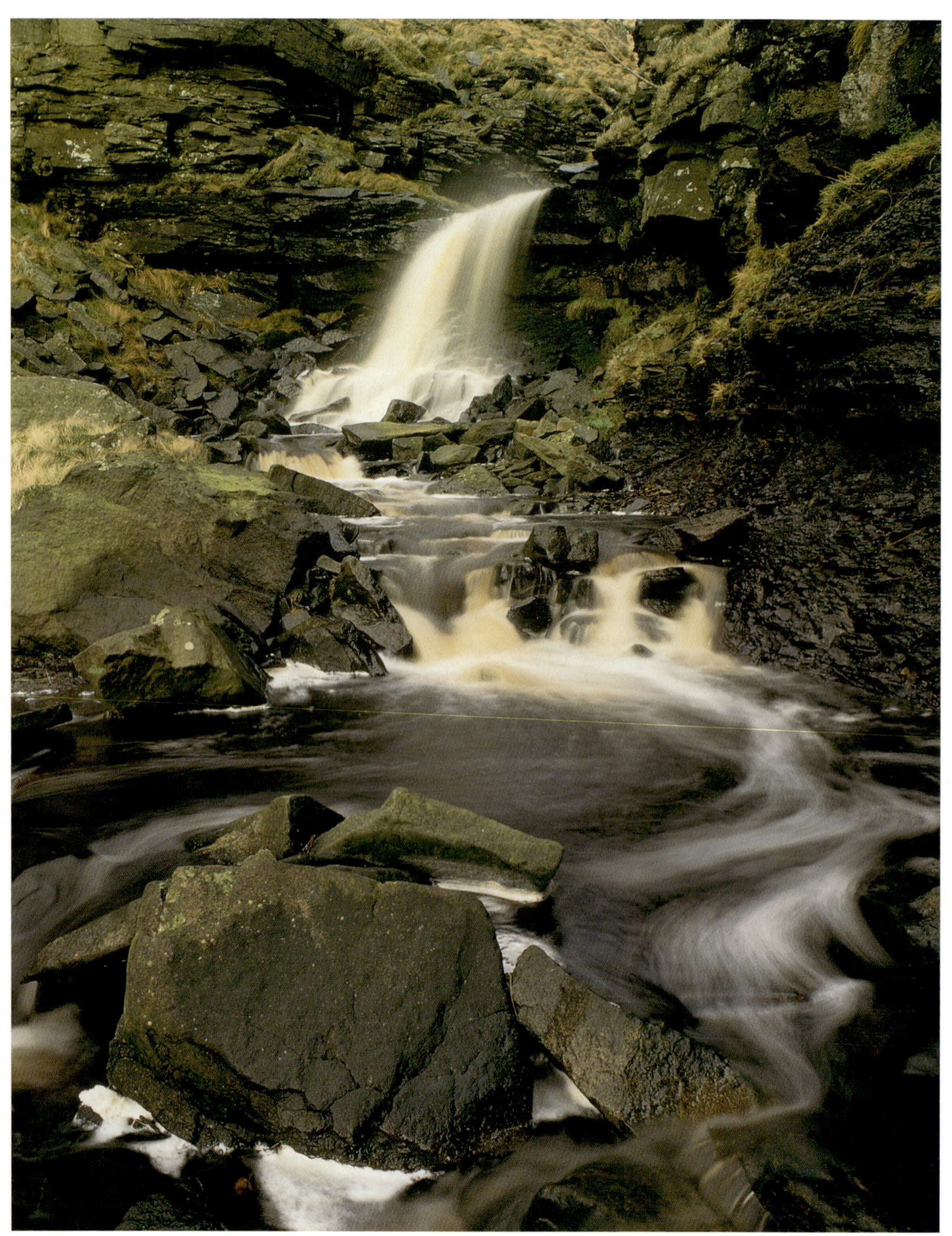

Abbey Brook cascade
The misty waters of the fast flowing Abbey Brook rush down from Howden Moors through a rocky ravine high up in Abbey Clough in the Upper Derwent Valley.

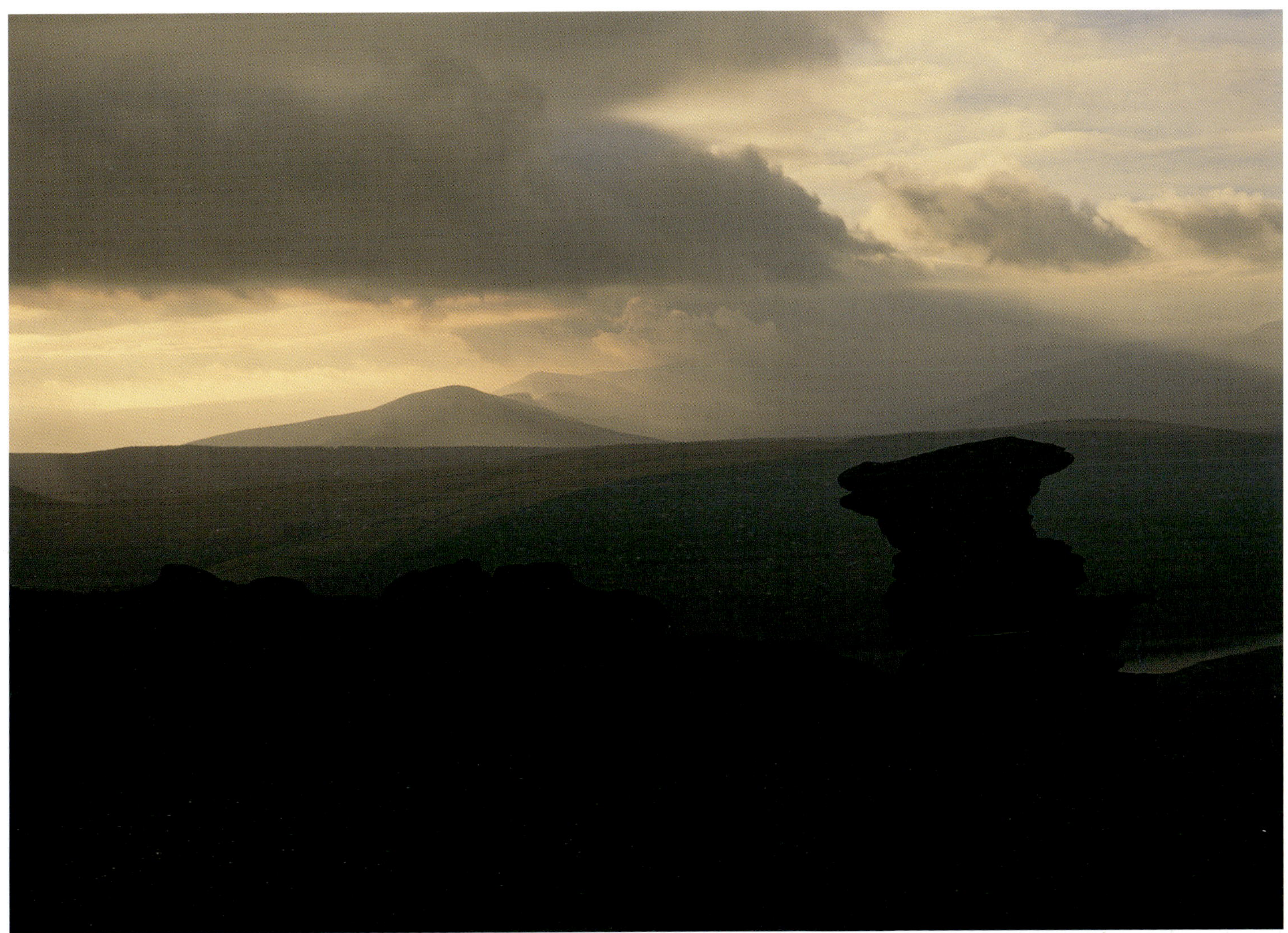

The Salt Cellar
The sun sets behind Win Hill, with the eroded tor of the Salt Cellar on Derwent Edge acting as a foreground.

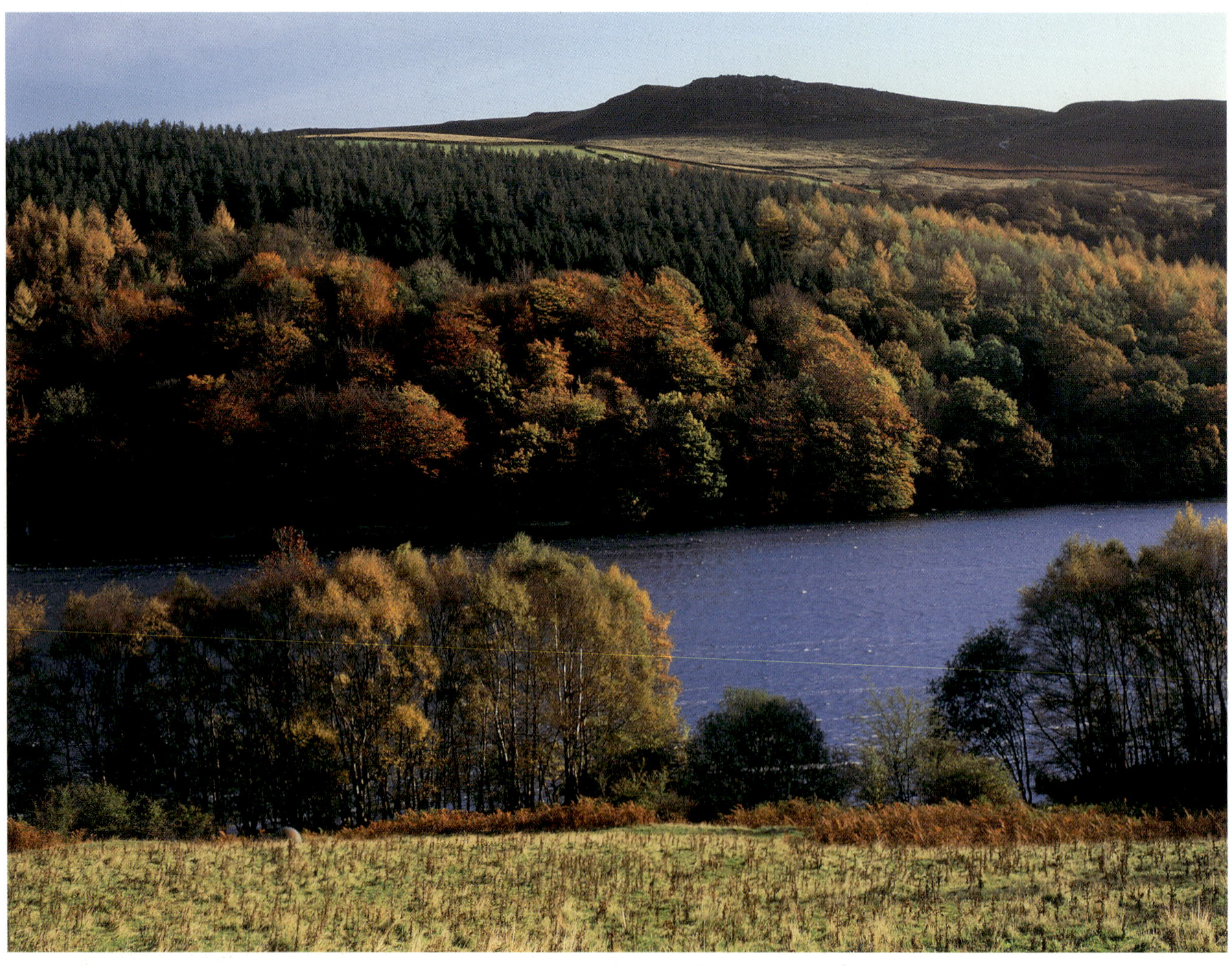

Ladybower Reservoir
A vibrant mix of autumn colours add charm to this view across Ladybower Reservoir to the tor-topped Derwent Edge.

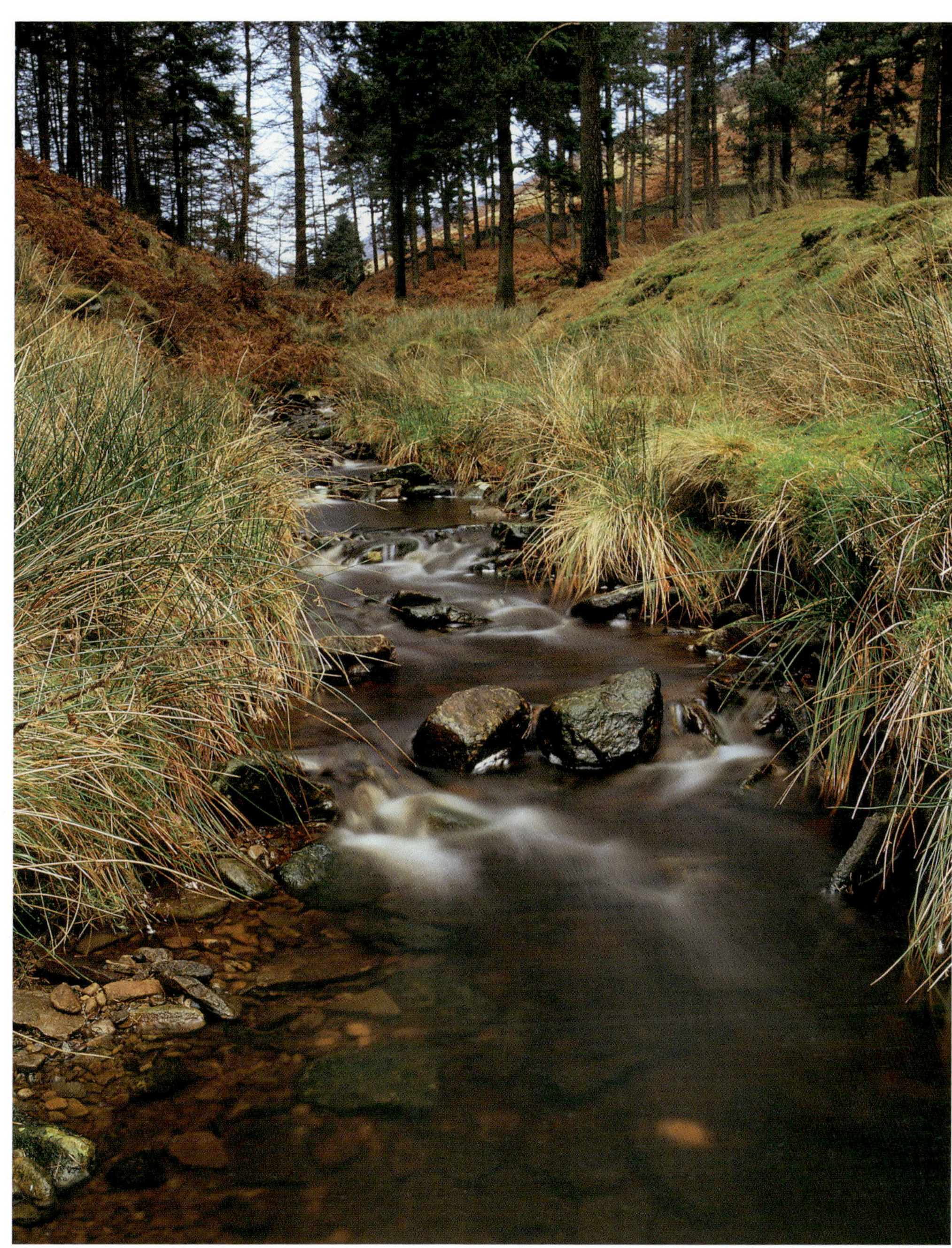

Tumbling stream
A stream tumbles through a wooded glade below Linch Clough in the Upper Derwent Valley.

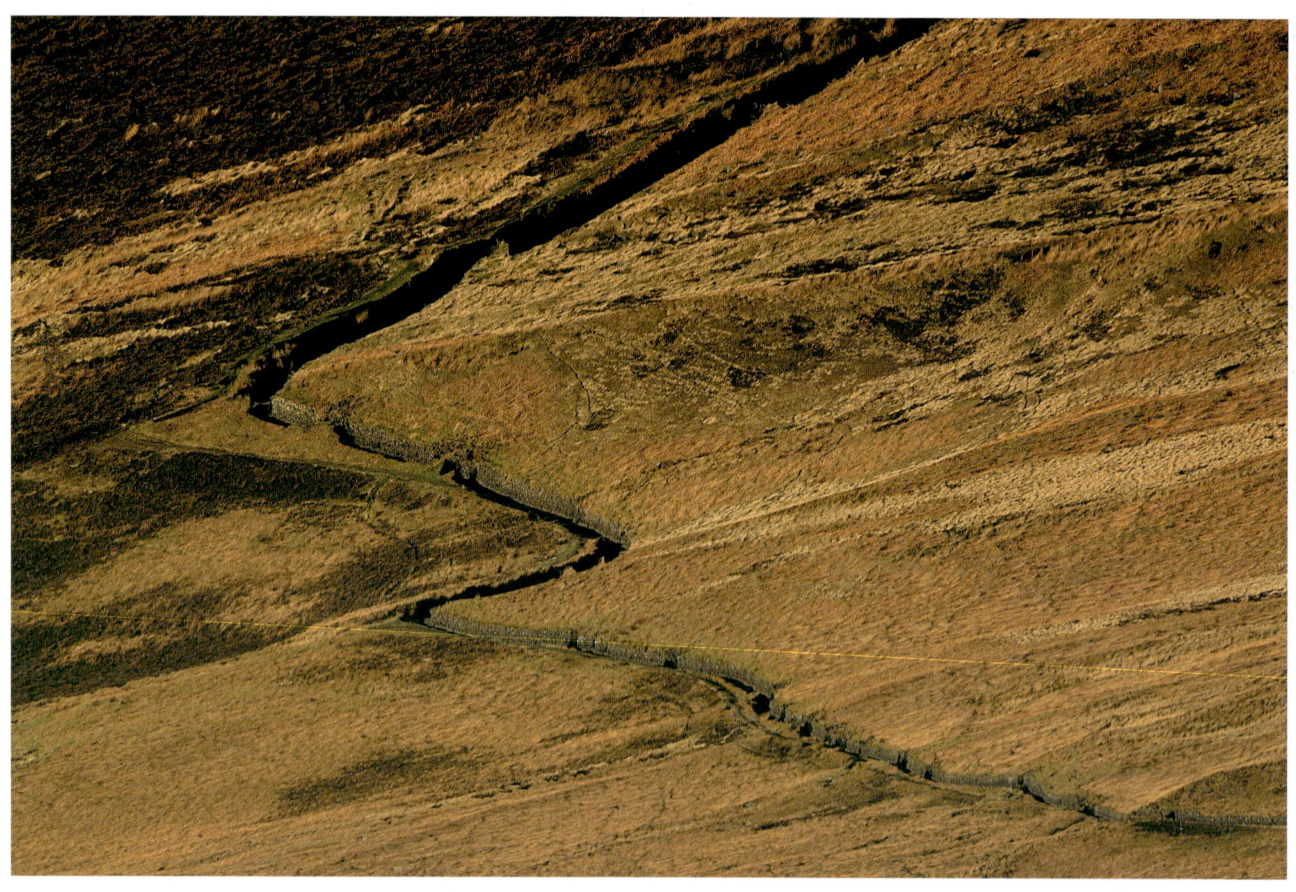

Snaking wall
A gritstone wall snakes its way across the bracken-covered slopes below Derwent Edge.

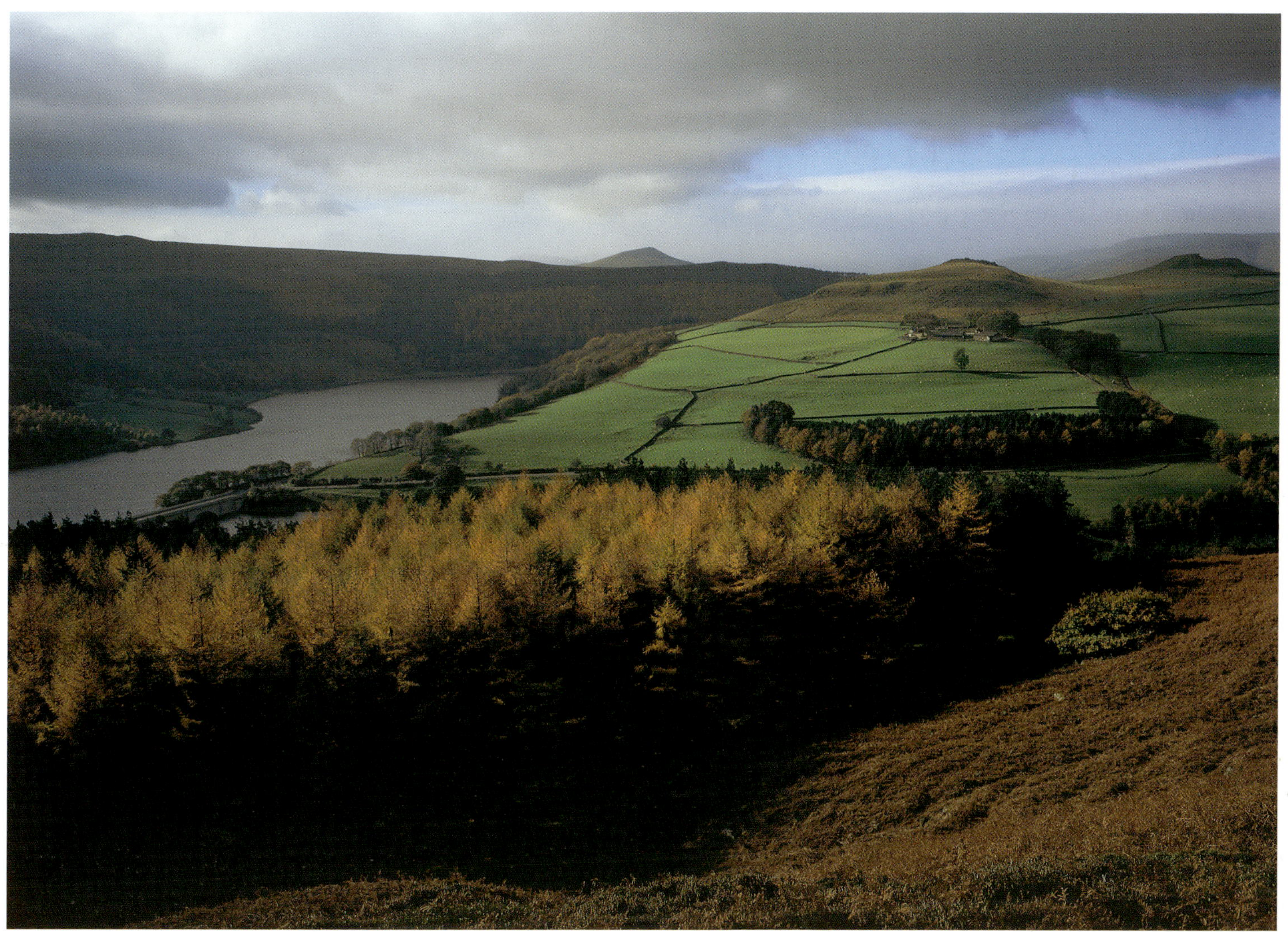

Autumn splendour
A patch of sunshine picks out the green patchwork fields around Crookhill Farm in this view over larch trees to Ladybower Reservoir and the Woodlands Valley.

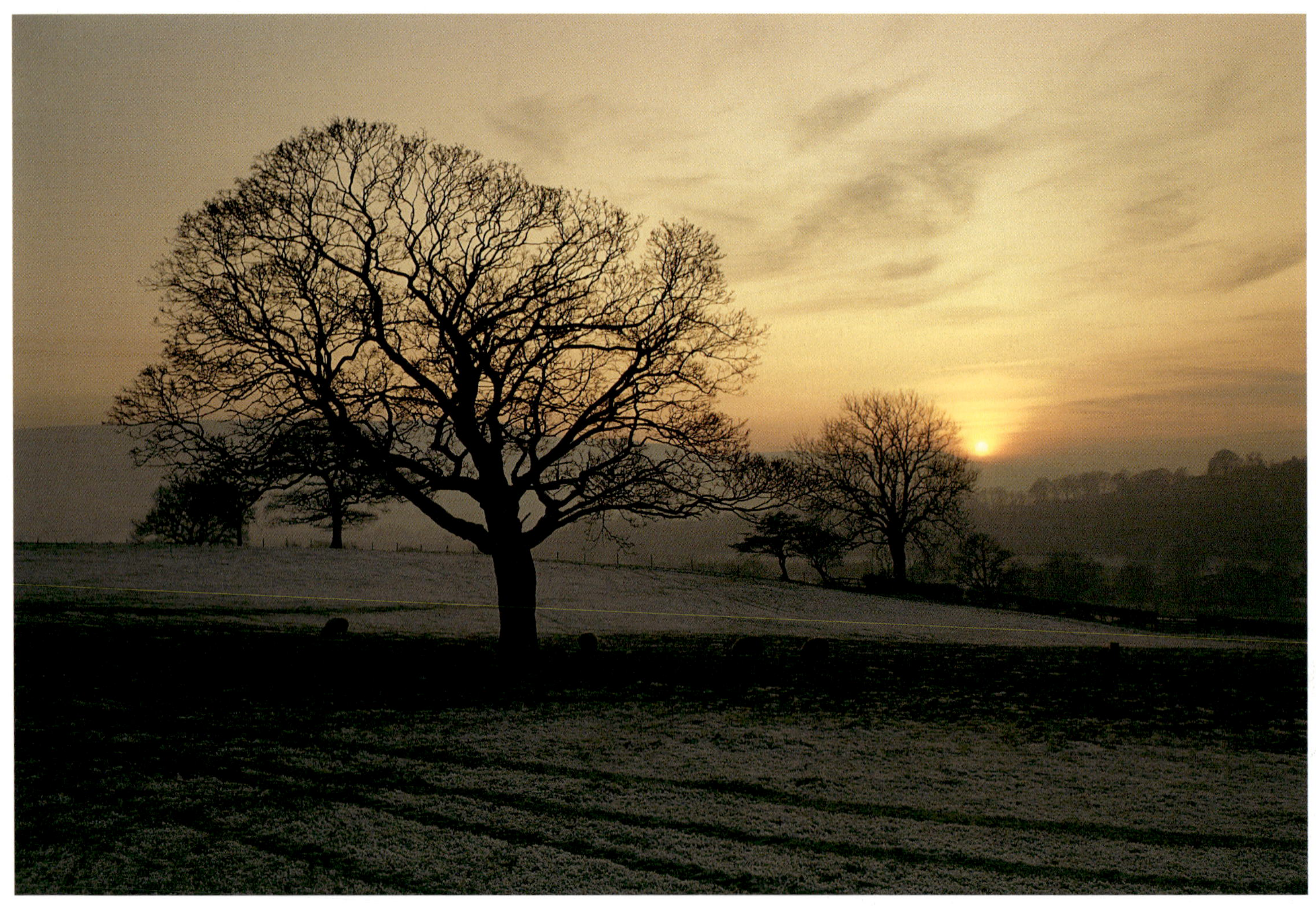

Frozen trees
Trees frozen in the icy grip of winter as the sun sets beyond the Derwent Valley.

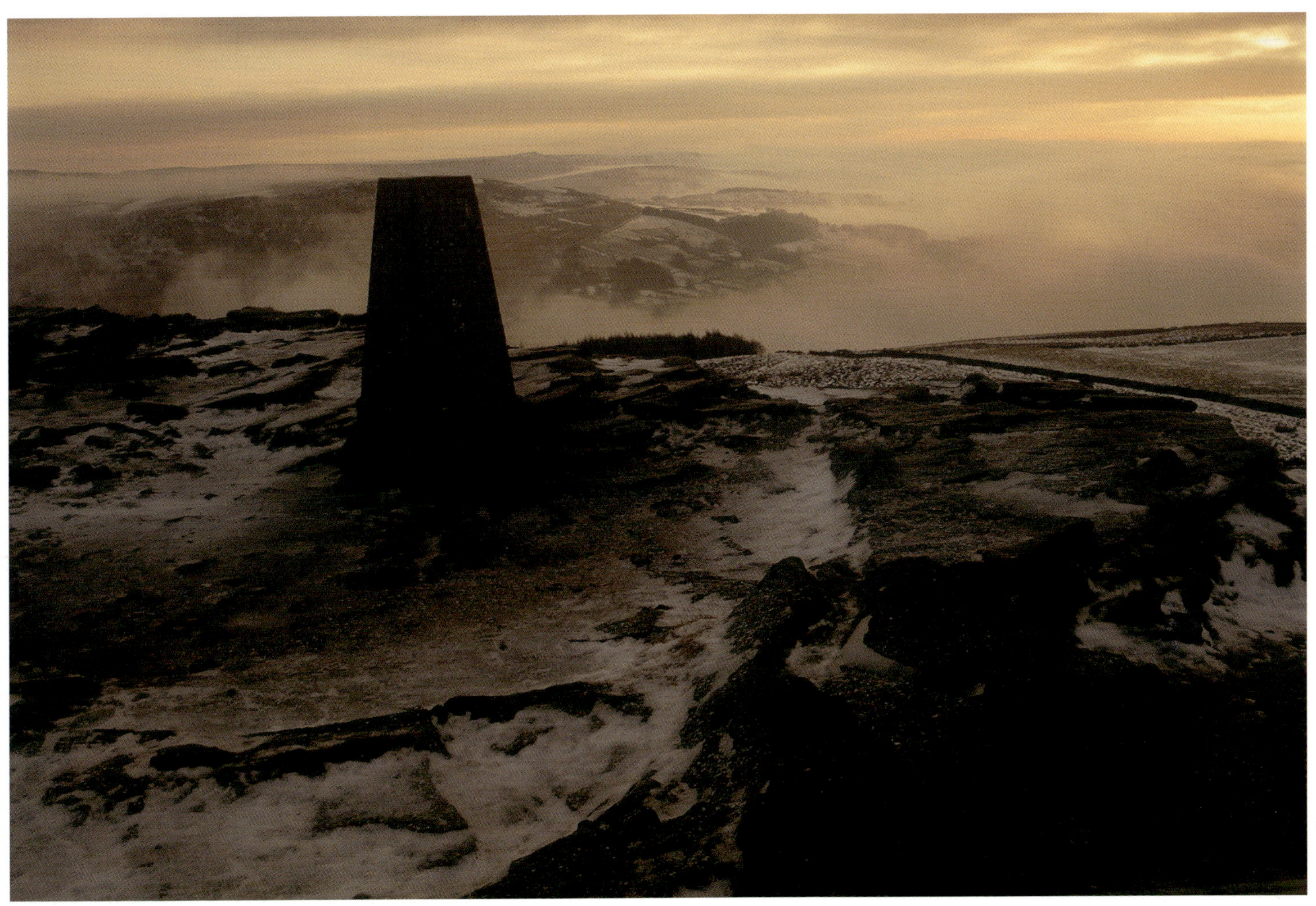

Win Hill sunrise
Looking eastwards from Win Hill, as the sun rises over the mist-filled Derwent Valley.

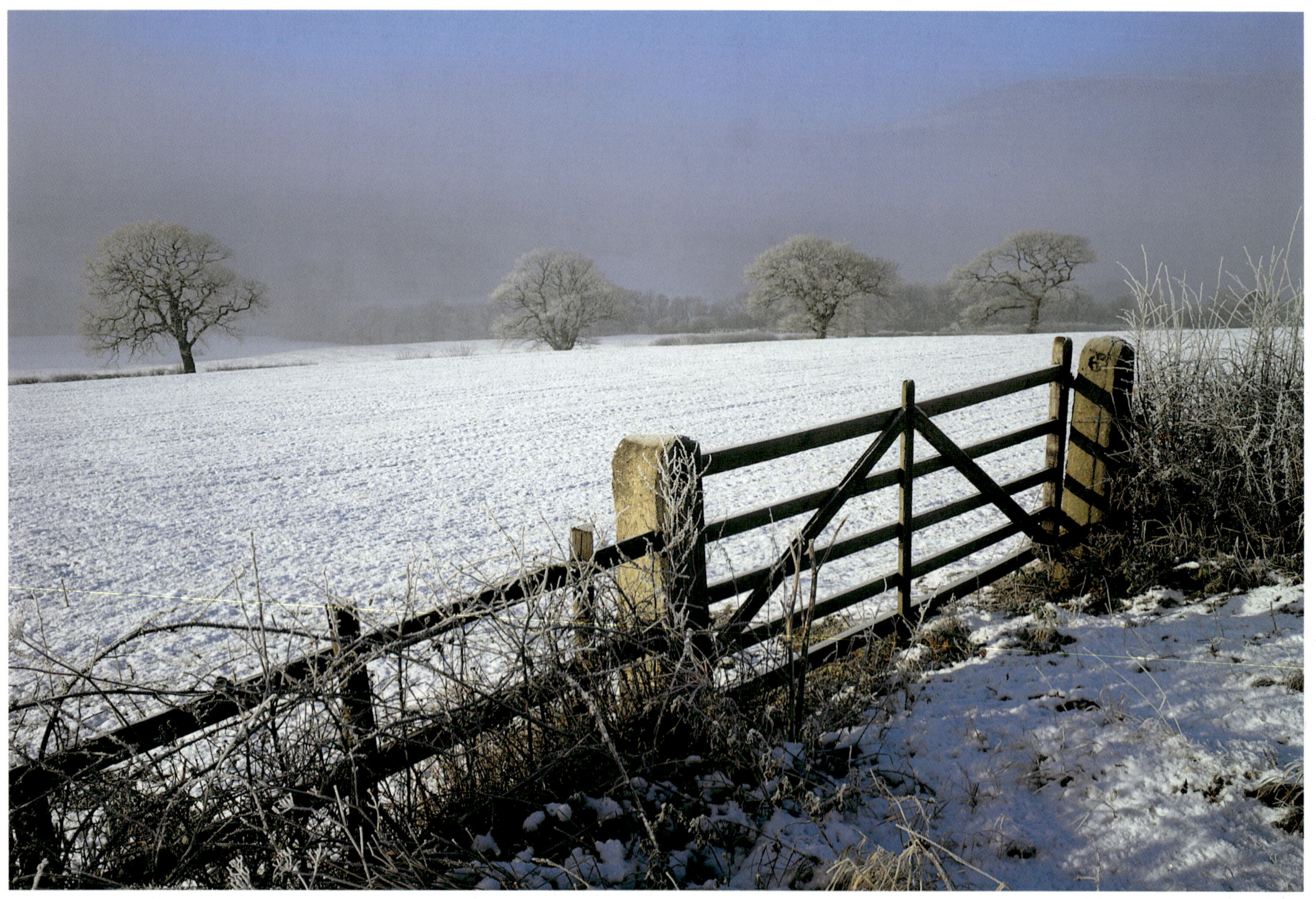

Morning mist
Mist slowly evaporates in the weak winter sunshine over fields near Bamford. Win Hill rises in the background.

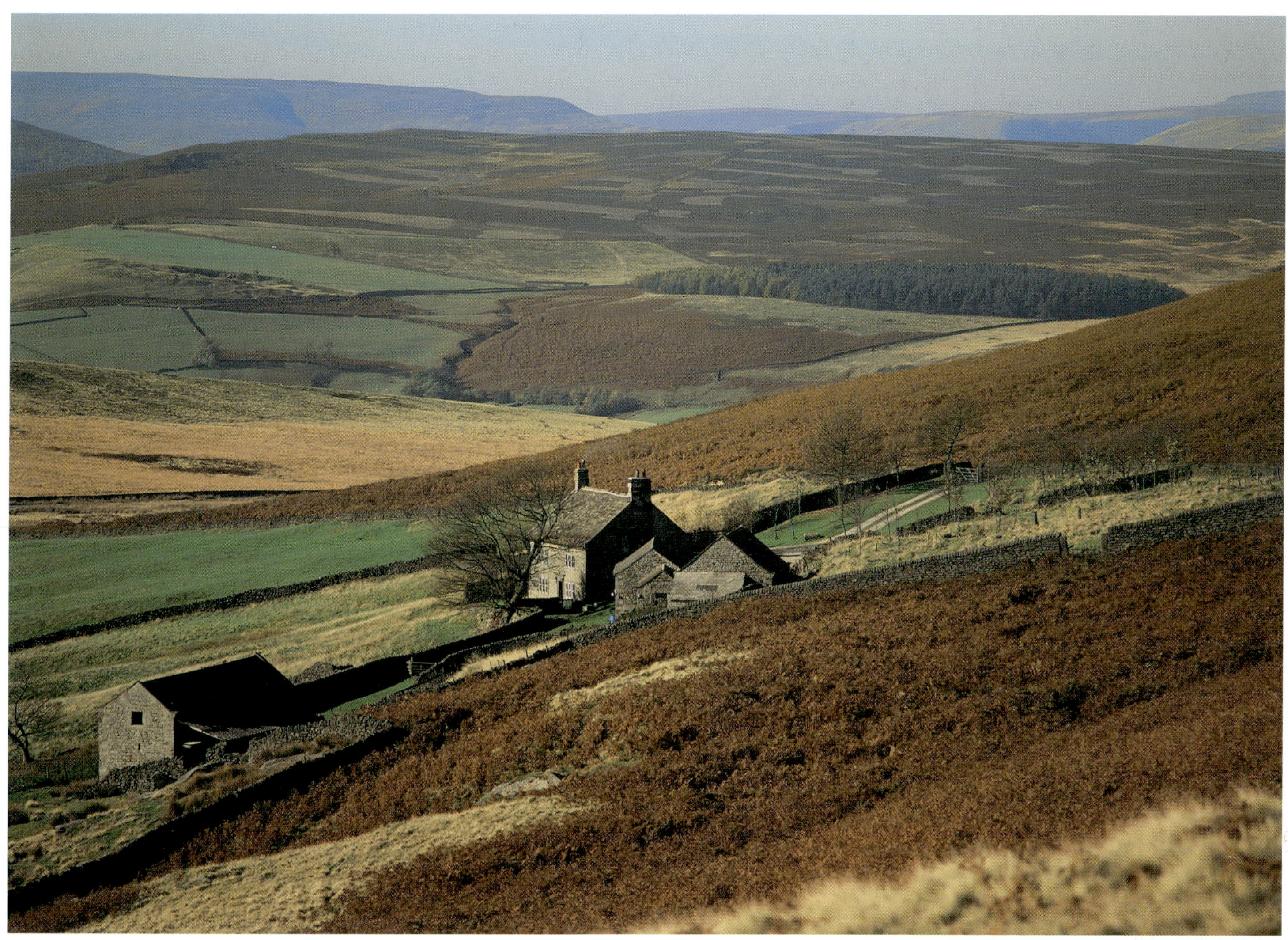

Overstones Farm
Nestling below the escarpment of Stanage Edge, Overstones Farm forms a lovely foreground for this view up the Derwent Valley to Win Hill and the distant Kinder Scout.

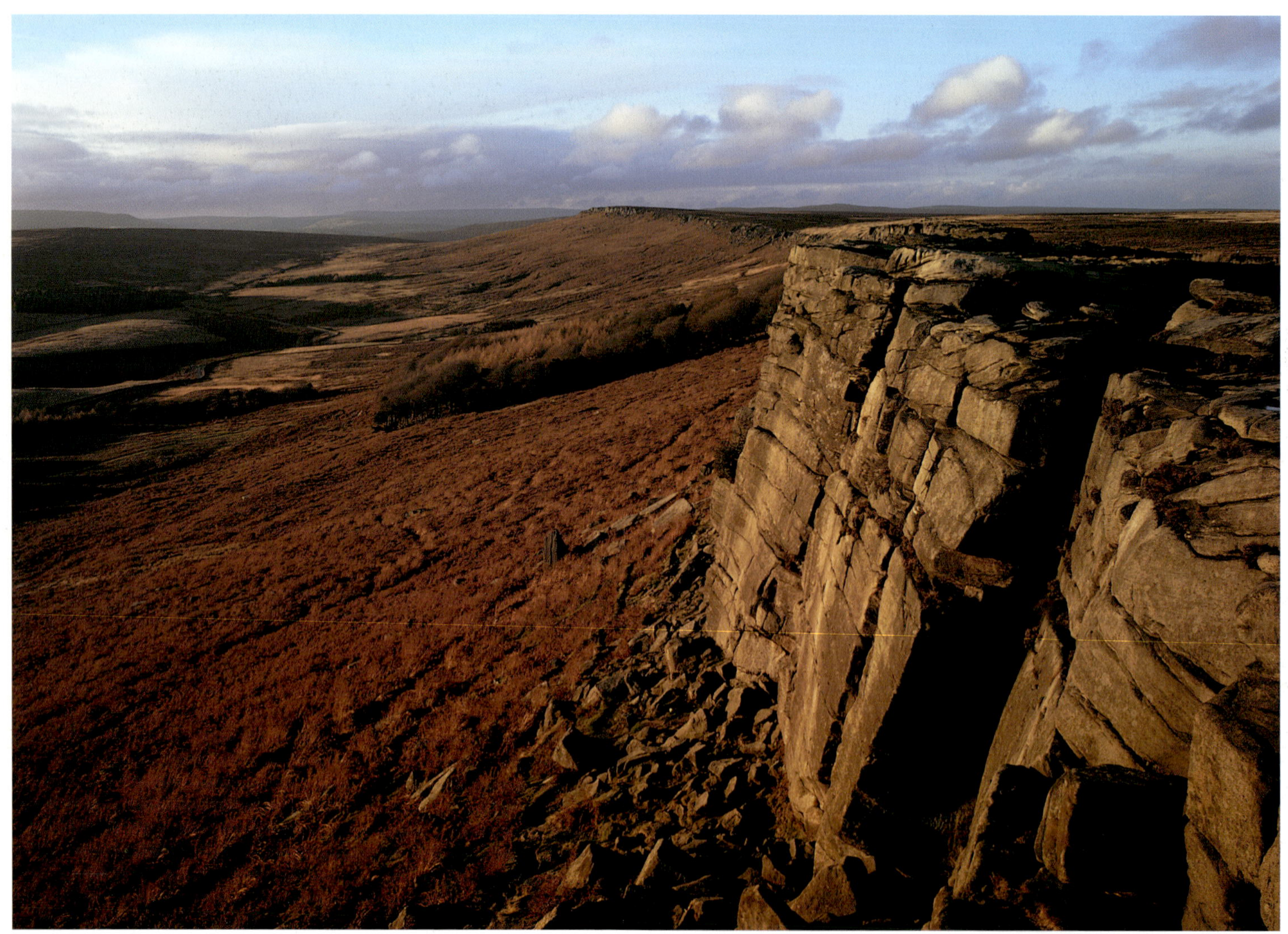

Autumn evening on Stanage
The gritstone buttresses of Stanage Edge overlook golden bracken slopes lit by the rays of the setting sun. These grey, gritstone buttresses on the eastern flanks of the Peak District are a Mecca for rock climbers.

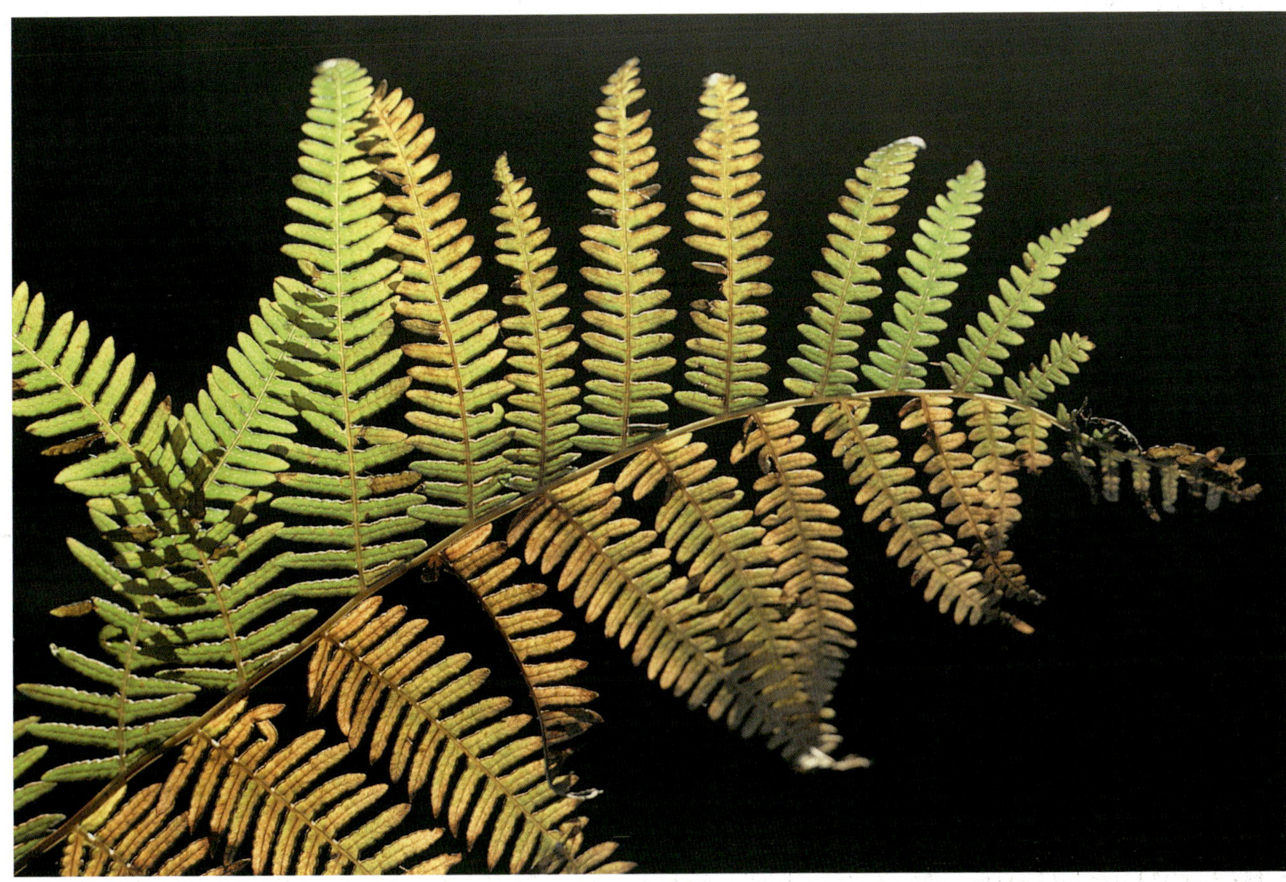

Turning bracken
Backlit bracken, so much a feature of the landscape below the gritstone Eastern Edges, starts the transformation into its golden autumn colours.

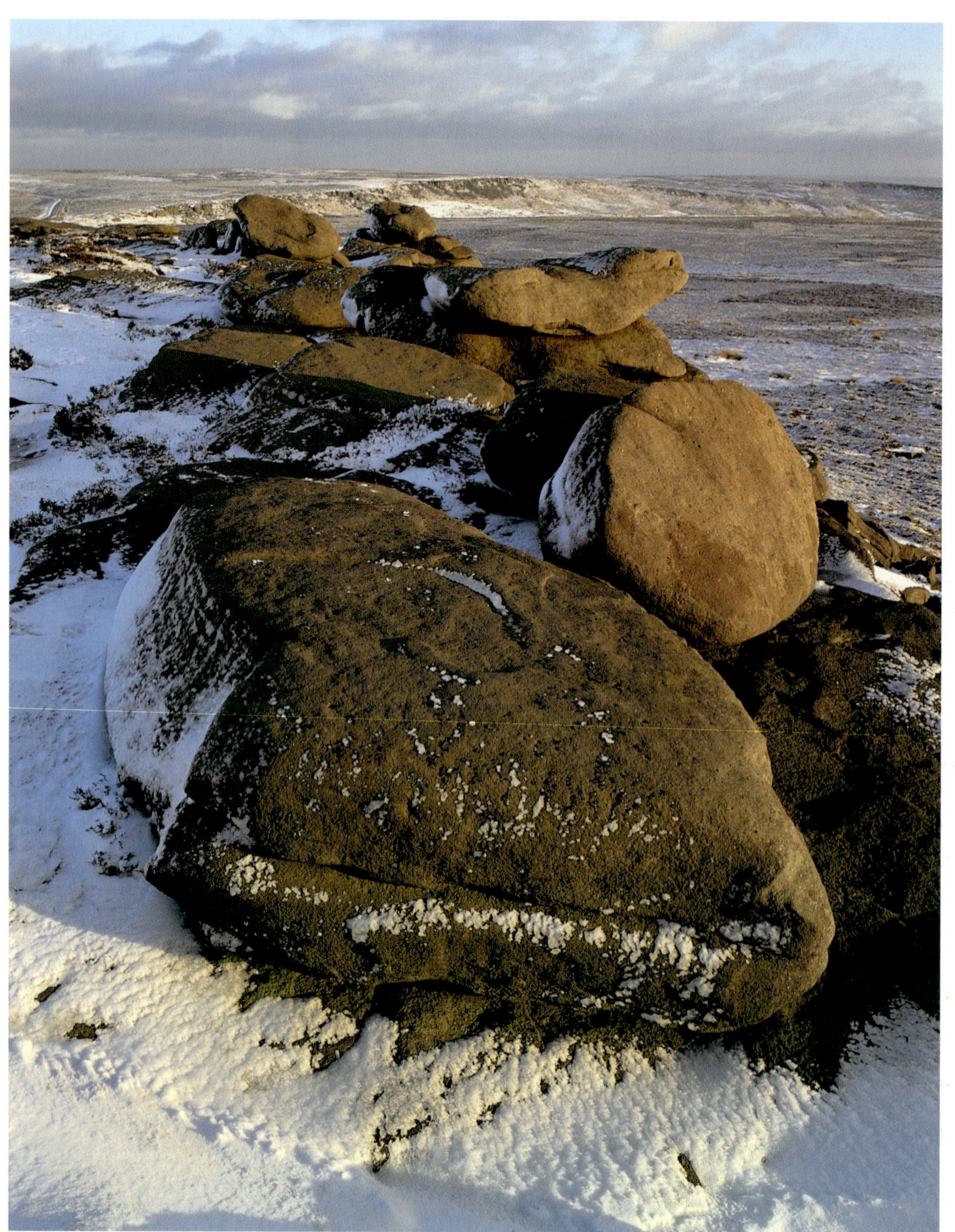

Iced rocks
The light of the setting sun adds a touch of warmth to icy gritstone boulders in this eastern view from Stanage Edge to Burbage.

Right: **Abandoned millstones**
Abandoned stacks of millstones or grindstones below Stanage Edge. Hewn from gritstone using simple hand tools, the production of these stones was once an important Peak District industry.

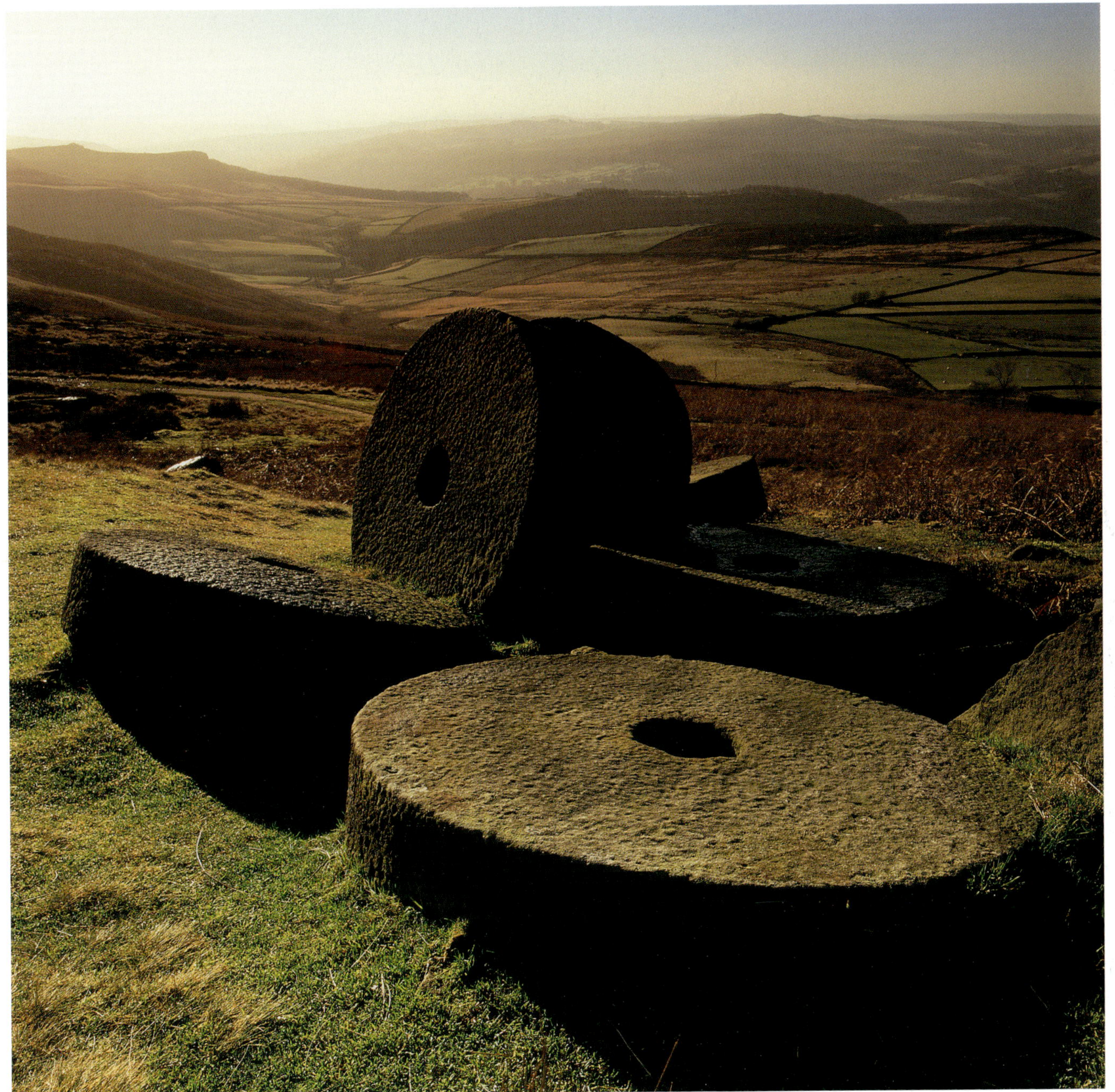

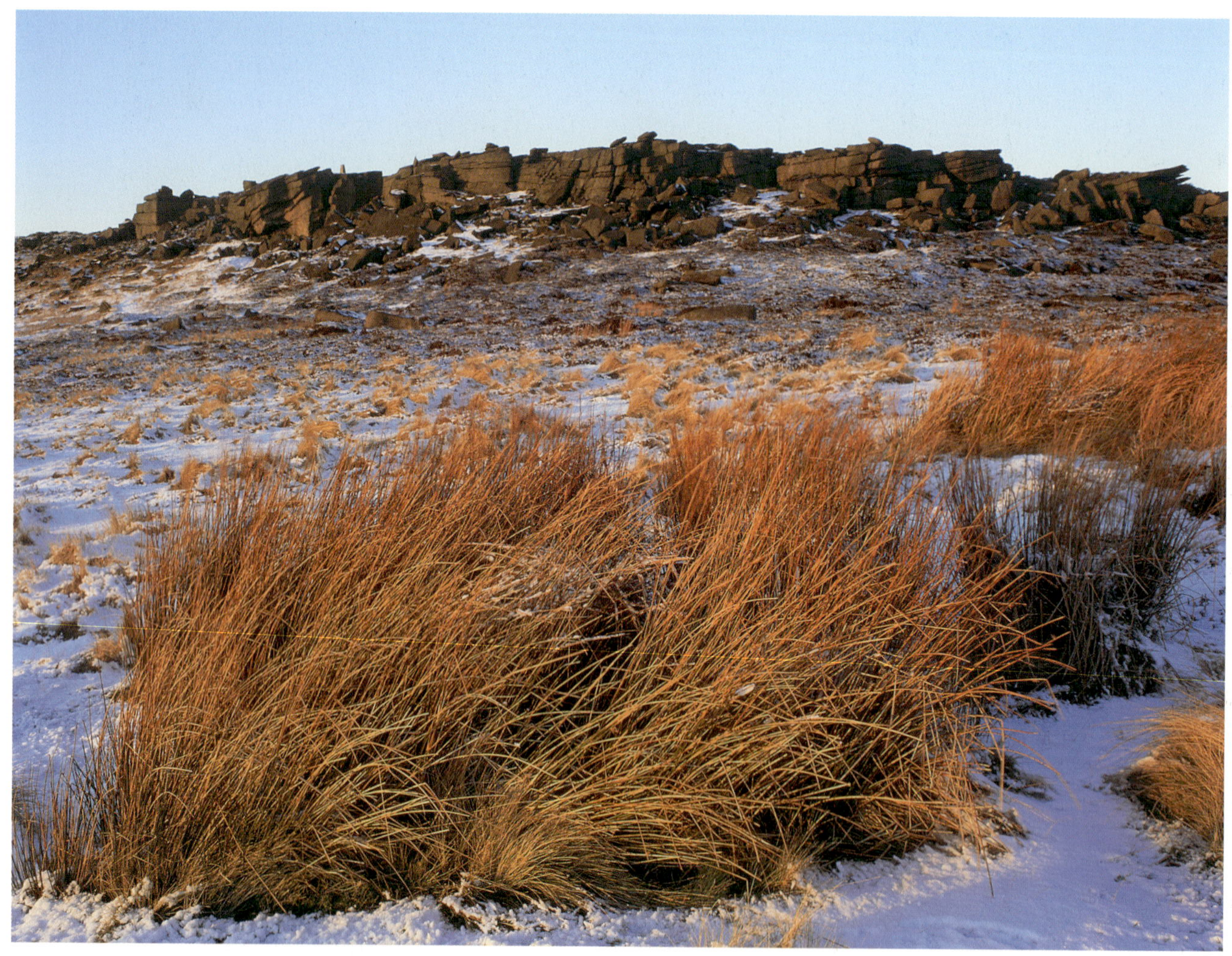

Winter grasses

Brown grasses stand out in this cold winter scene below the buttresses at the eastern end of Stanage.

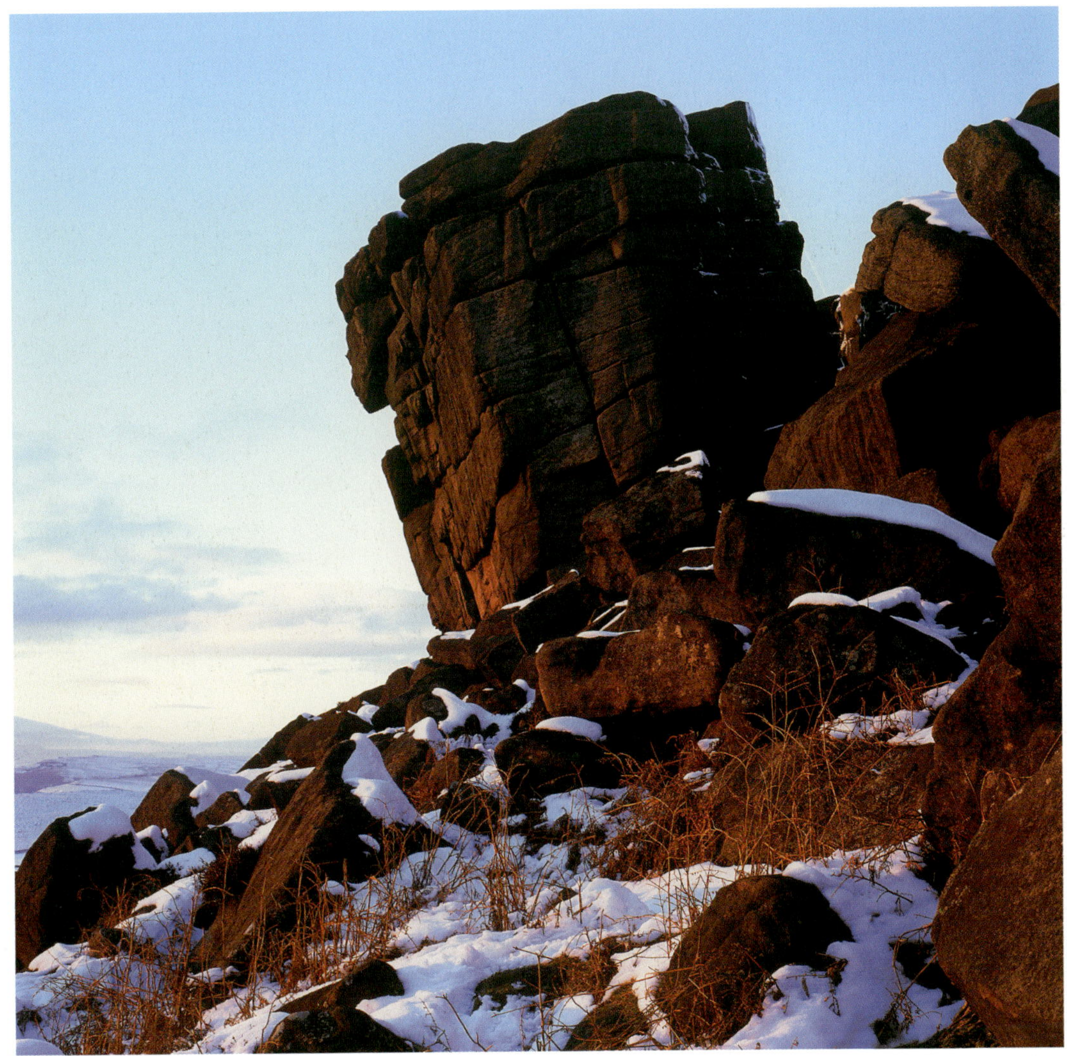

Leaning block

Late evening sunshine adds a warm glow to the huge leaning block at Higger Tor, the most prominent of all the gritstone outcrops on Hathersage Moor.

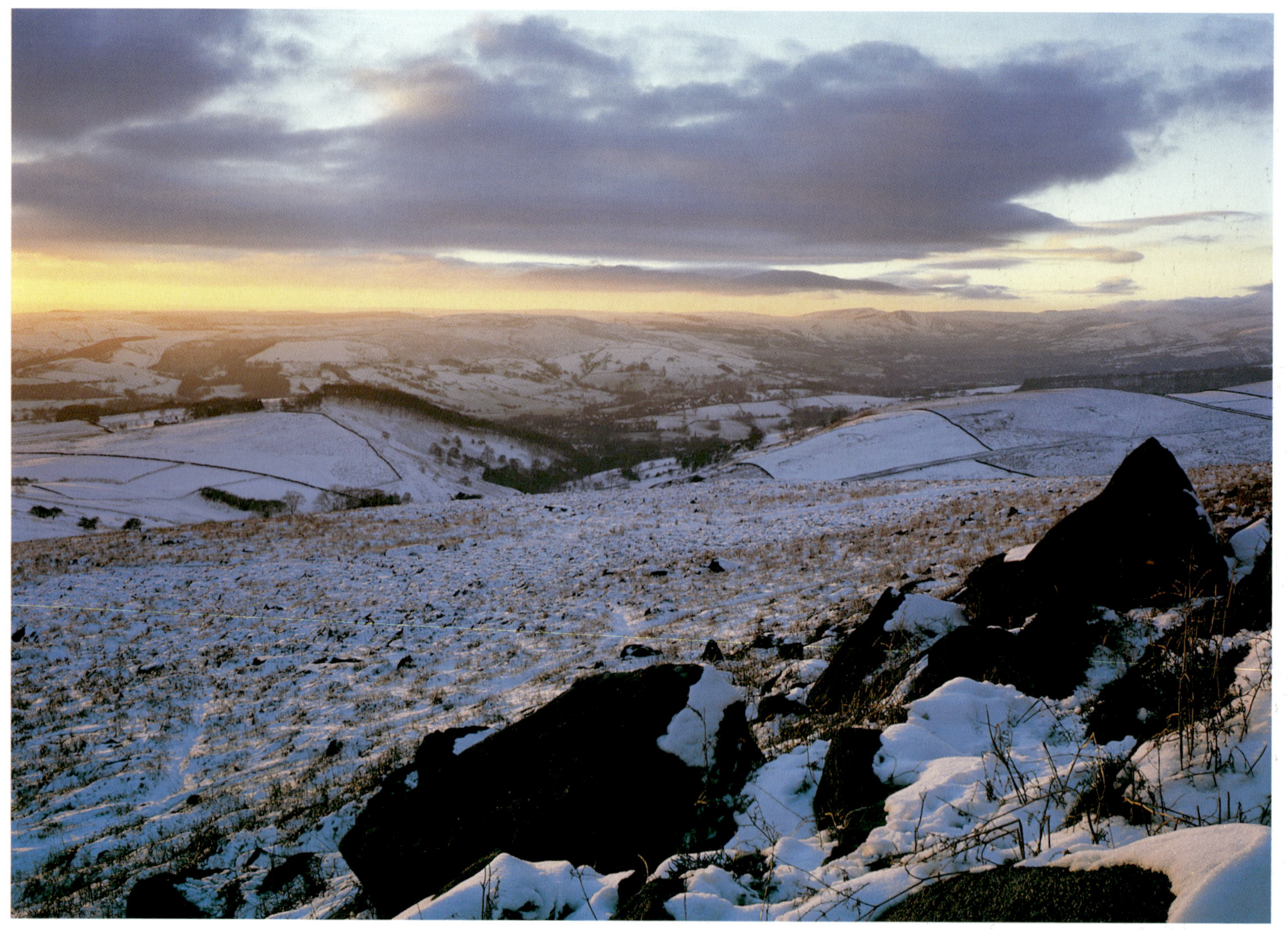

Derwent sunset
A winter sunset across the Derwent Valley, captured from Higger Tor.

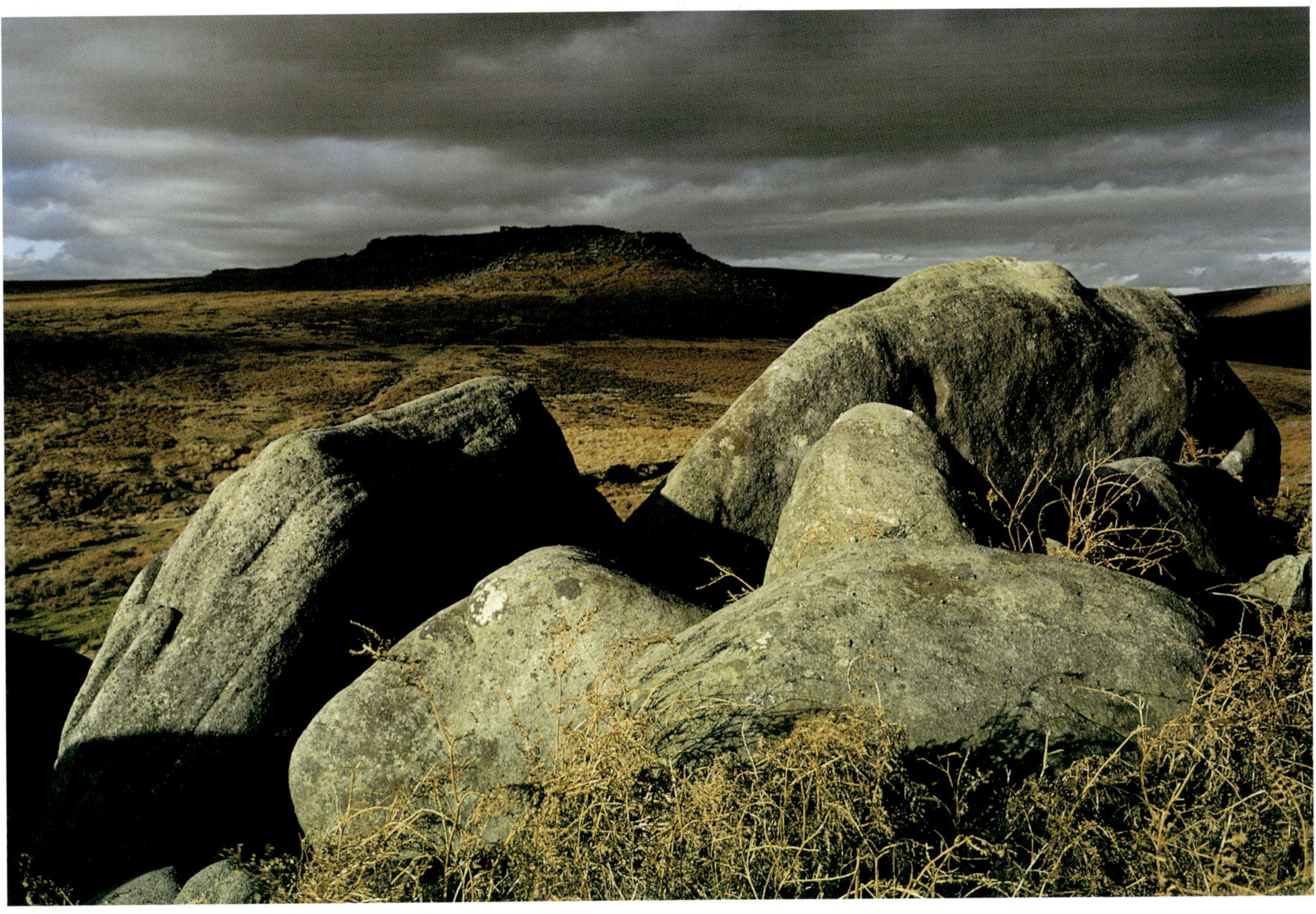

Carl Wark
Storm clouds over the craggy ramparts of Carl Wark set on the skyline above the burnished copper bracken of Hathersage Moor. This enigmatic prehistoric fortification may date from the Neolithic period.

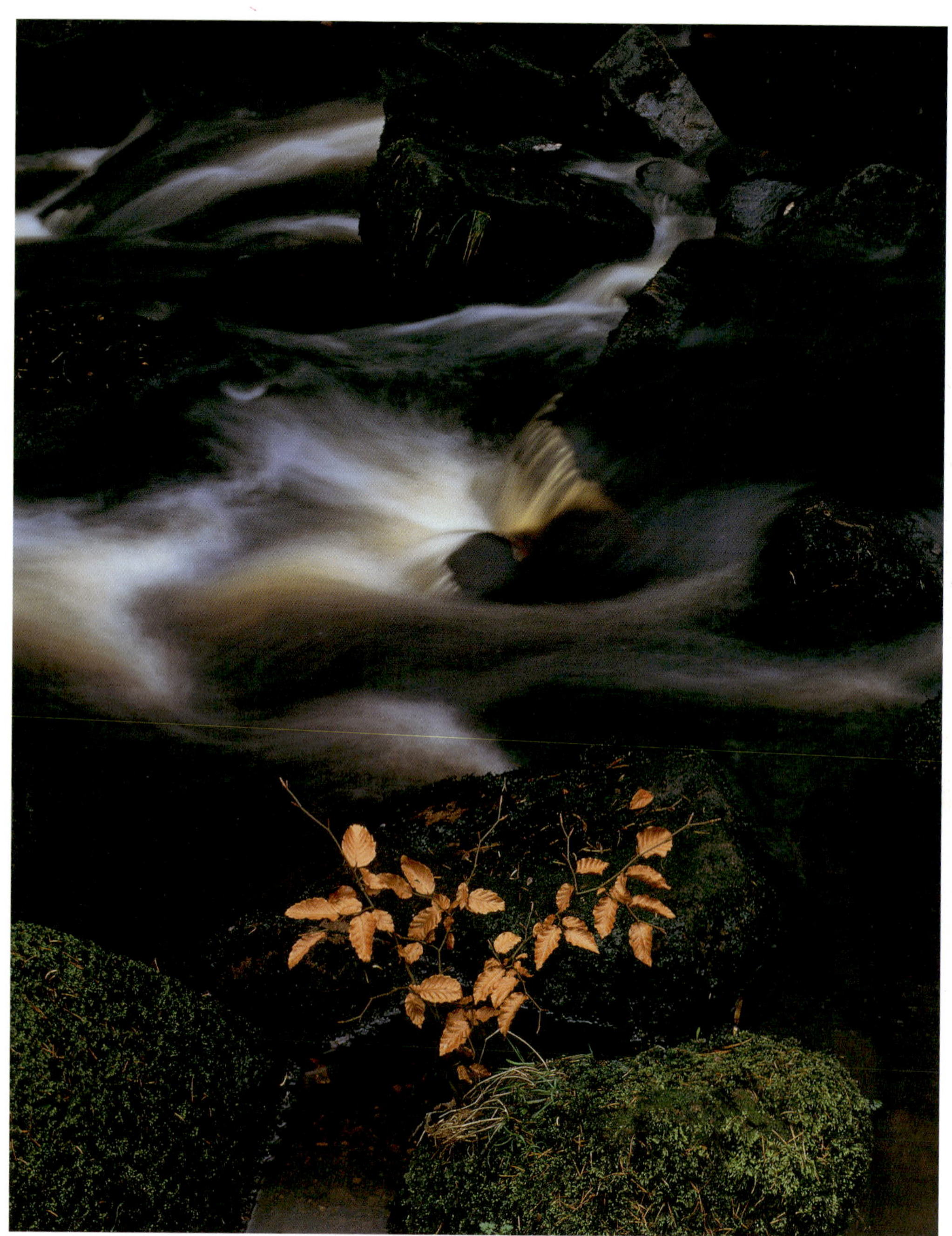

Precarious beech
A small beech tree grows precariously among mossy boulders beside the fast flowing Burbage Brook in Padley Gorge.

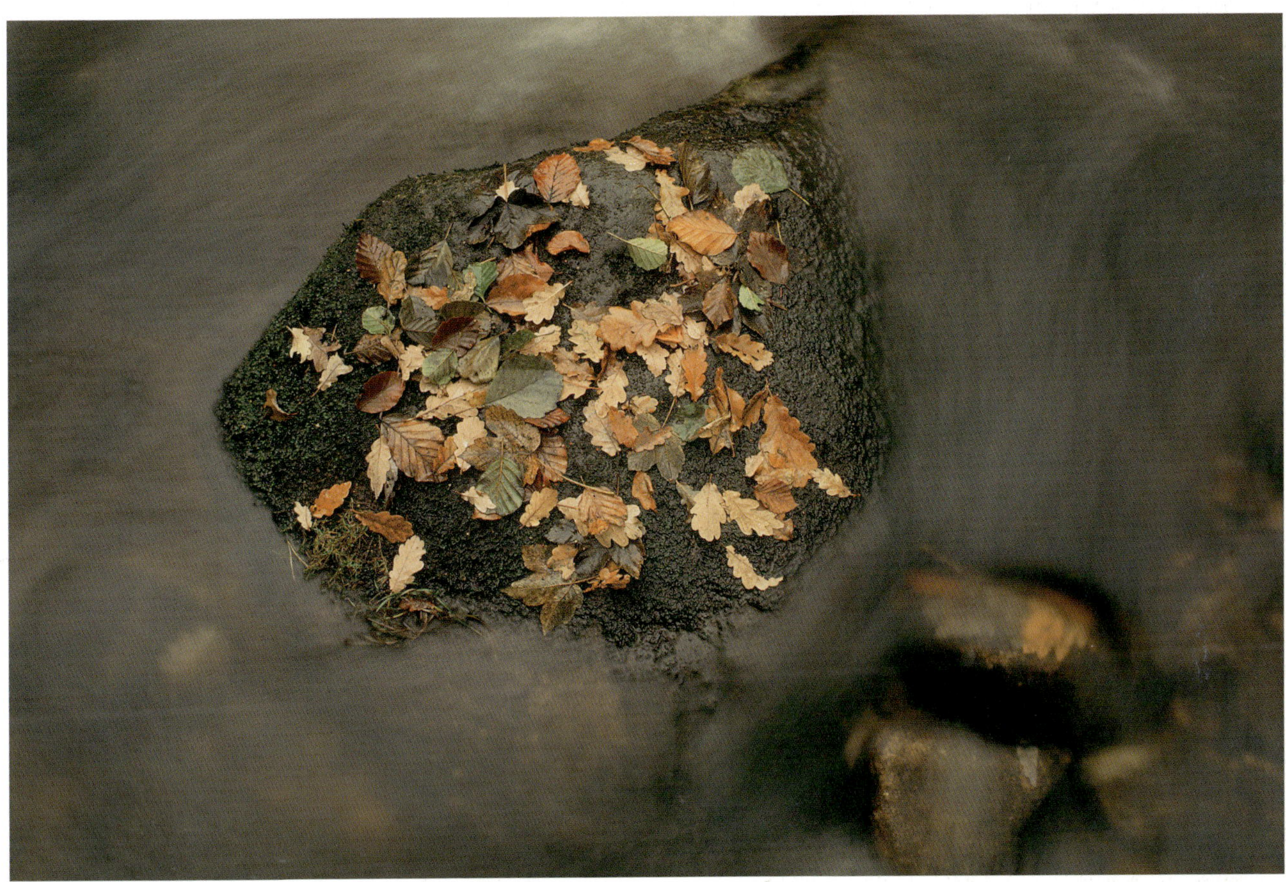

Silky motion
Autumn leaves are highlighted as Burbage Brook flows silkily around a mossy boulder.

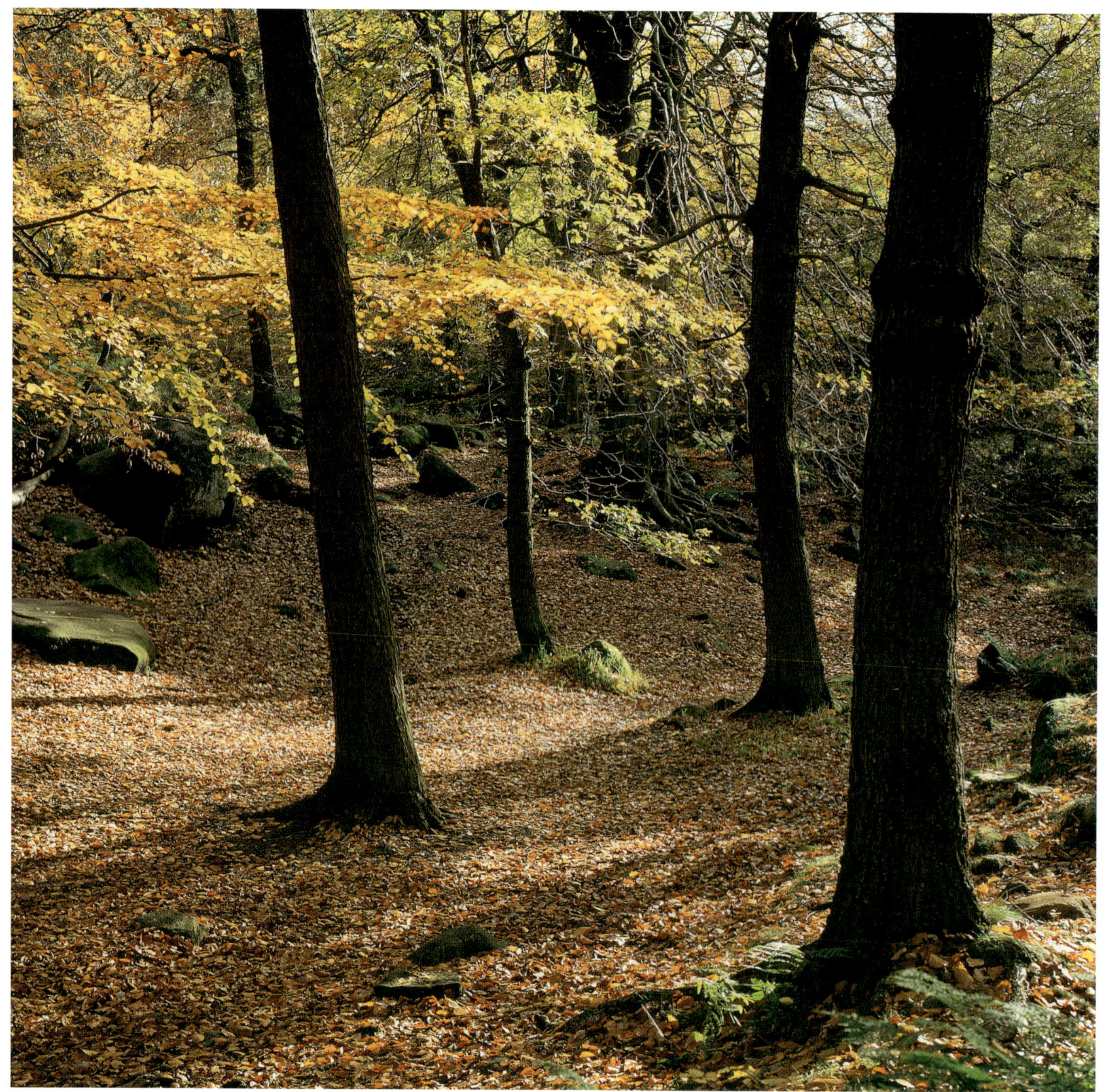

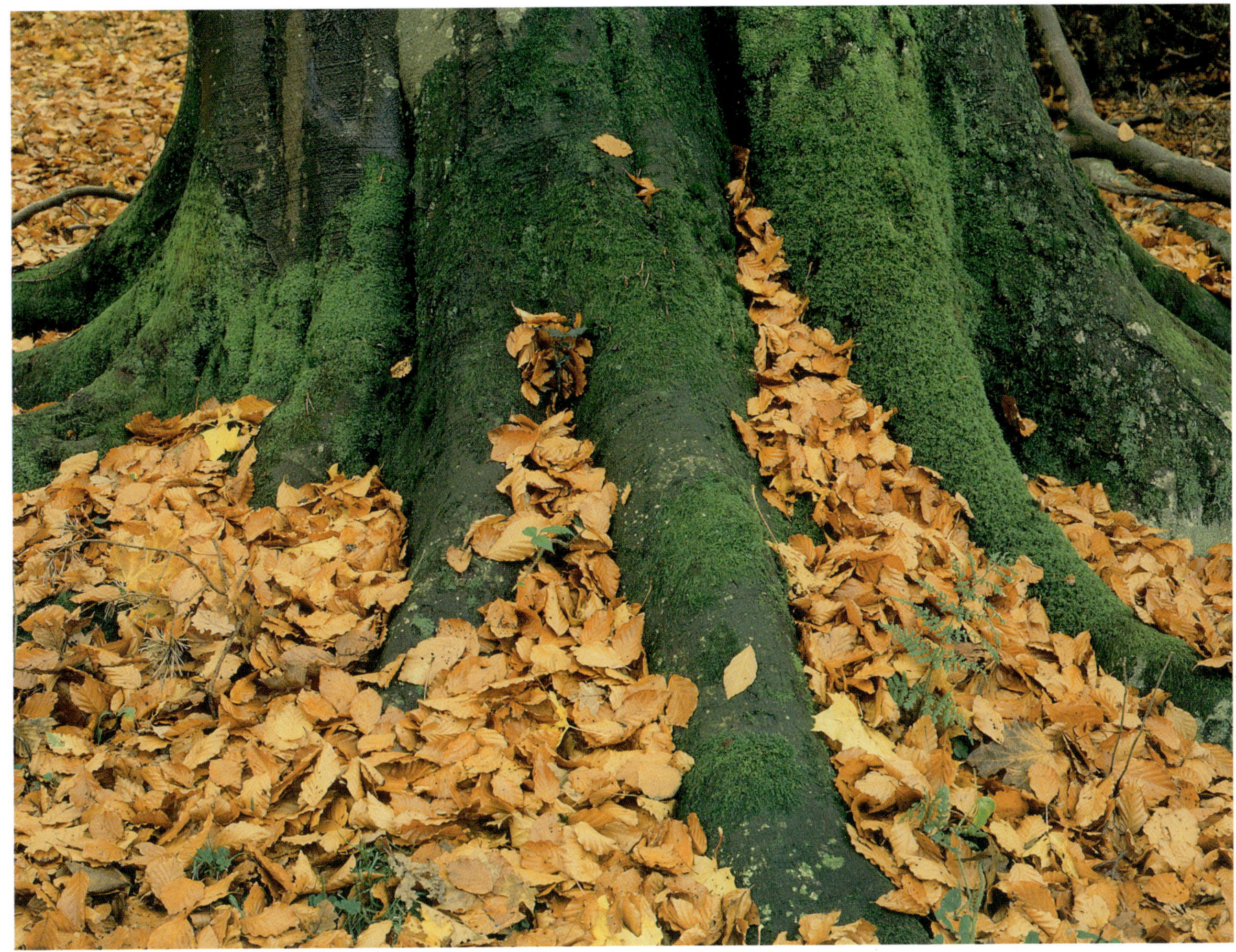

Beech fingers
A moss-covered beech tree dips its finger-like roots into a sea of fallen leaves.

Left: **Autumn majesty**
A tapestry of colour of ancient beech trees in Yarncliffe Wood, Upper Padley Gorge.

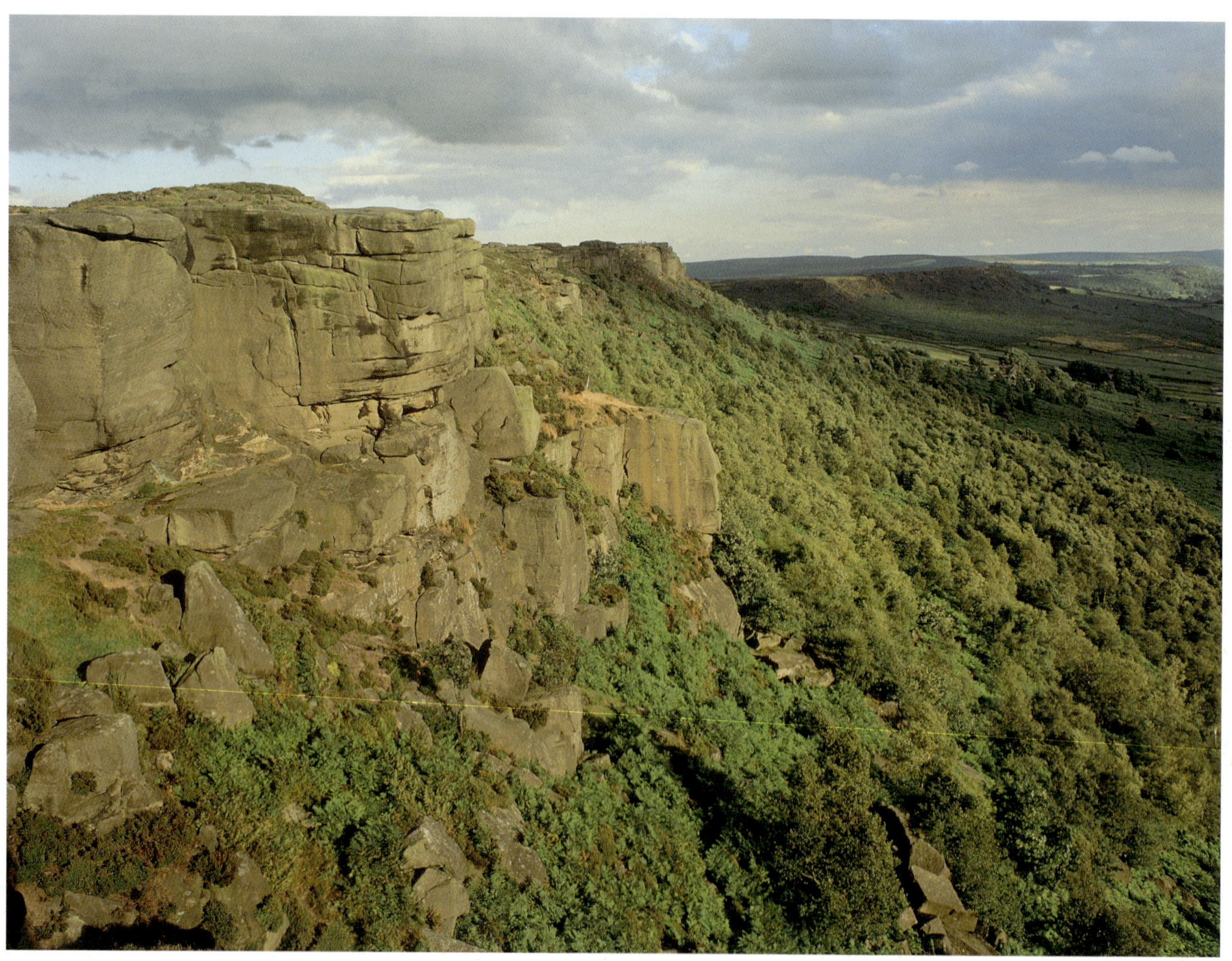

Curbar Edge
Looking south-east along Curbar Edge to Baslow Edge and Chatsworth, as storm clouds drift across the landscape.

Right: **Sunlit boulders**
Evening light on gritstone boulders above Curbar Edge, with the moors of Kinder Scout and Bleaklow visible on the distant horizon.

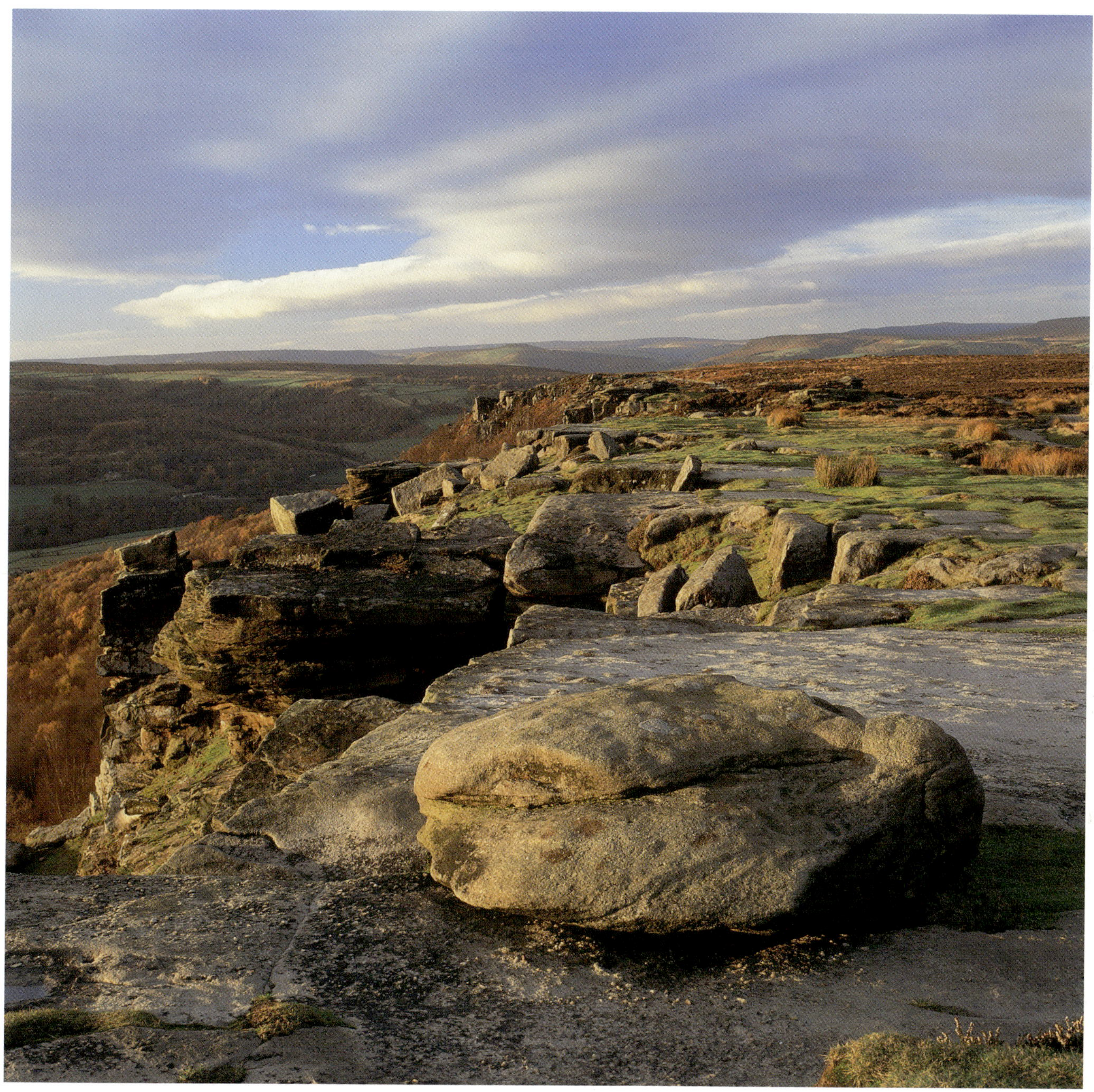

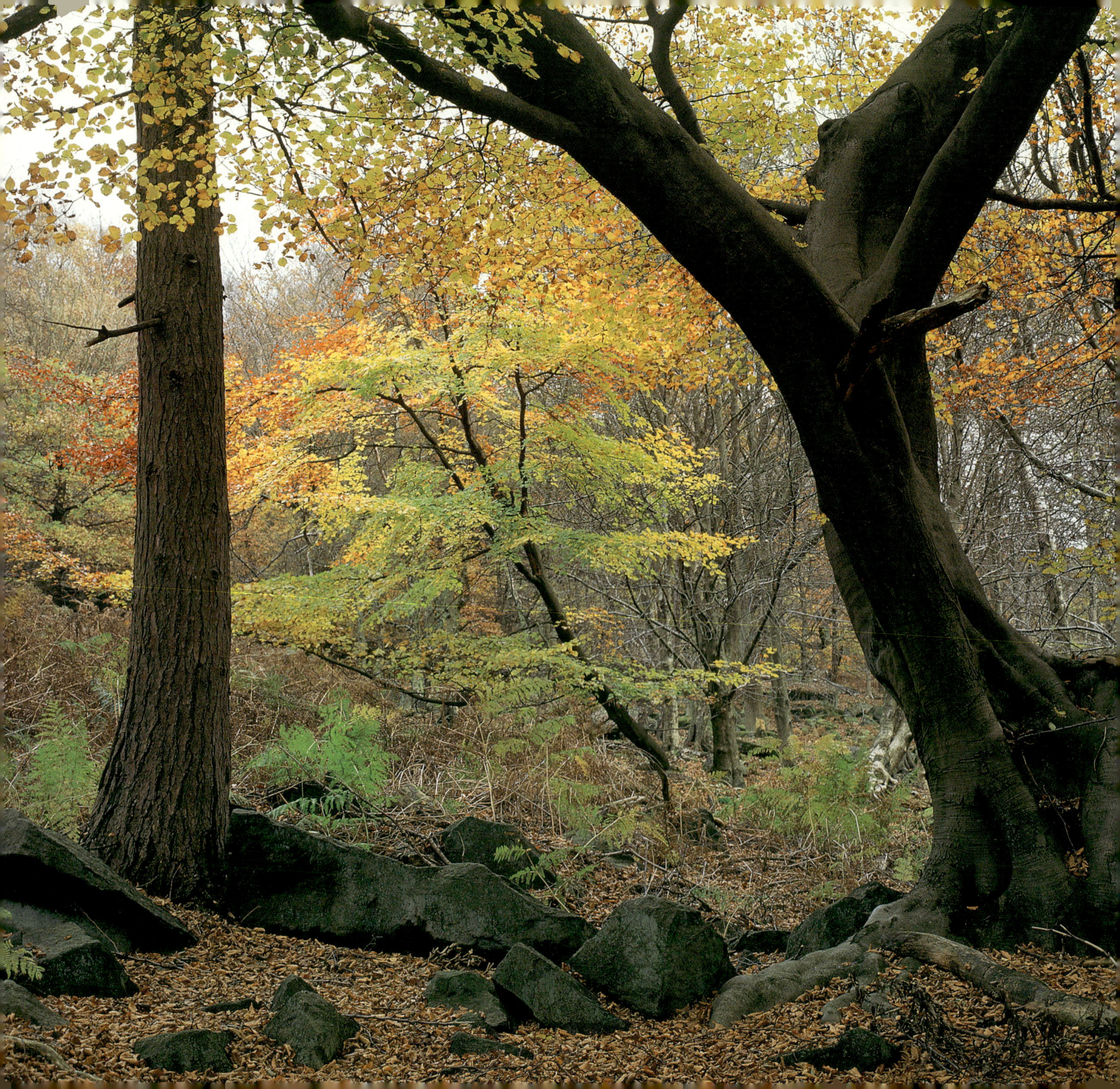

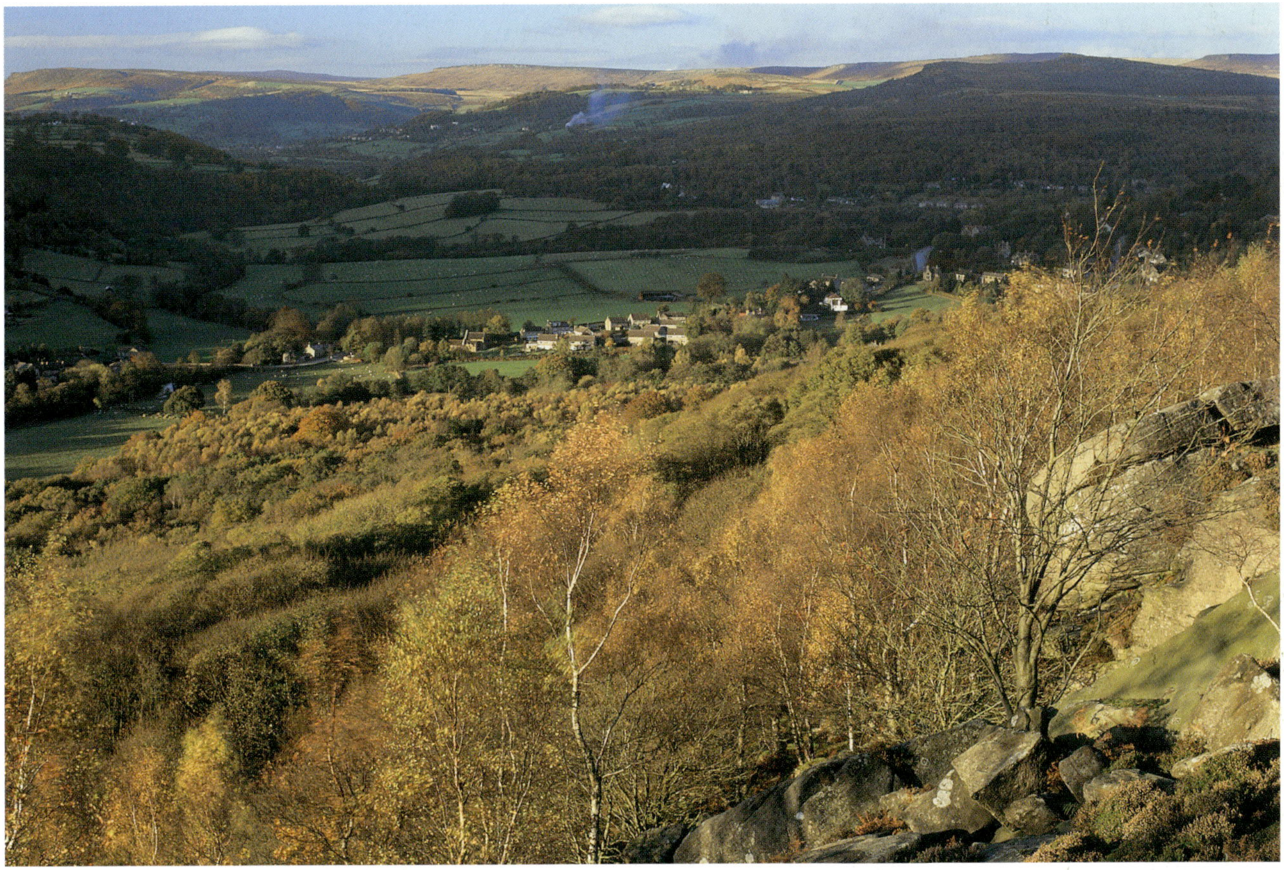

Overlooking Curbar

Warm evening light brings out the rich autumn colours of the wooded slopes of the Derwent Valley, overlooking the village of Curbar.

Left: **Autumn splendour**

A leaning beech tree set in a burst of autumn splendour in the woods overlooked by Froggatt Edge.

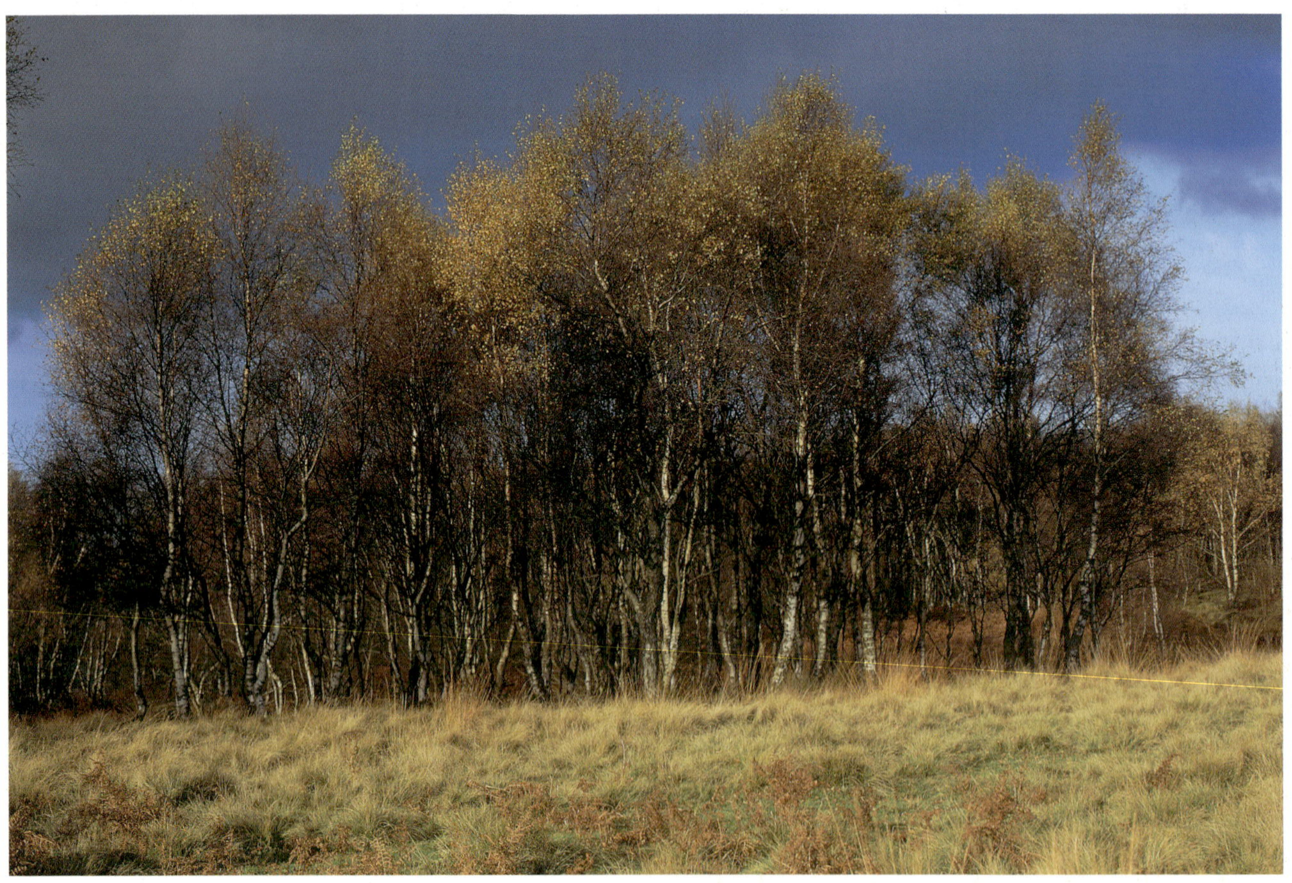

Froggatt birches
A storm approaches a group of silver birch trees on the top of Froggatt Edge near a small, hidden Bronze Age stone circle.

Right: **Ancient woodlands**
Ancient woodlands of oak and silver birch in their autumn glory below Gardom's Edge, east of the village of Baslow.

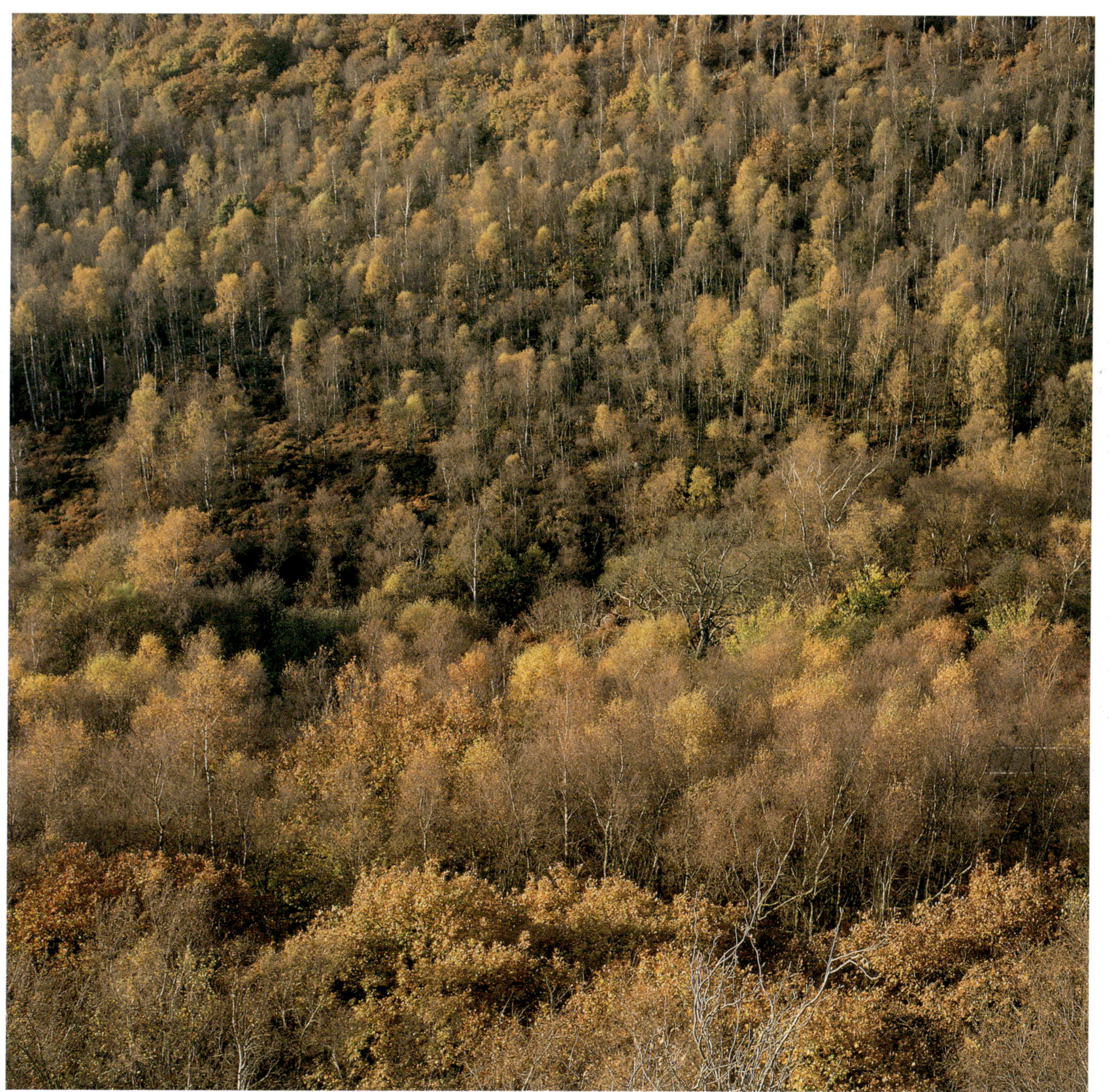

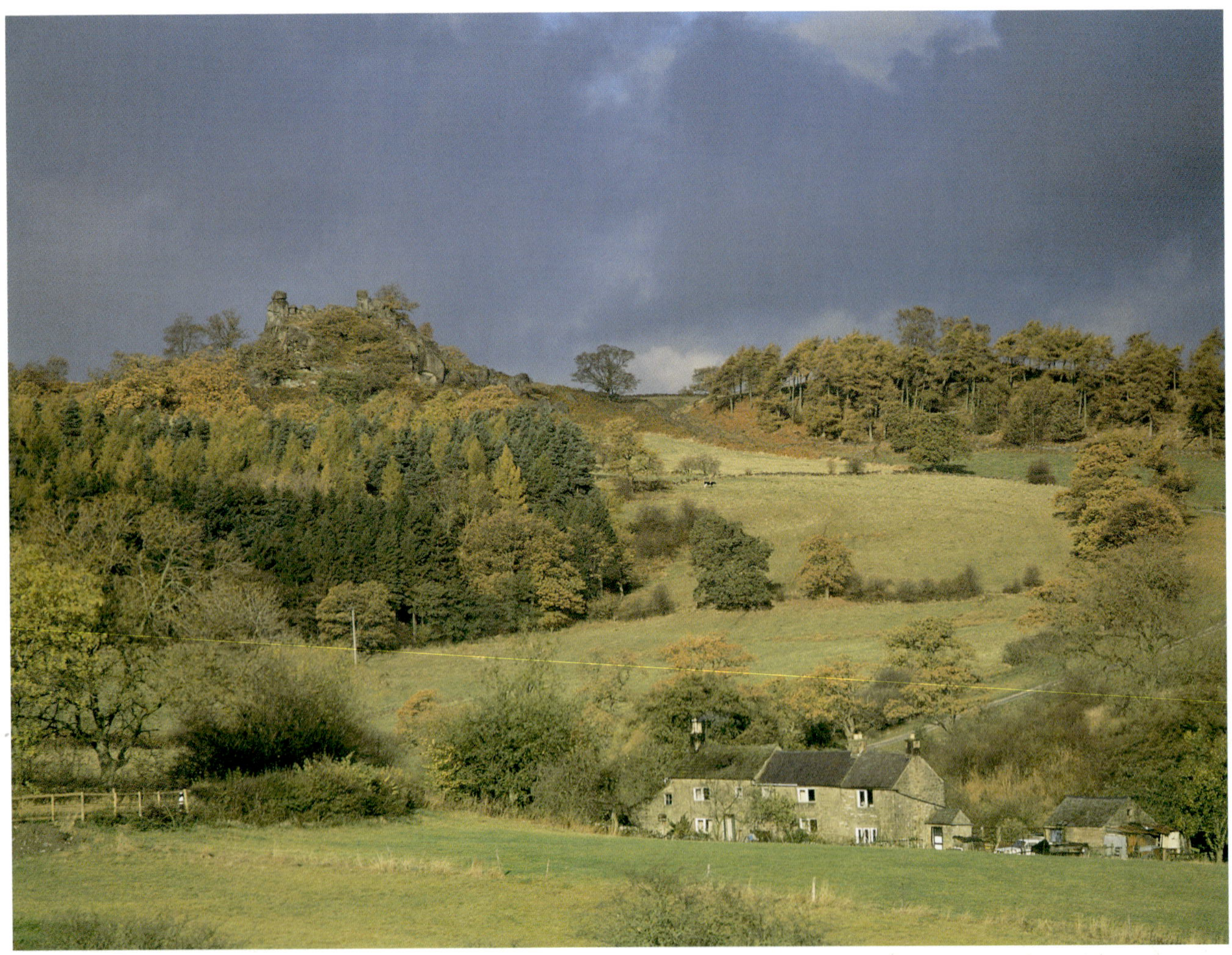

Dudwood Farm
Looking north to Dudwood Farm, with the gritstone pinnacles of Robin Hood's Stride on the wooded skyline on the edge of Harthill Moor, to the west of Birchover.

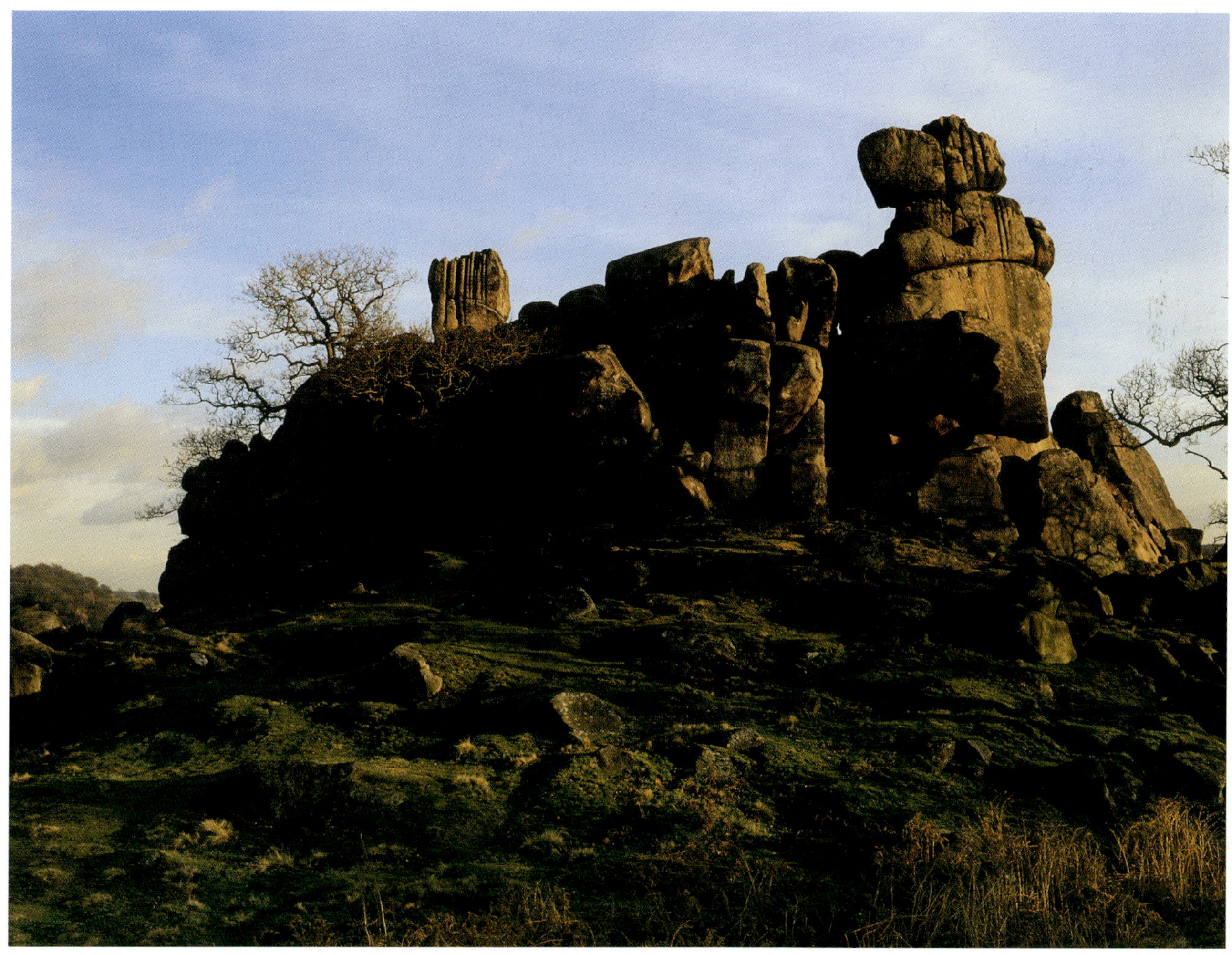

Robin Hood's Stride
The setting sun picks out the distinctive gritstone outcrop of Robin Hood's Stride on Harthill Moor.

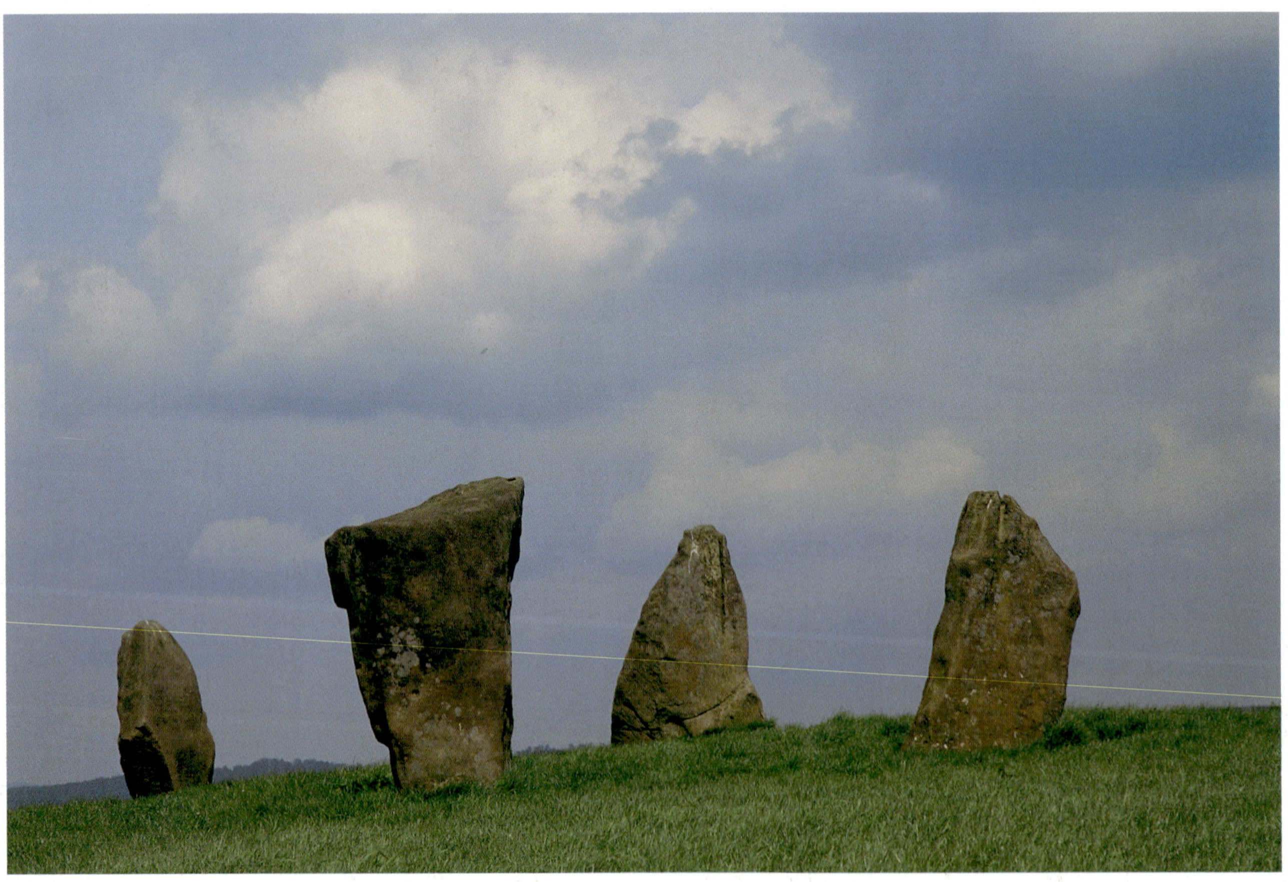

Stone circle
The four remaining monoliths of the original nine dating back to the early Bronze Age which formed a stone circle on Harthill Moor.

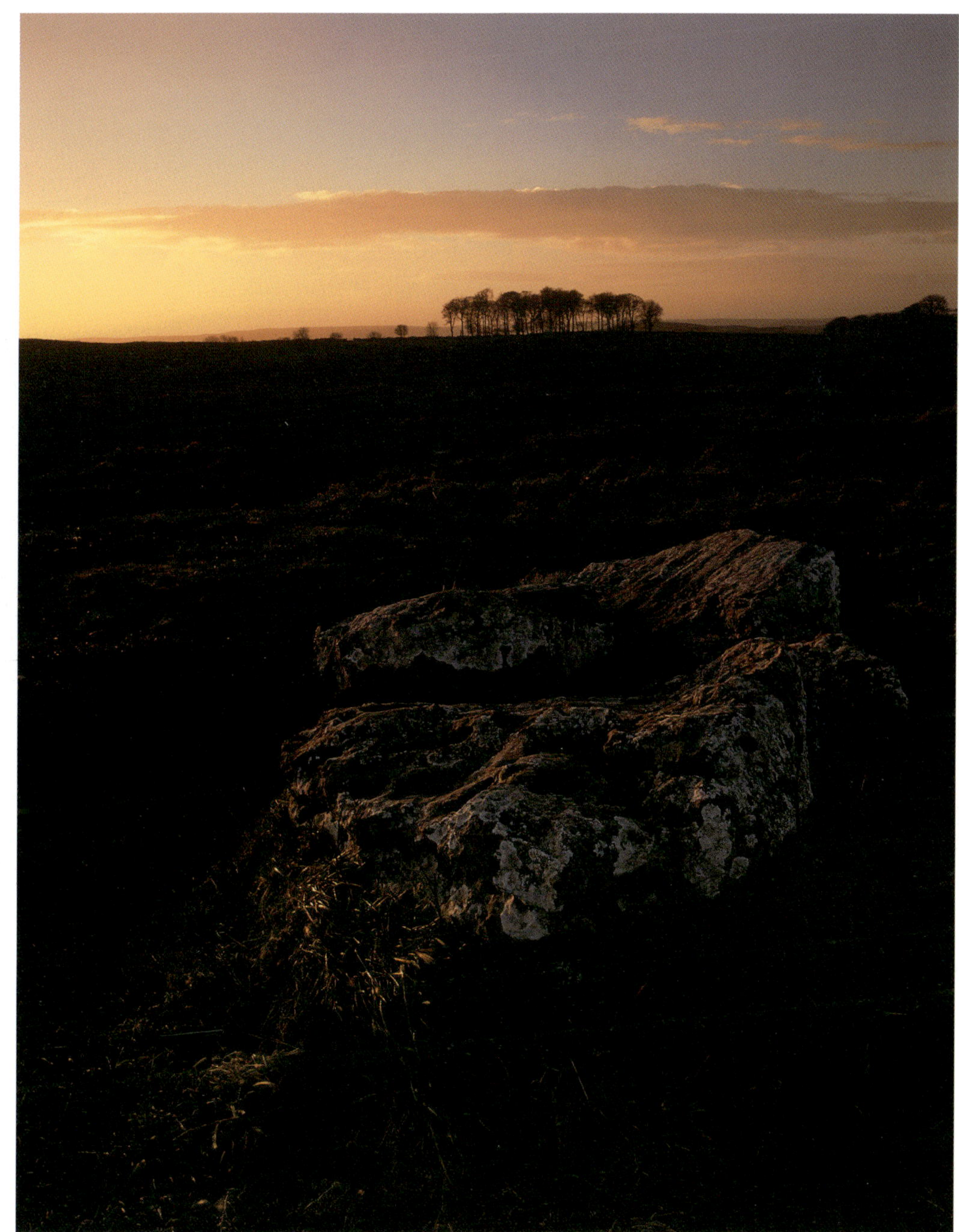

Fallen stone
Evening sunshine spotlights one of the fallen blocks at Arbor Low Stone Circle near Parsley Hay, one of the most important prehistoric sites in the Peak District.

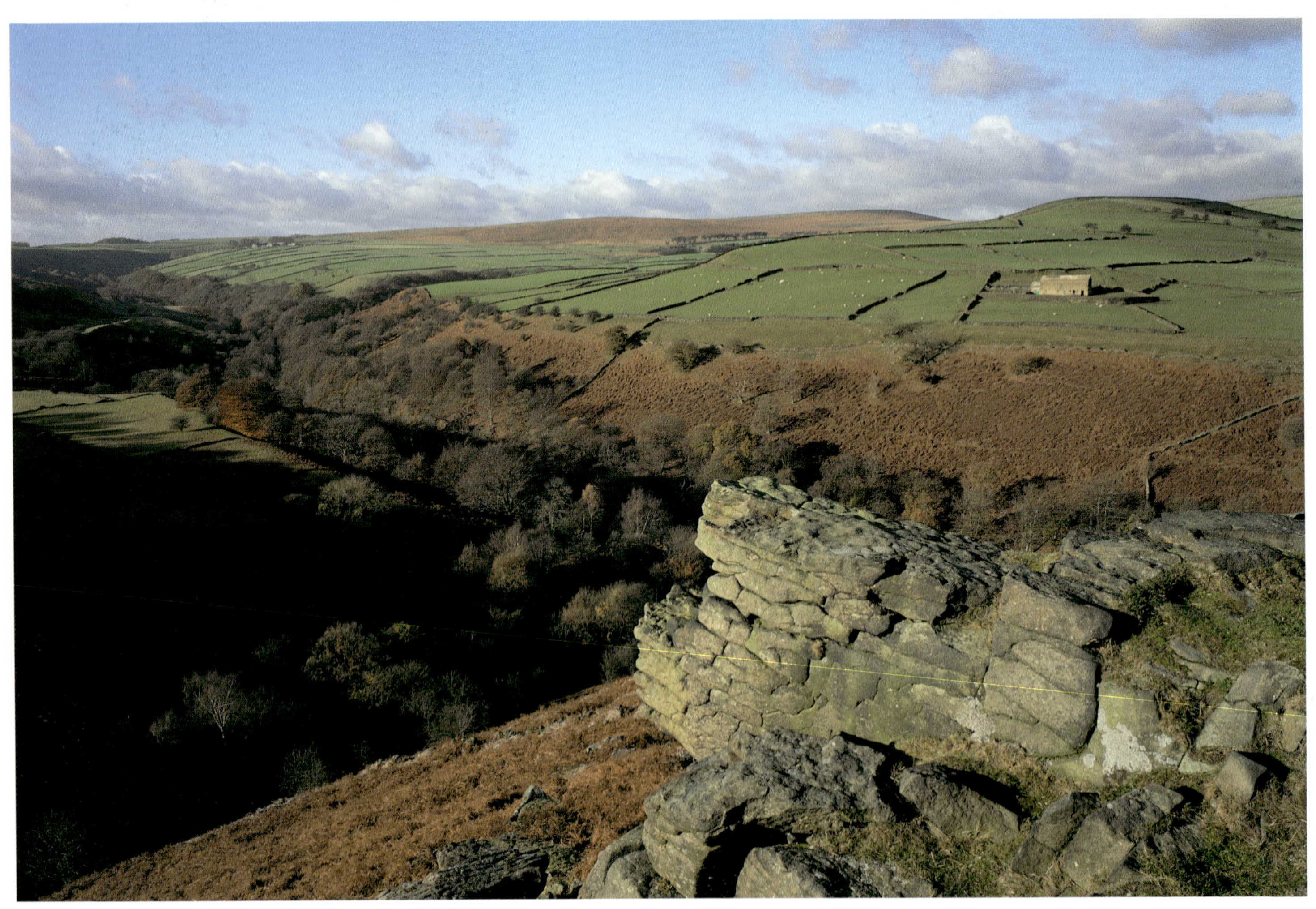

Bretton Clough
Looking out across the wooded Bretton Clough from the outcrop of Gotheredge.

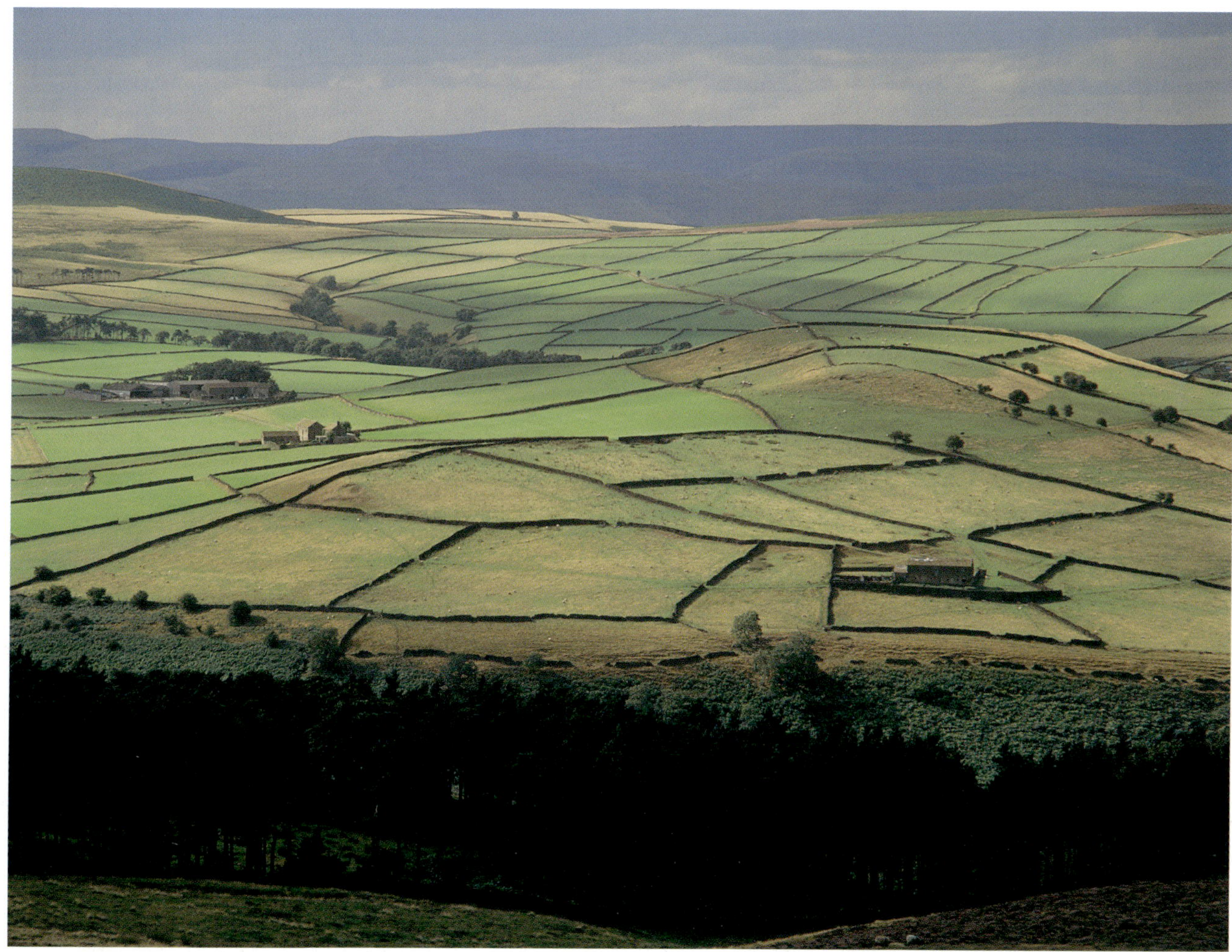

Field patterns
The patchwork walled fields of Abney Low backed by the moors of the Dark Peak are seen in this view north from the moors near the summit of Sir William Hill road.

Overleaf: **Winter sunset**
Night creeps gently across the Peak District.

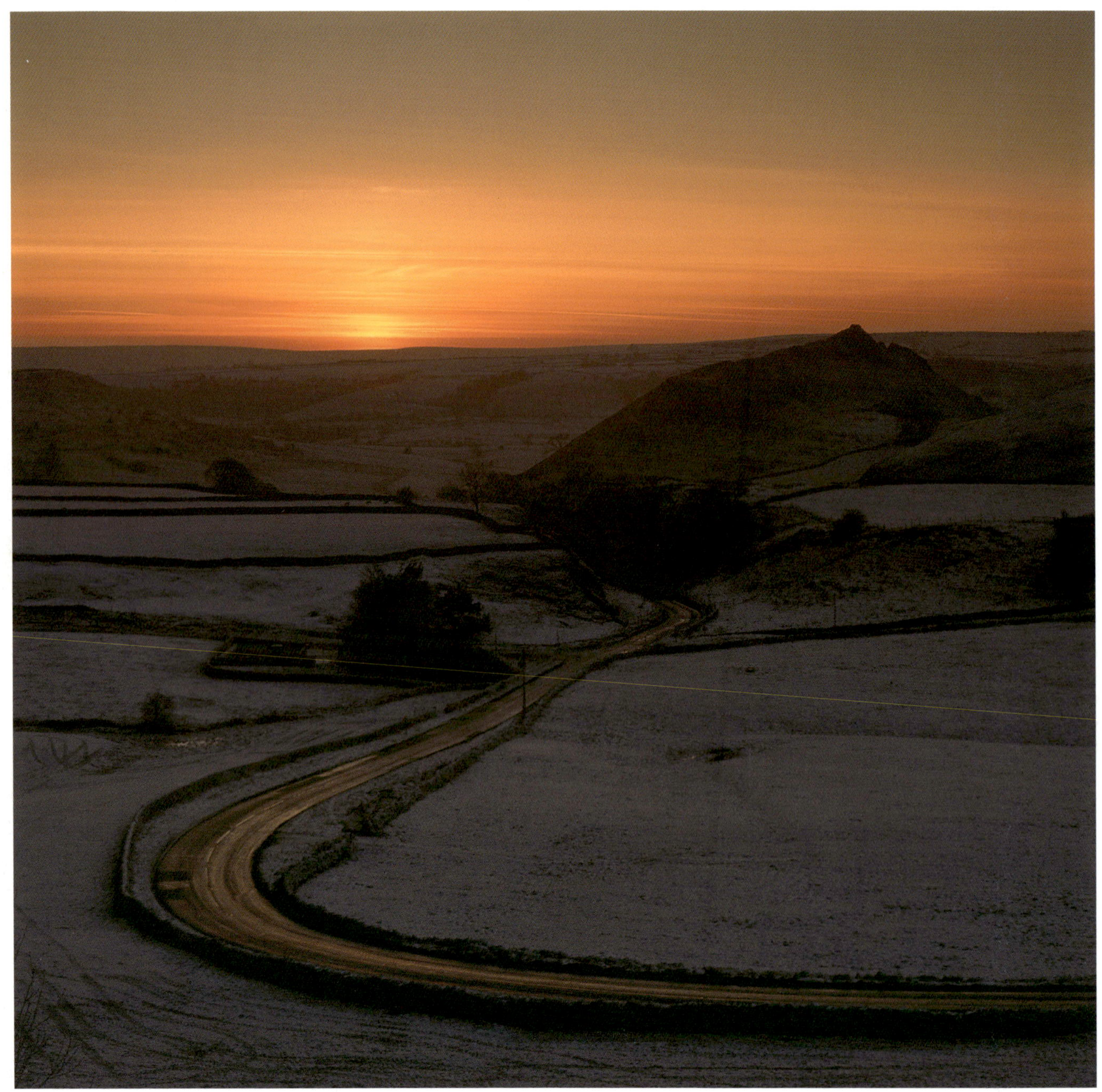